The Unconventionality of Church Leadership: It Works

Earlington W. Guiste, PhD

Evelyn B. Guiste, PhD

TEACH Services, Inc.
PUBLISHING
www.TEACHServices.com • (800) 367-1844

World rights reserved. This book or any portion thereof may not be copied or reproduced in any form or manner whatever, except as provided by law, without the written permission of the publisher, except by a reviewer who may quote brief passages in a review.

The author assumes full responsibility for the accuracy of all facts and quotations as cited in this book. The opinions expressed in this book are the author's personal views and interpretations, and do not necessarily reflect those of the publisher.

This book is provided with the understanding that the publisher is not engaged in giving spiritual, legal, medical, or other professional advice. If authoritative advice is needed, the reader should seek the counsel of a competent professional.

Copyright © 2006, 2015 Earlington W. Guiste, PhD, Evelyn B. Guiste, PhD
Copyright © 2015 TEACH Services, Inc.

ISBN-13: 978-1-4796-0488-3 (Paperback)
ISBN-13: 978-1-4796-0489-0 (ePub)
ISBN-13: 978-1-4796-0490-6 (Mobi)

Library of Congress Control Number: 2015908771

All scripture quotations, unless otherwise indicated, are taken from the King James Version. Public domain.

Scripture quotations marked AMP are taken from the Amplified Bible, Copyright © 1954, 1958, 1962, 1964, 1965, 1987 by The Lockman Foundation. Used by permission.

Scripture quotations marked NIV are taken from the Holy Bible, New International Version®, NIV®. Copyright © 1973, 1978, 1984, 2011 by Biblica, Inc.™ Used by permission of Zondervan. All rights reserved worldwide.

Published by

Dedication

This book is dedicated to a number of people who have played a significant role in the shaping of my life and career choice, and these are:

- Mrs. Josephine Guiste and the late Mr. J. Hayden Guiste, my parents, for their unconditional love and inspiration.
- Dr. Evelyn Guiste and Earlington E. H. Guiste, my wife and son, who are my pride and joy.
- Mrs. Janet King, Mrs. Lilia Stanford, Mrs. Dalia Israel, and Mrs. Judith Thomas, my dearly-beloved sisters.

My lifelong Christian brothers/sisters/friends:

- Brother and Sister Cordel and Ina Anthony and family; Brother and Sister Sylvester and Jean Charles, and Claude.

My dearest Christian mentors/brothers/friends:

- Brother Alpha Josiah (and family), the universally best MV or AY (Adventist Youth) and Pathfinder leader ever, and all the unforgettable memories, especially that college send-off party.
- The late Brother Alfred Richardson (and family), a courageous church elder worth imitating.
- The late Brother Cuthbert Prince (and family), a very classy church musician and choir conductor.
- Dr. Enoch James, Dr. Vincent Richard, the late Dr. Yvonne Richard-Ochillo, and Mr. Edson Jackson, my high school teachers.

- Mr. Eugene Marrow (principal), Mr. Richard Zoino (former Green Housemaster), and Mr. Michael Donovan (current Blue Housemaster) of the Brockton High School, MA. These three gentlemen have contributed to this book in significant ways that are probably unknown to them.

Last but certainly not least are Dr. David William of Harvard University and Steven Thomas, two dearly-beloved and well-respected Christian brothers who read and provided invaluable feedback on the manuscript that helped to shape the final product. My heartfelt gratitude to these gentlemen for their contribution.

About the Author

Earlington Guiste is a deeply dedicated and very loyal Christian who is married to Evelyn Joseph-Guiste (PhD) and wants to contribute something of significance to the growth and development of the Christian church. He was a teacher, principal, and former supervisor of a high school program. He is also a creator of eight board games, eight card games, a restructured numerical system to reduce the stress of learning to count, a restructured multiplication tables to facilitate easy learning and demonstrate the process through which multiplication products are derived and two booklets for children on the latter two.

He attended Caribbean Union College but received a bachelor's degree in theology and sociology with a minor in history from Oakwood College; a master's degree in religion and educational administration from Andrews University; and a doctorate in college and university administration and sociology of education from Michigan State University.

Evelyn Guiste is a graduate of Leeward Islands Teacher Training College with an associate degree in teaching. She received a bachelor's degree from Oakwood College; two master's degrees from Andrews University; and a doctoral degree from Michigan State University.

Contents

Dedication iii
About the Author v
Purpose of This Book 9
Book Structure 12
Introduction 17
Chapter 1 God and His Church 22
Chapter 2 Followership 77
Chapter 3 Jesus' Leadership 99
Chapter 4 Secular Leadership 124
Chapter 5 Church Leadership 150
Chapter 6 Planning for God's Church 197
Chapter 7 Conclusion 228
Appendix Plan Development in Local Churches 232

Purpose of This Book

This book is not a sweeping criticism of any particular church. It is not designed to be destructively critical or harmful, nor to send derisory signals about Christian churches, nor to derogate their leadership due to the fact that we live in an imperfect world and no organization is perfect, including the church. So whatever its defects may be, it is not as unique as it may appear. The defects are present in all churches. This, however, is not a plausible excuse for not taking the necessary actions, drastic as they may have to be, to redirect God's church toward the biblical ideals

The primary purpose of this book is based on the assumption that if church leaders, and followers too, have a biblically comprehensive understanding of the following—(1) who God is (the Son who is not only our Creator, Sustainer, Redeemer, and Sovereign King of His universe but also our Leader) and the One whose attributes His followers were called to mirror or represent to a dying world; (2) the origin, ownership, nature, structure, culture, mission, and underpinning principles of God's church and its operation; (3) followership principles, which are critical to know and implement in order for us to follow Jesus closely and be in a position to lead others to Him; (4) Christ's shepherd-servant leadership style and secular leadership principles in order to discern the critical differences for selective application and omission to and from the church respectively; and (5) strategic planning and implementation principles that are exceptionally important to the forward movement of God's church—they will be in a more advantageous position for the Spirit of God to work through them for the provision of effective leadership in God's church and the realization of its assigned mission. This book is designed to provide the said biblical information.

The clarification of the above-mentioned structural aspects of God's church will, to a great extent, provide some clear indications as to the type of followers we should be and how we ought to function in our relational interactions; the leadership style or model (shepherd-servant model) that is theologically and ecclesiastically relevant and applicable in it; and the demonstration that the wholesale application of secular leadership principles is fundamentally irrelevant, unacceptable, and unworkable due to the fact that the church is the body of Christ (an unconventional "organization" that functions like an organism) and not a secular conventional and/or bureaucratic organization.

Secondarily, the implied information is that the church has a perfect message (it came from God), but it is comprised of very imperfect people who are trying by the grace of God to develop the necessary organizational structures and gospel proclamation methods for the realization of the worldwide mission assigned to them (us), which is a continuation of Christ's ministry for the reconciliation of the world to God. This means that some of the assumptions underlying the structures, policies, operations, attitudes, and behaviors etc. are faulty and need to be revisited and changed respectively if the church will ever arrive or attain to that ideal state of maturity as He intended. It is, therefore, hoped that many of the bold statements made in this book will stimulate some critical thinking and rigorous discussion outside the box but within the parameters of biblical principles that are the guide to everything we do, and help us to arrive at more noble decisions for the advancement of the church and the fulfillment of the gospel commission to hasten the coming of Christ.

Last but not least, it seeks to provide some significant shepherd-servant leadership principles, attributes and functions that will help the church refocus its current assumptions, thinking, decisions, and actions as it attempts to teach the relevant skills and provide the needed experiences for the effective development of its leaders because they are not born but made. It should not be assumed that the natural imposition of the parental leadership role caused by the biological outcome of conjugal relationships is an indication that leadership knowledge and skills come with the territory. Many parents fail and do so miserably.

In like manner, many church members are elected and/or appointed to leadership positions with neither the knowledge of the processes involved in the accomplishment of expected outcomes, nor the skills and experience necessary for the effective realization of the church's mission or goals, yet they are expected to fulfill their roles/responsibilities with excellent leadership precision. When the performance does not meet expectations, and particularly if that leader(s) does not have sound political connections, say "goodbye" to the position(s) at the next election. This is not an indictment of the church in general, but it is a reality in many local churches. That needs to change through the provision or teaching of the appropriate and relevant shepherd-servant leadership knowledge/information (with some emphasis in the areas of biblically-based strategic planning) and experiential opportunities for the development of those needed skills and improved future execution of one's assigned responsibilities that will contribute to the effectuation of the church's internal and external mission.

All the ideals that God has in mind for His church are embedded in His Word. We, therefore, need to delve deeply into it, with the help of the Holy Spirit, in order to discover a more comprehensive understanding of His revelation about His divine attributes and anything else there is to know about Him, His church, leadership and followership in His church, His leadership model as was revealed through the leadership style of Jesus, and where the church needs to go in terms of a "destination" of which we are already cognizant, the Promised Land that Christ has gone to prepare for us. They are awaiting our discovery and correct interpretation, some of which will be revealed in this book, if we are willing to spend the time searching the Word with the assistance of the Spirit of God.

Book Structure

This book is fundamentally about ecclesiastical or church leadership. It includes the broad principles that may be applied to the whole gamut of all administrative levels, from the local church to all branches of church administration. And even though it does not include all the details of leadership, if those presented are applied effectively, leaders would improve their relationship with followers or church members and their performance relating to the effectuation of the gospel commission.

One may question the length of Chapter 1, which is a relatively detailed description of God and His church, in light of the book's leadership focus. It is the author's assumption that too many of our church members, including leaders, are unaware of the true nature of the church of which they are a part and in which they are providing a leadership service. There are many in the leadership spectrum whose conception of the church is that of an institution instead of the body of Christ, which is a brotherhood and a sisterhood. The idea here is that if one's philosophical and/or theological foundational premise is flawed, any deductive reasoning based on that misguided or faulty foundation will also be flawed. Also, if a leaders' philosophical conception of the church contradicts their theological understanding of it, they will be more apt to lead the church as conventional leaders rather than as unconventional shepherd-servant leaders.

This conventional approach is more likely than not to involve a partial or wholesale application of secular institutional leadership principles to the church, which would be conclusively irrelevant, unacceptable, and unworkable among brothers and sisters in Christ or in an organismic context. Leaders, therefore, must develop the correct philosophy that is based on the correct theological interpretation/understanding of the church and must fully comprehend the mission, nature, structure, function, and destination of, and develop appropriate structure to accommodate and/or facilitate the application of biblical leadership and followership principles. If this knowledge is lacking, not even the most skillful leader will be able to lead the church in the correct path to its predetermined destination, heaven at last.

This is the case because, to a large extent, the nature and purpose of organizations, including the church, determine the type of leadership that is relevant, applicable, and acceptable in them. For example, a medical doctors' or lawyers' association that is generally comprised of colleagues will never accept leadership of an autocratic or dictatorial type. The church is comprised of brothers and sisters (Christ's family on earth), and it will never function well, or as God intended it to, with institutional leadership and a bureaucratic structure; nor will the Arms Forces of the United States or any other country be able to function effectively or with great efficiency with shepherd-servant leadership. This is one significant reason why, as some in the church believe, that the command-and-control leadership structure and/organizational bureaucracy suggested by Jethro to Moses is the acceptable and applicable type for our modern church. Fortunately, it is that model that was nullified by Jesus in His presentation of the nature of leadership in the church. This kind of leadership (Jethro's type) was good, applicable, and workable for people emerging our of slavery, but in a more sophisticated, educated, and enlightened modern church with brothers and sisters (in a democratic society), this would prove to be disastrous or unworkable.

Apart from the leadership issue, it is hoped that this chapter will provide some clarity to some of the misconceptions held about the church, and provide for a greater understanding of the origin, ownership, nature, structure, function and mission of the church, and utilize the knowledge to organize God's church for a much more profound revolution for Christ in this world as we seek to fulfill our mission and end our journey in the Promise Land. For further information on the church, it would be good to read an out-of-print book titled *A Theology of Church Leadership* by Richard Lawrence and Clyde Hoeldtke. This was a significant resource for this portion of the book.

Chapter 2 addresses some critical issues of followership within the context of the church. Critical because leaders are also followers and they must clearly understand how to follow in order to avoid following blindly and creating very adversely devastating circumstances for whole churches. It is also no secret that church members in general are very inclined to follow their leaders (especially pastors) blindly with disastrous consequences in many occasions. There are some members who believe that church leaders, especially pastors, are called by God and/ordained by men, and that everything proceeding from their mouths are from God and any questioning would be tantamount to questioning God. The reality is that church leaders are no different from any other member, they are sinners saved by grace. At times, they present their agendas as some direct revelation from God, but nothing could be further from the truth. It is the right of all members to question any proposal or presentation that they do not clearly understand or believe is not based on biblical principle. And those that have no biblical, legal, moral, or ethical basis should be questioned to the point of nullification. Although it is the right of members to question things, it should not be done in a manner to create confusion or disunity, but to ascertain the legitimacy and appropriateness of all requests and/or presentations.

In addition, church followers need to understand their leaders in reference to their philosophy, theology, needs, vision and style, and assess or measure what they do based on biblical principles to determine if they are following Jesus. Anything that falls outside the perimeters of Christian principles should be rejected as inappropriate for church application. Church leaders are not CEOs or bosses, but they should be respected, and that respect is mutual, so both followers and leaders must collaborate their efforts to get things done. Neither is to be allowed to impose his/her will on any other; God's will is to take precedence at all times.

Leaders need to comprehend the needs, wants, and aspirations of followers, and endeavor to discover what makes them click in order to motivate them for the greater good of the whole church. As leaders take these things into account, their leadership will become more acceptable and that will make it much easier to lead. This should also provide the knowledge they need for the selection of new leaders and the changing of the guards since all are only on the stage of life for a short time. Developing a healthy working relationship with followers should create an atmosphere in which followers with certain technical skills can take the lead without the leader feeling threatened and reacting by blocking all opportunities for others to lead.

Good followership and leadership go hand in hand. There is no leadership without followership. They are both critical aspects of organizations, including the church, that must cooperate and work together for the realization of the purpose for which they exist.

Chapter 3 presents some exemplary functional attributes and practices of Jesus, the greatest of all strategic leaders and One whose practices and underpinning principles are worthy of replication and applicable to the church. All Christian leaders should seek to know as much as is possible about shepherd-servant leadership, which was personified in Jesus's life and use it as a guide in their leadership role in God's church. He was the Master Leader.

Chapter 4 provides information on successful practices of secular leaders. Much can be learned from them, but what they do and the underpinning reasons cannot be applied on a wholesale basis in the church because of the significant differences between the church and conventional organizations. An excellent source of information in this area is a book written by James Kouzes and Barry Posner titled *The Leadership Challenge*. This was a significant source for this chapter.

Chapter 5 provides an in-depth analysis of the shepherd-servant leadership model found in the New Testament that, when combined with that of Jesus', should be the standard model after which all modern-day church leaders pattern their leadership and by which all potential leaders are measured prior to their employment and/or election.

Chapter 6 is a response to my observation over numerous years in the church and on church boards. Almost without exception (although some churches are embracing new knowledge in the area of planning), leaders take the current calendars that are dotted with segmented programs and activities and transfer them to the calendar for the ensuing year, which I refer to as extrapolative planning. The end product to this process is the absence of goals and objectives to be achieved for the year and no link to any future long-term goals. With this model the church may achieve a temporary spiritual and emotional high from each planned program, but that quickly evaporates and an emptiness sets in because there is no connection between programs and no particular goal to be achieved for each program. A program is implemented, but at the end, one cannot account for any substantive achievement because there are no established criteria by which to evaluate the success of each program.

Unfortunately, some churches plan as the year progresses, and at the end of the year, there is very little to show for the time, money, and effort invested. In the end, the said churches make little or no progress over the years and find themselves either in a stagnant or retrogressive situation. In other words, there are many churches that are going around in annual circles without any definitive destination in mind.

Planning for the work of the church is a function of leadership, a biblical and Spirit of Prophecy mandate. The type of planning referred to is not one of an extrapolative nature, but one that will be most effective in getting the work accomplished. This chapter provides an integrative method of planning from a strategic perspective that should assist churches and leaders in the development of holistic plans for the realization of their mission. Such a plan provides direction(s) for your church instead of departments and groups heading off in separate directions/paths. With the entire church focused on and working toward the achievement of the established strategic plan, with the help of God, your church will become a progressive one. Leaders must take responsibility and be held accountable for the progress or stagnation of the church.

Remember, a general does not go to war without a strategic plan to win, and a church engaged in a spiritual warfare needs a plan and the Holy Spirit to win the war. The criticality of planning strategically cannot and must not be underestimated, but a plan of this nature will only be words on paper unless leaders work consistently for its implementation. Further detailed information on strategic planning may be obtained from a major work written by Leonard Goodstein, Timothy Nolan, and William Pfeiffer titled *Applied Strategic Planning: A Comprehensive Guide*. This was highly referenced for the writing of this chapter.

Introduction

It is a truism that organizations/institutions rise and decline based on the quality of leadership deployed in them. In other words, with all things being equal, credible/ effective/excellent leadership is the most critically significant component in determining the success or failure of any organization. Conversely, mediocre/poor/ineffective leadership will ineluctably lead to failure. Therefore, based on the criticality of credible leadership for organizational success, no organization should tolerate the existence of ineffective leaders unless it has fulfilled its mission and is in the process of disintegrating. But why is credible/effective leadership so significant to organizations apart from the above-mentioned success factor?

Credible leadership is critical for at least two broad and fundamental reasons: (1) such quality leaders understand very clearly that organizations need specific "destinations," structures and directions, and that it is their responsibility to guide them through the path that leads to the ultimate purposes for their existence (with or without the members assistance, but better with it in an age of participation for psychological ownership reasons); and (2) they are cognizant of their role to supply the fuel/energy/motivation needed to get their organizations to their predetermined "destinations." Leaders of this caliber who provide the two above-mentioned critical services to their organizations are the ones who hover, like a helicopter, over their companies to ascertain the effective and efficient operations of all interlocking parts for the effectuation of their organizations' missions.

Unfortunately, the leadership literature seems to suggest that there is a scarcity of such credible leaders in organizations, and it is primarily referring to those in the apex of the leadership structure. If this is a true reflection of organizational leadership reality, it would be presumptuous of me to even think about the establishment of a repletion of leaders throughout all organizations, including the church, since one or two leaders cannot provide the credible leadership needed in organizations for the realization of their mission and/or transformation from their current state to a better ideal future state that will be beneficial to all involved.

At this juncture, however, it is appropriate to ask a very fundamental question, which is, what is leadership? Strangely enough, leadership has been defined in an exceptionally wide variety of ways in the literature (over three hundred and fifty definitions), but for the purposes of this book, it is defined as *the art of mobilizing followers to accomplish things by challenging their mindset and energizing them to action through the introduction of great ideas, principles and values (not through manipulation) that are beneficial to all.*

In a more fundamental sense, however, the word "leader" comes from the Latin word for "path" and implies that leaders know the "destination" and the path to it. Therefore, the leader acts as a guide and accompanies the followers in order to show them the path by staying ahead of them. He/she is the one who identifies the dangers and obstacles (alone or in collaboration with others) and leads those following away from the pitfalls for a safe journey, and, if it is deemed necessary, changes the course or path of the journey to safely reach the intended "destination."

The implication and/or assumption of the above definition and leader derivation are that leaders are in possession of the relevant and necessary knowledge, skills, and experiences needed to lead people from point A to B. In addition, credible leaders must clearly understand the mission, nature, structure, function, and all the underlying assumptions of the operations of the organizations they lead and have a well-developed vision and a plan for the realization of their mission. This means that leaders are to be insightful and courageous enough to change the structure and function and, if necessary, change the whole organizational culture to achieve its mission. If these things are needed and ignored due to the lack of knowledge, skills, and experiences in the leader, one can only conclude that such an ill-prepared leader will be leading his/her organization on an ill-fated journey to anywhere.

The aforementioned leadership information has relevance not only for secular leaders but also for ecclesiastical or church leaders because human leaders lead people whether they are of the secular society or affiliated with the church. Therefore, there will be commonalities that exist in both types of leadership as well as distinct differences due to the nature of conventional organizations versus that of the unconventional church, the body of Christ that functions like an organism and on organismic principles. An example of distinct differences between both conventional (secular) and unconventional (church) leadership lies in the fact that the former, presidents and/or CEOs of companies, receive their "marching orders" from board of directors and/or other governing bodies while the latter, church leaders, receive their directives from God through His Word and guidance from the Holy Spirit. This is the case because Jesus is the Owner, President, CEO, and Sovereign King of the church. He bought it for a staggering sacrificial price with His life and blood, and no earthly leader can claim or usurp the position of Christ over and in His church.

Another distinct difference is that church leaders do not develop and/or formulate any philosophical position relating to how they will lead out in and/or apply it to the church. There is a theology of leadership inherent in the Word of God that is based on the foundation principles underpinning the operations and leadership of the church. These are the same principles that form the functional perimeters within which church leaders ought to operate. Examples of these are love, patience, compassion, self-discipline, self-control, honesty, truthfulness, self-denial, benevolence etc. And to operate on these and the unwritten ones, as well as the high and noble expectations of a diverse people, is an exceptionally challenging role and requires tremendous amounts of patience, determination, and credibility due to the high moral and ethical standards bare mortal leaders are expected to uphold in the performance of their leadership responsibilities.

Another functionally significant difference between secular and church leaders is that the former are given grave responsibilities with commensurate positional power and authority to get the job done. In other words, inherent in their positions are (1) the necessary authoritative tools to influence or gain compliance from followers in the pursuit of their companies' goals, and (2) a status that is respected above any other in the organization. Conversely, church leaders also have grave and sacred responsibilities but are not accorded proportionate power and authority for the execution of the task due to the organismic nature of the church.

The church is a brotherhood and a sisterhood; no one has any authority or power over the other; power and authority are grass-root based; they reside in the membership, not in the leaders. But for some phenomenal reason, church members, inadvertently or advertently, have allowed church leaders to usurp their "power" and "authority" in spite of our Lord's description of the role of church leaders as "slaves" and "servants" of the people. This means that the status accorded church leaders is one below those whom they lead. Their fundamental role in the church is one of *service*. They are there to serve the people, not lord it over them. And it is not an authoritative or dictatorial imposition of the leader's will on the people under the guise of some God-given revelation to the leaders for the church. The fundamental biblical principle of love is applicable under all circumstances and in all roles in the church. Even though leaders may be able to hide their true motive for a time, it will eventually surface in the form of off-the-cuff comments or otherwise, and the true motive will be revealed.

The last significant difference that will be mentioned here is the ultimate goal of secular institutions/organizations/companies versus that of the church. For the former, the color of the ink on their balance sheet is the deciding factor in how they will continue to operate. All is generally well if that color is *black* because black in organizational reality is "green." On the other hand, the ultimate earthly goal for church leaders is not the color of ink on their books or balance sheet, although this is very meaningful to its operation, it is the *saving of souls*. This may not be the goal for many church leaders, but it the one that is mandated to the church by its CEO, Jesus Christ.

When I contemplate the commitment, passion, time, and resources credible secular leaders, in general, bring to their organizational table for the effectuation of their goals/mission, and that their mandate does not come from God but from corporate boards, I have often wondered why many church leaders do not bring a greater passion and commitment to the work of God in His church when their directives come from the Creator, Sustainer, and Redeemer of the universe, and with the understanding that the church's mission is of greater importance due to the "eternal destination" factor involved for all.

Jesus was both a Master Teacher and Leader. He selected twelve men of varied background and made them (through education and training in the school of life, better known as the University of Hard Knocks) into disciples—pupils/students, adherents, and believers in Him and the principles of His teachings. Thus, they became imitators of their Master and were commissioned to "go and make disciples of all nations, baptizing them in the name of the Father and the Son and of the Holy Spirit, and teaching them to obey everything I have commanded you. And surely I am with you always, to the very end of the age" (Matt. 28:19, 20, NIV). That is, to carry on His work in His absence, the making of other disciples. Inherent in this process is the latent expectation of leadership, because disciples are expected to play a significant leadership role in both living (exemplary) and the verbalization of their Master's teachings. Jesus not only transformed these men but made them into revolutionary shepherd-servant leaders.

The making of disciples, however, is not the responsibility of church leaders only, it is a function of all church members who are His modern-day disciples. This shared responsibility is one that should be executed with credible leadership skills. But how can church members perform such a significant role without receiving the necessary education and/or training for the efficacy of this mission. It is, therefore, the responsibility of the church, led by credible leaders, to provide the resources needed for the development of disciples and leaders in the body of Christ. When we consider the small percentage of our members who are engaged in soul winning with such phenomenal results, can anyone begin to imagine what the results would be with the introduction of a greater part of our membership becoming disciples and leaders.

We definitely need a spiritual revival, reformation, and revolution in the church before we can seriously consider any large-scale revolutionary action for Jesus in the world. And the changes needed should begin with the leadership of the church due to the significant role and influence played and exerted respectively by its leaders. Such a revolution should begin with the flattening of the church's organizational structure and the sharing of more leadership "power" with members, particularly in the local church. God's church is not an institution; it is not about power, authority and privilege, and the hoarding of these by individuals (including leaders) or groups. It is the body of Christ, a brotherhood and sisterhood, which should be primarily concerned with service and sharing the redemptive love of God with a dying world. This definitive understanding of the church is critical for the shaping of the type of leadership that will be deployed in it.

Chapter 1

God and His Church

If we, the body of Christ, are going to develop (that is, educate and train in terms of providing the necessary knowledge and skills) and assign the relevant, appropriate, or right type of leadership in God's church (the criticality of which cannot be underestimated), it is critically significant that followers, and probably more so that leaders, have a biblically comprehensive understanding of who God is (our Creator, Sustainer, Redeemer, and ultimate Leader); His ownership of the "vineyard" or church; the nature, structure, function, and mission of His church; and our role as leaders and followers in His church for the successful realization of its mission or the purpose for its existence.

The church is the unconventional "corporate" or organizational context within which ecclesiastical or church leadership takes place. It is the metaphorical body of Christ, a brotherhood and a sisterhood, and not an institutional bureaucracy that is controlled by superordinates who lord it over the subordinates. God is its Originator, Owner, "CEO," Sovereign King, President, Head, and Leader. He formulated/established its ideal and pure principles (directives that serve as the perimeter) within which His church is to function. Leaders/elders, therefore, are not heads of the church but part of the body. They are assigned as stewards/overseers of His "vineyard" and provide a shepherding service to the rest of the body that is based on the said God-given principles.

Church leaders do not develop their own philosophical perspectives and/or theological directives for the church but serve as stewards and shepherd-servant leaders. If these leaders, and followers as well, are going to perform their responsibilities in a lovingly effective manner, it is mandatory that they know the Owner of the "vineyard," including His attributes, principles, values, and character, because both His leaders and followers are admonished to "be ye therefore followers of God, as dear children" (Eph. 5:1). If one does not know the Owner through one's personal relationship with Him, it is virtually impossible to imitate such a mysterious God. And if one does not know the path to Him and eternal life, it is almost impossible to lead others to that destination.

In addition to knowing the Owner, leaders (elders) should know the "vineyard" or the church over which they were made overseers or shepherd-servants. Understanding its nature is critical since this, to a large extent, determines the type of leadership and followership and leadership-followership dynamics that should exist in the church. As was mentioned previously, if leaders falsely perceive the nature of the church to be one of a bureaucratic institution, they will lead as CEOs and see members as subordinates. Conversely, church leaders need to understand that all are equal at the foot of the cross. One's role or function in the church does not make that person, even the leader, a better Christian nor provides that individual with a higher status because all are brothers and sisters, a point that cannot be overemphasized. Thus, the superordinate-subordinate principle does not apply in God's church. The principles of love and equality undergird their relationship.

Leaders should also fully understand the purpose of the church and how to organize it for mission effectuation. The mission of the church is the driving principle that underpins its existence. Any aspect of the body of Christ, the church, that does not know the purpose of its existence has no justifiable reason to exist unless it changes its mission. The purpose or mission is the heartbeat of any organization, and the effective structuring and policy development in reference to the application of biblically based administrative and leadership principles will keep the heart beating on a timely basis for the effectuation of the church's mission. Leading for mission realization is the heart beat of what leaders do for the Owner of the "vineyard." Let us turn our attention to learn about the Owner of the church because whatever we do inside or outside the said church is done to represent Him and in recognition of His universal sovereignty, and for the vindication of His name. It is all about Him, our Sovereign King, and not about us.

God

God is a mysterious Being, and we, as human beings, in all our brilliance, who have delved deeply into the natural things that we can see, hear, touch, and experiment with, will never be able to fully comprehend God because He cannot be scientifically investigated and/or discovered. Job provides some confirmation of this in both of his questions and answers when he wrote, "Can you fathom the mysteries of God? Can you probe the limits of the Almighty?" He claims that "they are higher than the heavens ... deeper than the depths below ... longer than the earth and wider than the sea" (Job 11:7–9, NIV). Solomon, probably the wisest human who ever lived, compares our ignorance of the origin and path of the wind, and the formation of the human embryo in the mother's womb with that of not being able to "understand the work of God, the Maker of all things" (Eccles. 11:5, NIV). If we cannot fully comprehend His works, much of which is visible to us, it would be futile to even attempt to completely discover the ultimate Mystery of our universe.

Fortunately, the essence of who God is (His identity) is concealed in His character, and through His own volition, He has selected to reveal that which we need to know about Him through Moses and the other prophets, Jesus (through whom was a complete revelation), His disciples/apostles, and His Word, the Bible. His self-revelation is significant for us to probe in order to, at least, partially discover who He is for our understanding and representation of His character attribute to a dying world. But who is God and what are His expectations of us? I will attempt, in a very succinct way, to explore the Scriptures and provide some limited answers to the questions, inherent in which will be sufficient for us to know about Him and what He desires of us in reference to our role as disciples, leaders, and followers in His church on earth.

God the Father and the Holy Spirit are non-human entities who live or dwell in the good spirit world as is affirmed by John in his writing that "God is a Spirit: and they that worship him must worship him in spirit and truth" (John 4:24). Jesus possessed that same form or likeness to both the Father and Spirit until He chose to cloth His divinity with humanity through His incarnation and became one of us in order to identify with us, lived an exemplary life as an example for us, and died to redeem us from the strangle hold of sin, all of which is a profound mystery. That combination of human and divine will remain with Him throughout eternity. However, just the idea of an eternally omnipotent God becoming one with matter or flesh to suffer and die as a sinner, yet without sin, is something that is difficult to wrap one's mind around. But that is the length to which God went to redeem us, and this is truly a reflection of or an attestation to the quality of His character as will be revealed in this section.

God is the only eternally existing One. His existence is not caused by any force that is external to Him. The reason for His existence is inherent in Him. He is life and is the only One who experiences real and permanent existence. In Moses' experience with God on Mount Horeb when he was asked to go on a mission to Egypt to lead God's people out of bondage to a land that was flowing with milk and honey, Moses wanted to know whose name he should refer to as the One who sent him. God's response was

Chapter 1 God and His Church

that "I AM THAT I AM ... I AM hath sent me unto you" (Exod. 3:14). In essence, God is the Alpha and Omega, the beginning and end. Yet He has no beginning and no end. Everything has its source and beginning in Him. He is and lives in the continuous present. He is not affected by our time and space; He does not grow older or get younger; He is the same yesterday, today, and forever (Heb. 13:8), and Paul refers to Him as the "King eternal, immortal, invisible, the only wise God, be honour and glory for ever and ever" (1 Tim. 1:17; see also Rom. 16:26, 27).

He, God, is the only One who is light and lives or dwells in light where no mortal can approach Him except through Jesus Christ our Lord. According to John, "God is light, and in him there is no darkness at all" (1 John 1:5). He is a "consuming fire" (Deut. 4:24; see also Exod. 24:17; Heb. 12:29); He is the only God who transcends all that is human. That which is so critical to human existence—time, space, matter, energy, and information—has no impact on Him. He is infinite in every way, and it is in Him that all beings and things have their origin, support, and end. This God is *El Shaddai* or God Almighty with whom nothing is impossible (Mark 10:27); He is a great and awesome God (Deut. 7:21; Dan. 9:4; Neh. 9:31); He is the Source of real power and any power that humans perceive to possess can be taken away from them by Him in a flash. He is omnipresent, omniscient, and omnipresent, the everlasting Father and the "only Potentate, the King of kings, and Lord of lords" (1 Tim. 6:15). In other words, there is no other like Him in the universe.

God is holy. He is infinitely righteous, without sin or sinless, and has no inclination to sin. There is not a streak of light in Him that can be contaminated by evil. He is the only good and Holy One (Lev. 19:1, 2; Isa. 40:25; Hab. 3:3; Hosea 11:9; Mark 10:18) and He expects His people to reflect this special aspect of His character as is indicated to Moses (Lev. 19:2; Isa. 43:14; 1 Peter 1:15; Matt. 5:48). It is not that there is something inherently godlike about us which He expects us to demonstrate at His command. He will make us holy, if we are willing and ready to let Him through the presence and power of the Spirit of God, dwell in us, and work through us. He instructed Moses to inform "the entire assembly of Israel and say to them: 'Be holy because I, the LORD your God, am holy" (Lev. 19:2, NIV) and "sanctify yourselves therefore, and be ye holy: for I am the LORD your God" (Lev. 20:7; see also Isa. 43:14). And we begin to sense in a limited form what He means by this holy condition when He said in Isaiah 43:11 that "I, even I, am the LORD; and beside me there is no saviour" and that "I am the LORD: that is my name: and my glory will I not give to another, neither my praise to graven images" (Isa. 42:8). He is to be the central focus or our lives.

"God is love" (1 John 4:8, 16), and this statement is the expression of the full depth of God's being. He is the epitome of what true love is about. Love originated with Him and not from any other being or place in the universe. Therefore, if we think and say that we love, the Source of that love is to be recognized as coming from God and Him alone (1 John 4:8). That which is so fascinating about the quality of His love is the depth of its unconditionality. In spite of the fact that human beings have chosen to separate themselves from God to engage in things that are diabolically ungodly, He loves us and continues to pursue us in order to woe us back to Him. The depth of His love was clearly demonstrated in sending His Son, " his only begotten Son into the world, that we might live through him" (1 John 4:9). "For God so loved the world, that he gave his only begotten Son, that whosoever believeth in him should not perish, but have everlasting life" (John 3:16). In other words, He gave up the most precious Being, a part of His existence or who He is, Christ the Son of God, to become one with man through His incarnation, and to die a cruel, criminal death on a cross to redeem man from a destination of extinction.

God did not act in response to our love for Him, but because He loves us unconditionally. When we went astray, He kept on loving us, and He wants us to love Him and one another with the same depth with which He loves us. This was unequivocally confirmed by Jesus when He was asked by the Scribe about the first commandment of all and He proclaimed that it is to "love the Lord thy God with all thy heart, … soul, … mind, … strength: … And the second is … Thou shalt love thy neighbour as thyself" (Mark 12:30, 31). The second grand challenge is to love each other as Jesus loves us, which in the new commandment is stated as such: "A new commandment I give unto you, That ye love one another; as I have loved you … By this shall all men know that ye are my disciples, if ye have love one to another" (John 13:34, 35).

Other aspects of His character are that God is gracious, merciful, and compassionate (2 Chron. 30:9; Ezra 8:22; Deut. 4:31). He is the God of justice (Isa. 30:18; Ps. 7:11); the God who is patient or slow to anger (Jonah 4:2; Neh. 9:17; Nah. 1:3); He is "the faithful God" (Deut. 7:9; see also Deut. 32:4; Neh. 9:17); the One who generously forgives (Ps. 99:8; 1 John 1:9); He seeks not to destroy life because He is the Life Preserver, the One who does not take away life (2 Sam. 14:14, Ps. 68:20); He is truthful; it is impossible for Him to lie (Num. 23:19; Titus 1:2; Heb. 6:18; 1 Sam. 15:29); He opposes all those who are proud (James 4:6); and God is impartial, showing no favoritism to anyone (Rom. 2:11; Acts 10:34, 35; Eph. 6:9; Col. 3:25; James 2:1, 9).

The following seven things that God "hates" provide further insight into what His character is like: (1) haughty eyes, (2) a lying tongue, (3) hands that shed innocent blood, (4) a heart that devises wicked schemes, (5) feet that are quick to rush into evil, (6) a false witness who pours out lies, and (7) a man who stirs up dissension among brothers (Prov. 6:16–19).

In reference to the above limited character traits of God, the following is fundamentally a repetition of many of those attributes, but due to its origin, it is by far much more profound, credible, and authentic because it is a direct self-revelation pronounced by God to Moses. It was a result of Moses' request of God to teach His ways and reveal His glory to him.

> Then the LORD came down in the cloud and stood there with him [Moses] and proclaimed his name, the LORD. And he passed in front of Moses, proclaiming, 'The LORD, the LORD, the compassionate and gracious God, slow to anger, abounding in love and faithfulness, maintaining love to thousands, and forgiving wickedness, rebellion and sin. Yet he does not leave the guilty unpunished; he punishes the children and their children for the sin of the parents to the third and fourth generation. (Exod. 34:5–7, NIV)

As was mentioned previously, God informed Moses to instruct "the entire assembly of Israel and say to them: 'Be holy because I, the LORD your God, am holy'" (Lev. 19:2, NIV). This was God's expectation of His chosen people, the Israelites, not to be half or partially holy, but to be totally consecrated to Him. The end product of this process would be a clear demonstration and expression of His holiness in all aspects of their lives.

As "grafted" or spiritual modern-day Israelites (Christians; disciples of Christ), God has the same expectations of us—leaders and followers. He expects our complete loyalty, commitment, dedication, and consecration to Him, which in essence results in our imitation of God from a character perspective. In his letter to the Ephesian Christians, Paul instructed them to "follow God's example ... as dearly loved children and walk in the way of love, just as Christ loved us and gave himself up for us as a fragrant offering and sacrifice to God" (Eph. 5:1, NIV).

This notion of being holy, imitators of God and representing God's character to the world is confirmed by Ellen G. White, a modern-day prophetess, who wrote that "we are called to represent to the world the character of God as it was revealed to Moses." She continues to write that "this is the fruit that God desires from His people. In purity of their characters, in the holiness of their lives, in their mercy and loving-kindness and compassion, they are to demonstrate that the 'law of the Lord is perfect, converting the soul'" (*Testimonies to the Church*, vol. 6, p. 221).

From an intellectual perspective, this seems to be an extreme "tall order to fill," and it appears virtually impossible for any finite sinful human being to become an imitator of an infinite and divine God. Will we, as God's people, ever attain to this position in this life where we consciously and consistently, without any diversion, imitate in character our heavenly Father? Just as how a light bulb will never produce light unless connected to an electrical power source, it is impossible for us to reflect God's character without being connected on a consistent basis to the Source of those attributes.

Ellen G. White informed us (and as scary as this may sound to those who lack the necessary faith to believe in its possibility) that Jesus, who was/is a complete revelation of and perfect representative of God, "revealed no qualities, and exercised no powers, that men may not have through faith in Him. His perfect humanity is that which all His followers may possess, if they will be in subjection to God as He was" (*The Desire of Ages*, p. 664). This is an idea that was put forward by Jesus when He said in John 14:12, "Verily, verily I say unto you, He that believeth on me, the works that I do shall he do also; and greater works than these shall he do; because I go unto my Father."

If Christ was fully human as we are, how did He perfectly represent God's character to the world when we can hardly represent one of His attributes. In other words, what did Christ do that we are not doing? Ellen G. White claims that Christ

> was fitted for the conflict by the indwelling of the Holy Spirit. And He came to make us partakers of the divine nature. So long as we are united to Him by faith, sin has no more dominion over us. God reaches for the hand of faith in us to direct it to lay fast hold upon the divinity of Christ, that we may attain to perfection of character. (Ibid., p. 123)

These ideas of being "partakers of the divine nature" and "united to Him by faith," resulting in liberation from sin's domination over us and allowing for the perfection of character in us, appear theoretically and theologically sound but practically and humanly impossible.

To some Christians, however, these notions are intellectually and spiritually feasible and attainable through our total submission to God. Some are part of a movement in our church who are preaching and teaching total submission only to Christ and He will take care of the rest. In dialoguing with some of them, I have not received, up to this point in time, an explicit enough definition and/or exposition of what it means to be totally submitted to Christ in practical terms without any effort on our part, or is that the effort? If we are to fully represent God's character to the world, the image of God has to be reproduced in us as a clear demonstration of our character transformation and this will not be realized without some effort on our part. Ellen White confirmed this idea when she wrote that "those who are waiting to behold a magical change in their characters without determined effort on their part to overcome sin, will be disappointed" (*Selected Messages*, book 1, p. 336). This serves as a confirmation of James' faith/works theology, principle, and an affirmation of our belief as Adventists on this issue.

The essence of all this is that God has revealed to the human family His character attributes for our finite comprehension of who He is—loving, holy, good, merciful, just, truthful, gracious, faithful, forgiving, patient, impartial, and so much more. He abhors liars, false witnesses and those who shed innocent blood, plan wicked schemes, and are quick to stir up dissension. Paralleling this self-revelation of God is His expectation for His people's loving and willing acceptance of a replication of His character attributes in their lives by the power of the Holy Spirit and their determined effort in order for them to fully represent Him to the world. Impossible? No!! God has provided a Power Source for us to plug into by faith, and if we comply, the power will be ours for character transformation and genuine representation of who He is to the world. He did it for Peter and Paul and numerous others. He will do it for us also.

Such character changes will not be realized unless we begin in earnest to shine the probing light on ourselves and conduct an objectively genuine evaluation of our current spiritual condition in order to compare it with God's expectations/standards for us. This process should provide some insight into the gap that exists between where we are and where we need to be. Some gaps will be wider than others; however, the important thing is not how wide your gap is but how willing and ready you are to make some needed and difficult changes/choices, by the grace of God, that will lead to your total loyalty, commitment, and surrender to Him. Such a transformation will provide, for both individuals and the collective body of Christ, the attraction and credibility in the eyes of the world for the effectuation of a genuine and successful revolutionary movement for Jesus that will usher in the completion of the gospel to all the world and the coming of our Savior, Jesus Christ. What a magnificent day that will be in the history of humanity! Until then, both followers and leaders, all His children, are called to represent His character attributes to the world and that is a significant reason enough to know who God is as is revealed in His Word.

God's Church

The church, the metaphorical body of Christ, is the organizational context within which spiritual shepherd-servants lead and those who are shepherded follow. Fortunately, all church members function in the roles of leaders and followers. Many who do not perform prominent leadership roles in the church are leaders, whether it is in their homes (fathers, mothers, and even siblings), classrooms, Sabbath Schools, jobs, groups, and other organizations. There is, however, One who is our ultimate Leader, and whether we are leaders or followers in the church, we are all followers of Him, Jesus Christ our Lord. In addition, the members, both leaders and followers, are the church, which make it critically important for all to have a comprehensive understanding of its nature, structure, function, and mission in order for them to be aware of the organismic principles that undergird the operation of the body. It is even more critical for those who are providing a shepherd-servant leadership service to have a comprehensive and god-fearing understanding of all components of God's church, due to the enormity of influence exercised by leaders and the negatively serious consequences that may result from a lack of that right biblically-based knowledge and application about and in the church respectively, and leaders' incompetence.

> Not only groups but individuals may seek to reshape the church after their own desires. Certain lay persons, entrenched in power, come to look upon the local church as a personal possession, blocking all change and perpetuating ineffective or unchristian practices. Some ministers continually refer to 'my church' in their conversation and mean it literally. They dominate everything from routine handling of money to designing a new building. They try to use the church to win admiration for themselves as gifted leaders. (Lindgren, *Foundations for Purposeful Church Administration*, pp. 29, 30)

Much truth has been dispensed in this passage by Dr. Lindgren, and he should be applauded for his courage to express these sensitive shortcomings in the church. These are serious issues that are normally "pushed under the rug" and not addressed in any objective and/or systematic manner. People who are cognizant of the sensitivity of these emotionally-laden issues make conscious decisions to avoid any public expression or dialogue involvement for fear of being labeled "trouble makers," resulting in social ostracism and denial of any opportunity to serve in any aspect of church ministry. In addition, there is a general lack of information concerning the parameters of the minister's role and his/her authority/influence and how members should relate to him in a way that is honest and avoids the "wrath of God." There are also many misconceptions about the church in reference to its nature, structure, function, and mission. This chapter will present a picture of the church primarily from a biblical perspective.

Origin of the Church

Due to the fact that this section of the book is not dealing with the evolutionary history of the church, I will briefly mention God's selection of Moses for a special mission to Egypt in Exodus 3 and that which he was later instructed to build in Exodus 25–27. According to the biblical record, God had seen the affliction of His people or "church" and heard their cries of anguish in the state of their Egyptian slavery, and decided to "come down to deliver them out of the hand of the Egyptians" (Exod. 3:7, 8). So He selected Moses as the human instrument through whom He would perform some exceptional miracles that eventually led to the liberation of His people and a forty-year journey through the wilderness that brought them to their destination, the promised land of Canaan.

During their lengthy journey, God instructed Moses, in verses 8 and 9 of Exodus 25, to have the children of Israel build Him a dwelling place amongst them when He said, "Let them make me a sanctuary; that I may dwell among them. According to all that I shew thee, after the pattern of the tabernacle." This was to be a holy place, or sanctuary, and a dwelling place for God amongst His people, and it was built according to the specifications provided by Him. The said structural specifications were a replication of the heavenly sanctuary and thus the beginning of an earthly physical structure known as the sanctuary or God's church on earth. It was built for Him, and even though it was constructed by man, God owned the sanctuary. He is its Originator, Owner, Chief Executive Officer, and President. And as the Originator of the original blueprints, He owns the "eternal copyright" on the sanctuary or Old Testament church, which cannot be taken away from Him. But this does not mean that His people were excluded from the building, because it was His intention for the children of Israel to meet with Him there at His dwelling place (Exod. 29:42–46) for instruction and worship, and eventually with their tithes and a variety of offerings. The original structure was a portable one that was transported or carried on the journey in the wilderness by the Levites and set up where they rested before moving on. The sanctuary eventually became a permanent or fixed structure under King Solomon and was known as the temple.

God's covenant with His people, His "church," was that in exchange for their obedience, He would make them His "treasured possession [out of all nations]. Although the whole world is mine, you will be for me a kingdom of priests and a holy nation" (Exod. 19:5, 6, NIV). In addition to this glorious promise, God was going to raise their status to becoming "the head [of all nations], and not the tail; and thou shalt be above only, and thou shalt not be beneath" and "all people of the earth shall see that thou art called by the name of the LORD" (Deut. 28:13, 10). It is my deepest conviction that the same promise God made to Israel is applicable to His modern-day church as is indicated in 1 Peter 2:9.

There is great uncertainty concerning the identification of what is truly the church of the Old Testament. Is it the sanctuary building? Is it the people called Israelites? Or is it a combination of both people and the sanctuary structure? It is my definitive conclusion that the sanctuary building with the presence of God in the Most Holy

Place made it the most important entity in Israel, His church where the people came to meet with Him. And it is probably from this idea of the holy God dwelling in the sanctuary building that has carried over into the New Testament times and applied to all church buildings as being holy.

Fast forward to the New Testament. Unlike the Old Testament in which there is no specific designation of a church, in the New Testament the word "church" is a translation of the Greek word *ekklesia* (transliteration), which means "a called out" people, or those who have been called out of secular darkness into the marvelous light of Christ. It was used in New Testament times for any called assembly for public meetings, and it was the same word utilized by Jesus and New Testament authors to refer to His church and its various designations such as the following:

1. **A single house congregation** of Christians coming together in loving fellowship for worship, instruction, and other experiences. The church was, therefore, the coming together of two or more Christians for the above purposes. Jesus referred to this concept of church when He said, "For where two or three gather in my name, there am I with them" (Matt. 18:20, NIV). Although this text does not refer directly to those coming together as a church, we have always interpreted it with that meaning in mind. Paul, however, was more specific and direct in referring to the church as the coming together of Christians when he wrote, "I hear that when you come together as a church, there are divisions among you, and to some extent I believe it" (1 Cor. 11:18, NIV).

2. **Several local house congregations** in a particular geographic area. This idea is expressed in Acts 5:11 (NIV) after the death of Ananias and Sapphira, which created an atmosphere of fear in the church, "Great fear seized the whole church [all the churches] and all who heard about these events." Another text supporting this concept of the church is Acts 8:3 (NIV) in which Saul, who became Paul, "began to destroy the church. Going from house to house, he dragged off men and women and put them in prison."

3. **The universal combination of all Christian people as a single church**. This universal concept of the church is expressed by Jesus in the following text in which He stated, "And I tell you that you are Peter, and on this rock I will build my church, and the gates of Hades will not overcome it" (Matt. 16:18, NIV). This text has been misinterpreted for centuries and, therefore, deserves at least a brief explanation. The Greek word *Petros* used for Peter means a small stone, but the word

used by Jesus for rock is *petra,* which means a huge rock or bolder in reference to Himself, not Peter, as the foundation of His church. Jesus did not intend to build His church on a sinful human being. Without Him, we are nothing more than shifting sand and what an unstable foundation that would have been. The other text supporting the above-mentioned concept of the church is written by Paul in which he stated, "Do not cause anyone to stumble, whether Jews, Greeks or the church of God" (1 Cor. 10:32, NIV).

The central idea referred to in the above three meanings of the church is that anywhere God's people are assembled (local house church, modern church building, under a tree, etc.), there is His church. Each house church in the New Testament was referred to as the "church of God." Paul, in 2 Corinthians 1:1, addressed the Christians of Corinth as "the church of God which is at Corinth." A modern-day example would be the people of God assembled for worship, instruction, and/or other experiences, etc. in the city of St. John's, Antigua, West Indies. They are the church of God in that geographic area or locality. The point is that the word *ekklesia* is never used in the New Testament to refer to a church building made of concrete, wood, and/or steel that contains pews or chairs; nor is it the budget, financial reports, or bureaucratic structure. According to William Barclay, the *Seventh-day Adventist Bible Commentary,* and the author, the church of God, by definition, is the men, women, boys, and girls who have accepted Jesus as their Lord and Savior, and have responded to the call to come together as a community of believers in a fellowship of redemptive love and live their lives in a responsively redeeming relationship with Jesus and one another.

These are people who made the decision to allow the Spirit of God to dwell in them and influence their thought processes, as well as control their actions, resulting in a totally different lifestyle from that of the world. Therefore, unless these conditions and changes exist and are effectuated respectively, the church of God is virtually nonexistent (Barclay, *The Mind of St. Paul,* p. 240; *Seventh-day Adventist Bible Commentary,* vol. 10, p. 303).

This is not to suggest that members coming into the body of Christ or His church are joining a perfect body or community of believers. The community consists of fallible people who have determined to live, by the grace of God, a totally different lifestyle compared to the one they lived in the world. And to be very realistic, the church, according to Ellen White, is "enfeebled and defective, needing to be reproved, warned, and counseled" but "is the only object upon earth upon which Christ bestows His supreme regard" (*Testimonies to Ministers and Gospel Workers,* p. 49).

The Structure and Nature of the Church

Metaphorically speaking, the church of God has a two-tier structure. The two components are (1) head and (2) body.

Head

Christ is the foundation of His church: "For no one can lay any foundation other than the one already laid, which is Jesus Christ" (1 Cor. 3:11, NIV). He is Owner of the church because He bought it with His blood (Eph. 5:23; Acts 20:28), and "he is the head of the body, the church" (Col. 1:18, NIV) because "God placed all things under his feet and appointed him to be head over everything for the church, which is his body" (Eph. 1:22, 23, NIV). From a New Testament perspective, therefore, the question of the church's ownership/headship was settled by God, and Jesus through Paul.

So why do we so frequently, according to Lawrence Richards and Clyde Hoeldtke, "treat the pastor and/or other leaders as though they are really the head of the church" (*A Theology of Church Leadership*, p. 275). Christ and Christ alone is the Owner and Head (President and CEO) of the church, yet He took a basin and towel and washed the dirty feet of His disciples (unspeakable humility). He performed the role of a servant as a demonstration of the significant value and indistinguishable worth of serving. As a Servant-Leader and Head, no human being, leaders nor followers, can legitimately usurp this unique position of Jesus in reference to His church.

But what did Paul mean when he claimed that Christ is the Head of the church? Did he mean that Jesus is Ruler, Dictator, and/or Commander-in-Chief who dominates the body because He is Head? A brief exploration of headship in the Old and New Testaments is in order for a clarification of this concept of headship. According to Richards and Hoeldtke, the word used in the Old Testament for head is *r'osh*, which has several usages, a few of which are heads of families (Exod. 6:14); heads of militaries (Judges 11:11); and heads of tribes (2 Chron. 5:2). An analysis of *head* in the Old Testament indicates that the word was applied to human leaders who by virtue of their birth or station (or position) were endowed with great power and authority in these hierarchies that were similarly organized to our modern-day institutions.

An excellent example of the application of this concept of headship is found in Exodus 18:21 in which Moses became the head or leader of the Israelites. He in turn delegated judicatory authority to selected leaders of a lower status to identify and solve problems of a less serious nature, with the most serious cases reaching the

"Supreme Court" of Moses for final adjudication. It is safe to conclude that headship in the Old Testament was of the command-and-control model with leaders having the power and authority to command and control through the delegation of authority (Richards and Hoeldtke, *A Theology of Church Leadership*, p. 16).

Conversely, Jesus introduced/ushered in a new headship/leadership model/paradigm of unprecedented distinction that is fundamentally different to that of the Old Testament, and this is foundationally significant to the organizational structure and leadership within the church. In the New Testament, the word (transliteration) for *head*, according to the two above mentioned authors, is *kepole* (*kephale*), and it is used to designate a person's physical head, a cornerstone. It is used to identify Jesus as the Head of the church and His relationship with it, the body. This idea was expressed by Paul when he wrote, "Wives, submit yourselves to your husbands as you do to the Lord. For the husband is the head of the wife as Christ is the head of the church, his body, of which he is the Savior. Now as the church submits to Christ, so also wives should submit to their husbands in everything" (Eph. 5:22–24, NIV).

But why would Paul make such an unprecedented comparison between the headship of the husband in a marital (husband/wife) relationship to that of the headship of Christ to His church when the husband did not purchase the wife with his blood? The answer is found in Ephesians 5:23, a previously used text, in which Paul admonished husbands to love their wives as Christ loves the church. Christ's love for the church was/is so pure, unconditional, and intense that He gave His life in submission to the Father for its redemption. Submission (*hypotasso*) was not performed out of fear, but "in the sense of voluntary yielding in love" (Richards and Hoeldtke, *A Theology of Church Leadership*, p. 19, see also pp. 16–19). Two ideas are exceptionally clear here, the depth of Christ's love for the church and His role in it salvation. Christ as Head is not a function of dictating and/or imposing His will and desires on the church, but one of providing direction and redemption through His transforming power. His headship was exemplified in the servant model personified in His humility with a basin and towel.

In the process of being our Servant and becoming our Savior during His itinerary on earth, His relationship with His disciples and others was not based on authority, power, and/or privilege, nor was any of these an issue. It was based on love, and when He called anyone or when people were drawn to Him, it was into a loving and redemptive relationship, not one of authoritative command and control. If Christ did not exercise any power or authority, nor expected any special treatment, why would any church leader or husband ever think of invoking any claim to biblical authority (such as "I am the pastor") over God's people or his wife respectively? It appears to me that if the role of Christ in reference to the church is one of providing un-authoritative direction, redemption, and transformation, I am assuming that the role of the husband should be very similar in nature. Husbands should function as saviors in the relationship with their wives. They should seek to protect, build up, serve, and care for in a redemptive manner as the wives submit to them in a mutually beneficial and loving relationship. In addition, husbands, as Christians, are to submit to their wives in the context of the body members relationship as is stated by Paul in Ephesians 5:21 in which he advised the Ephesian Christians to "submit to one another out of reverence for Christ" (NIV).

Headship in the New Testament is very different from that of the Old Testament. It is not lordship, dictatorship, command, and control, but one of leaders exercising the role of saviors in terms of loving, caring, self-giving, protecting, and redeeming for the transforming good of those being served. There is no indication that *head* or *headship* refers to leaders (shepherd leaders) in the body of Christ. Therefore, everything leaders do, according to James Means, should be done "with the supreme consciousness that Christ is the Head of the church and we are his servants here to accomplish his work" (Means, *Leadership in Christian Ministry*, p. 68). It is our individual responsibility to learn to look to Jesus, the Supreme Head of the church, for direction and guidance through His word and the Holy Spirit, and not necessarily to human leaders because their leadership role cannot be substituted for the headship role of Jesus over the church.

In Jesus, we are "neither Jew nor Greek, neither slave nor free, nor is there male and female, for you are all one in Christ Jesus" (Gal. 3:28, NIV). We are one in Him, yet we have a variety of roles to perform in God's church and no one role can claim "monarch of all I survey"; no role is given a command-and-control responsibility; no role is given a lordship function to lord it over God's people; and no role can claim the headship of Christ in an attempt to usurp any of His prerogatives because none of us is like Him. We are all sinners and at the same level at the foot of the cross. In addition, God has called us into a deep, intimate, loving, and redemptive relationships with Him and each other, not one of lord-leaders and servants-followers respectively. This should be our guiding principle in the body of Christ. His lordship only must be lifted up!

Body of Christ, His Church

Christ is the Head and we, the church, are the metaphorical body. Why are we referred to as the body of Christ? There is an underlying principle to this reference, and it is the "organic unity" of the body. In 1 Corinthians 12:27 Paul wrote: "Now you are the body of Christ, and each one of you is a part of it" (NIV). In Ephesians 5:30

he reiterates the body concept of those who have accepted Christ as Lord and Savior when he wrote to the Ephesian Christians, "for we are members of his body." If we are the body and Christ is the Head of the body, it follows that we are, in a figurative sense (could it be in a literal sense in that the Spirit is united with us, thus providing the link to Christ), linked to each other and united with Christ in the body through the presence of the Holy Spirit which is a consequence of our total submission to Him. If Christ is the Head, He is the intellectual and spiritual Source of the body that should accept and follow His directions and guidance only as are outlined in His Word and confirmed by the Spirit.

Head-Body Connection

There is a great amount to be gained when we stay connected to the Head (Christ) and much to lose when we disconnect. Jesus declares in no uncertain terms that "I am the vine; you are the branches. If you remain in me and I in you, you will bear much fruit; apart from me you can do nothing" (John 15:5, NIV). This is an unequivocal statement of body members' relationship of total dependence on Him, the Head of the body and the One who controls all body functions, something that cannot be delegated to any body part/member. The maintenance of that connection with the Head is critical for the survival and spiritual maturity of the body. It is not an off-and-on thing that is done today and not tomorrow. It is to be maintained on a continuous basis as Jesus did with the Father when He was here on earth and as Paul wrote about "dying daily" in Jesus. It is this consistent connection with Him that will cause us to think, act, and say things (including our body language and attitude) differently compared to the world. We will be in harmony with His word. We are the *hagios*, or saints, who are spiritually minded and different from those who are secularly oriented (this idea of saints will be given greater attention later).

But how do we maintain our connection with Him? The following notions are things we talk about as Adventists, but we seem not to put genuine priority on any of them: (a) daily Bible study; (b) consistent communication through prayer, meditation, and reflection; (c) worship, thanksgiving, and praise, and (d) being responsive to the Spirit's pleading. Some may think that this type of connection is too ideal and unrealistic based on the innumerable responsibilities that saturate our busy lives in this modern and complex world. As Christians, however, we need to emphasize and place priority on, not the ephemeral, but things that pertain to our eternal destiny. God must take center stage in our lives, or there will be a disconnect that leads to the unspiritual.

Paul warns against those with "hollow and deceptive philosophy, which depends on human tradition and the elemental spiritual forces of this world rather than on Christ" as well as "anyone who delights in false humility and the worship of angels" (Col. 2:8, 18, NIV) because such a person is puffed up with idle notions and has "lost connection with the head" (verse 19). There is no doubt that as Christians, if we do not maintain our connection with Christ through our total submission to Him, things will subtly creep in to create an unspiritual mind. The battle between good and evil is for the mind, and when it is captured by evil, there goes the soul. We must guard the avenues of our souls by guarding those of our minds.

The Body (Church) Function

When we come together as a church, how are we to relate to one another in our various functional roles? From a biological perspective, we are cognizant of the divisions of the human body into cells, organs, and systems that are of distinct size, shape, and function, separated but linked to each other for the sharing of oxygen, nutrients, and waste extraction for the survival of the whole body. In other words, the parts of the body are not independent and unrelated, but interdependent and interrelated because they must function cooperatively for their own survival and that of the whole body. This means that all parts are important and play vital roles for the growth and development of the body. It is, therefore, obvious that the body functions on the organic (organismic) unity principle, and it is after this organic model that Paul intended the church to pattern its operations. Paul wrote, "So in Christ we, though many, form one body, and each member belongs to all the others" (Rom. 12:5, NIV) and "just as a body, though one, has many parts, but all its many parts form one body, so it is with Christ" (1 Cor. 12:12, NIV).

In spite of our size, height, racial, ethnic, and cultural differences, when body members come together as a church, no one is inferior and no one is superior. No one is more important than the other; we all have significant roles to perform in the building up of the body and sharing the love of God to each other and non-body members. This means that even those members who are perceived to be weak and play less important roles are indispensable and should be treated with "special honor" (1 Cor. 12:22, 23).

Members of the body of Christ are required to function in a similar manner to the parts of an organism, harmonious in nature for the benefit of all and based on the all-important principles of love and unity. Neither individuals nor groups of members are given the prerogative to operate in a manner that controls other members. Remember, the Head is the only part with the authority to exercise any control over the body or church, and He does not do so in a controlling sense. This is the fundamental reason why the body of Christ should not be classified as an institution. Institutions are comprised of hierarchical structures and member rankings that are designed to give power and authority (control) to the few over the many.

If the church is organized and operates on the bases of institutional principles, it "robs us [Christian lives] of our awareness of the supernatural" due to the shift in foci on the maintenance of the institution and all that it entails, and "the more we tend to view the church of Jesus as an institution the more we minister in the institutional mold. But the church is not an institution. And we are not its managers" (Richards and Hoeldtke, *A Theology of Church Leadership*, p. 75). When the church functions as an institution, it ceases to function in like manner to an organism as Paul intended. And there are some clear indications that our church is organized and functioning on some quasi institutional principles. The ranking of church officers, especially the elders in the local church being ranked as "the highest and most important" in the body, outranked only by the pastor; and that a conference/mission/field committee is not permitted to "confer on a local church elder the status which is granted to an ordained minister to serve other churches as elder" (*Seventh-day Adventist Church Manual*, 16th ed., pp. 47, 49), is by implication a provision of power and authority granted to these individuals over the local church based on their "positions."

The authority of church leaders will be dealt with later in this book, but for now, let us go back to ranking and its consequences. One of the very serious consequence of ranking is the failure of the church to fulfill its purpose due to bureaucratic infighting, destructive power struggles, and parochial politics to ensure that certain individuals and groups are placed in the top "positions" in order to maintain control of the church and its limited resources. During these insidious processes, conflict is produced that results in vexation, animosity, and prolonged bitterness that in turn kills creative thinking while alienating and frustrating many. This situation leads to disharmonious/unhealthy relationships and failure to focus on the true goals of the church. It was Wofford and Killinski who wrote that "the church is failing to fulfill its purpose largely because it has ceased to be an organism." They go on to write on the same page that "a church in which one person preaches, a few teach, and a few others work in administrative ministry, but the vast majority simply listen, learn, and follow without," strangely "becoming functioning members of the body, is not an integrated organism" (*Organization and Leadership in the Local Church,* p. 134).

Another serious consequence of position/office ranking is the spirit of self-importance that many leaders attribute to themselves as well as that importance that is perceived and provided by members. This type of thinking leads body members to look to human church leaders instead of to Christ, His Word, and the Holy Spirit for direction and guidance. Under such circumstances many followers/members are very reluctant to make any decision before seeking the approbation of leaders, even if the decision may be potentially beneficial to the body. Many grand opportunities to move the church forward are missed because many perceive the control of leaders to be too strangulating and decide against doing anything for the church.

I hope we never get to the position of a railroad company with a branch and agents in India. An agent was reprimanded on a few occasions for making independent decisions that were beneficial to the company but fell in the controlling category of headquarters' responsibility. One day, the said agent sent a telegram to his superior at headquarters which read, "Tiger on platform eating conductor. Wire instruction."

What the church needs today is not ranking for control purposes, but leadership/followership training throughout the church, because genuine Christian leaders understand how to follow intelligently and lead effectively when either occasion arises because we are all leaders and followers, and equal at the foot of the cross. Positions mean nothing to God, His interest is in our character development.

The Underpinning Principle of Body/Church Function

Paul uses the imagery of the human body function in his metaphorical description of the unified manner in which the body of Christ (the church) ought to operate/function. The underlying principle of this picture is the *unity of the church*. But how is the church to make this principle a reality in its life when there are so many personal and systemic factors that appear to be both a natural (sheep and goats in the church) and manmade outgrowth of people coming together in some organized way which keep the human family and many churches divided? The evidence is exceptionally clear that a united church is a powerful testimony to the world that God sent His Son to reveal His love through Christ's sacrificial death on the cross (John 17:21). So how do we, as a body, transcend these personal and systemic potential dividers in order to achieve a more acceptable unified state?

As was mentioned earlier, Paul likened the human body function to the operations of the church, and if the church is going to function in an organismic manner, its members "need close and intimate relationship" because "in an organism, only those cells that are in intimate relationship with each other can share their resources or heal their hurts" (Richards and Hoeldtke, *A Theology of Church Leadership*, p. 48). This kind of organismic sharing and member involvement, and a sense of equality among them in terms of the value placed on the contribution and worth of each member to the building up and advancement of the body are critical

Chapter 1 God and His Church

to the maintenance of a unified state. Equality of value/worth and contribution based on each member's gift, no matter how small or great, is the operative idea.

No matter what the role is of each member, none is of greater value or worth in God's sight. Therefore, according to Paul in 1 Corinthians 12:14–16, the eye cannot say to the feet, "I have no need of you so I will pluck myself from the body and go on my merry way." The eye will not survive independently of the body. It needs to remain in an intimate relationship with the body to receive the necessary oxygen and energy for its growth and development. In like manner, a church member cannot withdraw from the body and expect to share in its resources that are vital to each member's spiritual survival. All need to be in that critically redemptive and intimate relationship, united in spirit and working in harmony in order to experience the gift of unity that the Spirit offers to the church.

A prerequisite to this type of relationship is the genuine body demonstration of equal concern for all members that will facilitate the entering into the experiences of one another and truly sense what each other is feeling in order to show real compassion. Paul's advice is that "there should be no division in the body, but that its parts should have equal concern for each other. If one part suffers, every part suffers with it; if one part is honored, every part rejoices with it" (1 Cor. 12:25, 26, NIV). What Paul is saying is that the parts of the human body are so intimately linked to the head that if one part becomes dysfunctional and is hurting due to a diseased condition the whole body or all other members will experience the said hurt. In like manner, if church members are linked to the Head (Jesus Christ) and one another, it becomes virtually impossible for them not to sense the hurt and joys of other members. Body members who genuinely love and deeply care about each other will reflect it not only in their words but in spirit and conduct. Church members who genuinely love God, one another, and non-church people will base their thinking and behavior on the principles of the Word and will not show favoritism but will demonstrate equality of concern for all as difficult as this may seem to institute. Remember that the grace of God is sufficient to achieve anything.

When we cultivate healthy relationships based on the unconditional love of God for all human beings and particularly for body members through the indwelling of the Spirit, when we, in essence, decide to apply the word of God in its entirety to the totality of our lives, we will experience the fruit of unity that is so critical to the advancement of God's cause on earth, that "the world may believe that you have sent me" (John 17:21, NIV).

Christ, the Head of the body, prayed very sincerely and passionately for the unity of the church. In John 17:11 Jesus, in His prayer to the Father, prayed for His current disciples "that they may be one as we are one" and also for those "who will believe in me through their message, that all of them may be one, Father, just as you are in me and I am in you. May they also be in us so that the world may believe that you have sent me" (verse 20). In verse 22 He continued: "they may be brought to complete unity. Then the world will know that you sent me and have loved them even as you have loved me."

There is something compellingly attractive about a united group of people that grabs one's attention and interest. This heightened interest may be based on the inherent beauty and intrinsic value of unity as compared to the unattractive nature of conflict and division in our global society. Whatever the reason(s), Jesus introduced in His prayer the significance of our relationship with Him and each other. A genuine connection with Him will result in the internalization of His principles and their reflection in our lives—thoughts, words, and actions—as we relate to both Christians and non-Christians. Church members who are united with Him and one another send a clear and powerful message to all people about the love of God and the redemptive mission of Christ to our world.

In addition to sending a powerful message, God is displeased when church members (His children and earthly family) are at "war" with one another and involved in a wrong course of action. Ellen White wrote, "The sin of one man discomfited the entire army of Israel. A wrong course pursued by one toward his brother will turn the light of God from His people until the wrong is searched out and the cause of the oppressed is vindicated" (*Testimonies for the Church*, vol. 3, p. 519). That which is even more troubling is the expectation that a church functioning on organismic principles makes us more vulnerable due to our willingness to be open in the sharing of our lives and, therefore, much more aware of each other's spiritual growth and shortcomings. This in turn makes us responsible for each other, and God will hold us, as a church, accountable for the secret sin(s) of members as He held Israel for the sin of Achan.

Ellen White writes in no uncertain terms that "for one man's sin the displeasure of God will rest upon His church till the transgression is searched out and put away." She concluded that "with humiliation and searching of heart, let each seek to discover the hidden sins that shut out God's presence" (*Patriarchs and Prophets,* p. 497). This task is much easier to accomplish when a church understands the significance of being united in Christ and is willing to pursue the right course of action to maintain God's ideal in reference to unity in His church.

Unity, therefore, is paramount in Christ's body (the church) and every effort (at almost any cost) should be made to preserve it. This should be uppermost in our consciousness, and vigilance should be the order of the day because where two or three are gathered, the Spirit is there to bless but the evil one is also there to upset. And when we allow the evil one to use us to upset the unity of the church, the destructive consequences may take years to erase or resolve.

The criticality of the state of church unity is expressed by James Means in the following statement: "Church cohesiveness is more important than any possible decision on an issue. The loss of church unity is disastrous to public testimony and to interpersonal relationships" (*Leadership in Christian Ministry*, p. 87). Inherent in this statement is Means' understanding of the high value of church unity. He gives more credence and preference to it over the church's decision on any issue it will make in the course of its operation and mentions two of the serious consequences of disunity as negative public testimony and unhealthy interpersonal relationships.

Jesus alluded to the serious consequences of the loss of unity when He mentioned in Luke 11:17 about a divided kingdom and house, the end results being ruin and destruction respectively. Ellen G. White corroborates the consequences of a divided church in *Testimonies for the Church*, volume 5, in which she wrote that "divisions in the church dishonor the religion of Christ before the world and give occasion to the enemies of truth to justify their course" (p. 239). The late William Barclay takes the idea of a divided church even further in his book *The Mind of St. Paul* when he wrote that "when a church is divided in spirit and in heart, when bitterness has invaded its fellowship, when the unforgiving spirit has caused breaches which remain un-healed, the church ceases to be a church, for a church is no church unless it be a brotherhood" (pp. 240, 241).

If Barclay is correct, and I sincerely believe he is, then there are many churches that are, in essence, not true churches but social clubs because their operations are so political in nature that they can probably be sadly classified as political organizations. But how do these churches move from this politically quasi state of being church to one of unity, at least, in spirit, objective/goal and beliefs, without members striving for supremacy that plagued the disciples of Christ when He was with them on earth? The following are critical to the maintenance of church unity in addition to much of the aforementioned.

Equality of the Saints/Members

Inequality is rampant in the church. There exists amongst the saints, racial, ethnic, national, socio-economic, and educational differences/barriers, but in Galatians 3:26–29, Paul affirmed the equality of all saints (males and females) and declared the transcendence of unity in Christ over these socio-political and sexual barriers. I assume that Paul clearly understood the serious consequences of such barriers and that the disenfranchisement of people leads to resentment, anger, bitterness, division, and rebellion/anomie that will tear asunder the very fabric of any group or society, including the church. What is disturbing about this quasi caste system in the body are:

1. that many saints are cognizant of their existence but seem to accept them as part of the natural order of things in the church;

2. that too many members are fearful to raise them due to the sensitivity of these issues and the socio-political consequences associated with them, and so they are left unquestioned and pushed under the rug;

3. that there are some brave souls (this is extremely disturbing) who dear to or are bold enough to raise those issues and suffer the wrath of those in the "power structure" of the body; and

4. that the beneficiaries of these artificial barriers (and this is most disturbing) not only accept and cherish, and leave the issues unaddressed for fear of losing the privileges associated with them, but also that they are used at times as psychological weapons to maintain the status quo.

Where there is no equality, where some people are treated as inferior to others, where the above-mentioned barriers are utilized as blocks to saints' interaction, healthy relationships, issuance of social invitations and office denial is an unequivocal indication of the absence of true love. And where there is no love, there will certainly be no equality; and where there is no equality, there will be no justice; and where there is no justice, there will be no peace and *unity*. The absence of these creates a psychological sense of emptiness and despair, and leaves a vacuum that provides the breeding ground for dissension, conflict, suspicion, political divisions, and the eventual destruction of the body spirit, as well as many leaving the church for a lack of difference in behavior between the church and our secular society. It is important to remember that:

> The secret of unity is found in the equality of believers in Christ. The reason for all division, discord, and difference is found in separation from Christ. Christ is the center to which all should be attracted; for the nearer we approach the center, the closer we shall come together in feeling, in sympathy, in love, growing into the character and image of Jesus. With God there is no respect of persons. (White, *Selected Messages*, book 1, p. 258)

She goes on to write that when we look to Calvary and see the Royal Sufferer bearing the curse of the law for us "all national distinctions, all sectarian differences are obliterated; all honor or rank, all pride of caste is lost" because the light shining from the throne of God on Calvary extinguishes the manmade separation flames of "class and race. Men of every class become members of one family, children of the heavenly King" (Ibid.). As Christians, we have voluntarily accepted to become members of the united family of God in which all are treated as equals regardless of their educational, financial, socio-economic, racial, or ethnic standing in society. This will not materialize by osmosis, but by focused, concerted, and consistent effort from both leaders and followers in their attempts to eradicate all the subtle, blatant, structural, and cultural barrier symbols that have been transplanted from the world to the body of Christ.

A few examples of these are systemic/clergy/personal pulpit ownership; first lady; head tables in which a certain class of God's children are allowed the freedom to eat all they want while others are "forced" to stand in line and served limited food; special parking spaces for "church officials"; ranking of church officers; exclusive invitations to dinners and other social events while the disenfranchised are excluded, etc. These systemic and social trappings provide the holders of certain positions with a sense of superior worth and importance over others, which results in a psychological defeat and sense of unworthiness for those who are consistently excluded. The need for change in these and other areas is urgent, but it will not be easy to begin the processes of thinking and implementing Paul's notion of "preferring one another" over ourselves or even loving our neighbor as ourselves. His grace is sufficient!

Election

This is one of the most divisive processes undertaken in local churches on an annual basis and throughout the administrative divisions of many church organizations, although less so at the latter level. It is during this time when many church members and some on the nominating committee go deep-sea fishing to retrieve many of the mistakes (sins) of those whom they want to deny certain offices, and they use their "catch" as leverage to accomplish their pernicious desires/plans. My perspective on this issue is that if a member knows of improprieties of other members and refuses to follow the biblical injunction in order to restore those members, or refuses to request assistance in so doing, that those individuals should be denied the opportunity to communicate any such information to the committee during elections. This is not to suggest that serious infractions of biblical principles should not be investigated and appropriate actions taken in the spirit of love and compassion, but such members should not be allowed to use the election process as a political tool or means of exposing the sins of others in order to block their chances of holding certain offices when there was sufficient opportunity for restoration prior to the elections.

The following election experience may appear to be an aberration, but similar ones exist in numerous churches that employ the same system of electing church officers. It is included in this book as an example of what can happen (but should not be allowed to occur) in churches when members are not properly informed or do not buy into the established definition or explanation of the nature of the body of Christ or the church. Or when members do not submit to the influence of the Spirit of God and ignore both the biblically foundational principles and precepts upon which they should order their lives, and the established policies that are designed in good faith and with noble intentions of producing relatively smooth and fair elections.

When the said good-intention electoral system is implemented, there is always the possibility for unfair charges to be voiced at both the leader and system particularly when the rules are not followed, and all "hell can break loose" even in the church because such members are also emotional beings, and when not under the influence of the Spirit, they are liable to do almost anything. I know of certain elections in which provocative things were said that evoked such negative feelings, some members became engaged in physical altercations or fights.

The aberrant election I referred to in the above paragraph is one that should never be allowed to occur in any church. It involved (and this is the short version of it) a relatively well educated pastor who was young and inexperienced. On many occasions he referred to his position as the pastor of the church as an invocation of his authority to get his way by saying, "I am the pastor," and when one is engaged in such a declaration of his/her position for intimidation purposes or for the submission of one's opinion or will to that of the pastor's "superior" will, he has very little left. He manipulated the steering committee process to eventually stack the nominating committee with his supporters, but he only partially succeeded. When a meeting was called to nominate the officers for the new year, five (a majority) of the nine-member elected nominating committee were absent, yet the pastor and the remaining members selected the entire slate of officers in one setting or meeting and took it to the church as the work of the nominating committee. The church, being unaware of the diabolical process, voted to accept the names as officers for the ensuing year. Subsequent to taking that vote, the pastor walked off the pulpit area without informing the church that he had been transferred and would not be returning as the pastor of the church. Unfortunately, fourteen months have elapsed since he left, and the church has not even begun to recover from the division created by that arrogant disregard for the right of the elected majority on the nominating committee to participate in the selection of the officers.

Several significant principles were violated, and they are as follows:

1. **Jury principle** – Nominating committees do not have quorums, the reason for alternates. This means that the number of members voted on such a committee must be present for the committee to do its work, even if one or more alternates has to be included.

2. **Fairness principle** – In order for the process to be perceived as fair, the rules or policies that govern the electoral process must be implemented and not circumvented.

3. **Right–doing principle** – This is clearly stated in James 4:17, "Therefore to him that knoweth to do good, and doeth it not, to him it is sin." No further explanation is needed.

4. **Honesty principle** – By not informing the church of the number of members who were excluded from performing the assigned task for which they were elected, the impression was given that the appointed nominating committee had fulfilled its responsibility as was expected. The exclusion of this information was probably unintended, but it was still deceptive.

5. **Love principle** – If the love of God existed in some small portion in the hearts of the leader and minority committee members such an action would never have been pursued.

When things go wrong, whom do we blame? We are generally inclined to blame the leaders and forget to examine the faulty system that may be contributing to the problem in significant ways. There are no perfect systems, but some by design inherently work better than others based on the nature of the organization in which they are implemented. By their very nature, however, electoral systems are problematic due to the inherent element or principle of competition. An election that is designed to select candidates and elect one (or many) to an office(s) that is perceived to be inherently powerful, always involve some form of competition. Whether the system is intentionally designed to eliminate such a principle from the process does not mean that it is extracted from the minds of those participating in the election.

Inevitably, there will always be some level of dissatisfaction due to the fact that there will be a winner(s) and loser(s), and no one enjoys losing. And if the dissatisfaction crosses the threshold of what is considered acceptable by too many members, there will be trouble. The church is supposed to be an unconventional body in which members do not compete against each other but cooperate as a matter of principle with one another for the realization of the church's mission and the vindication of God's name. Any competitive process, programmatic or electoral in nature, that produces or encourages unhealthy reactions should be eliminated from church activities. Do not take any established system for granted. Evaluate and/or assess all programs that are creating negative outcomes and replace them with more cohesive and beneficial operations.

Although the system may be faulty, we are still very inclined to focus on and blame our leaders when things go wrong. Inevitably, leaders bear the brunt of responsibility for making sure that things are done decently and in order regardless of the nature of the system. They are required to implement the principles and policies in the administration of the affairs of the church, and when courageous and enlightened members perceive political shenanigans, they will not keep quiet or submit their will to that of the leaders. Spiritual leaders are required to lovingly yet courageously uplift the standards of the church in all circumstances, and when they fail to do so, they should be held accountable for their actions. Those who are willing to play the politically convenient games for their own or their supporters' benefit will soon realize the wrath of God emanating from many members. Always remember to stand firm on the principles of the word of God and He will stand with you.

In light of the significance of church unity and the problematic nature of the electoral process, it is time to give due consideration to the issue in order to develop a less divisive method or procedure. It cannot be overstressed that once the genie is out of the bottle, it cannot be retrieved. In other words, when we say destructive things about each other, the words cannot be taken back. When feelings are hurt, the emotional scars take longer to heal than physical ones. Church members under spiritual construction feel some of the same or similar emotions experienced by those involved in secular elections. When certain people are elected to offices solely for political reasons and for which they are not gifted/qualified, it is very difficult not to sense some negative feelings and question the process.

It is my position that less politically and/or emotionally-driven alternatives are available and should be implemented to preserve the unity of the church and vindicate God's name. These are as follows:

1. **Multiple Names Per Office Ballot** – If the current system is maintained, a ballot sheet should be provided with at least two names and a blank space to write in one's choice for each office/ministry. This is a way of providing God's people with the freedom to exercise their

discretion in their individual selection of those whom they think are most gifted for each office. By so doing, each member is given the opportunity to make a selection of one of the nominating committee's submissions and/or to submit his/her own choice. This approach should allow for less controversy because when the vote is counted, everyone would have had the chance to select a name or to submit one per office and not be completely locked into the block of names recommended by the said committee. If the names submitted and/or selected are eliminated in the process, there is no need to complain. In addition, there would be no need to make an objection and have the entire slate of names returned to the committee due to a question one may have about a single name, which gives cause to label the objector as a troublemaker.

2. **Voluntary System** – This idea changes the names of the church departments to ministries (e.g. Sabbath School Department to Sabbath School Ministries). This results in the literal and psychological elimination of the bureaucratic name association/implication and provides a more spiritual and caring overtone. Church members would be given the opportunity to volunteer their time and services in the ministries of their choice and for which they know themselves to be gifted. Someone would then be appointed to call the first meeting of each ministry once sufficient volunteers have filled the quotas. (Meetings could be staggered if there are crossovers or volunteers are in more than one ministry.) During each ministry meeting, leaders would be selected/chosen/elected to lead/guide each ministry in the realization of the church's goals. The leaders of the various ministries and others designated by the church would form the administrative board of the church and would be responsible for the formulation of suggested decisions, all of which would have to be ratified by the church body in fellowship sessions. It is my understanding that the implementation of one of the above methods would create a sense of greater individual involvement in the process and an atmosphere of electoral ownership and fairness which should contribute to attitude changes and greater acceptance of the results.

Unity and Relationship Building

Healthy Christian relationships that promote body unity and church progress are based on kingdom principles. This means that, if we are going to experience body/church unity as was expressed by Christ, we need to build more intimate relationships in which love, humility, gentleness, patience, mutual submission, and other kingdom principles are embraced and consciously applied in our interactions as we attempt to build up the body and effectuate unity. This to many may appear to be only theoretical and/or unrealistic due to the fact that there are both "sheep" and "goats," "wheat" and "tares" in the family of God on earth and that we are still living in an evil world. Many in the body may be inclined to take advantage of a situation of this nature in the church, but we are admonished to be as "wise as serpents, and harmless as doves" (Matt. 10:16). And if even a few behave like "sheep in wolves' clothing," let it be. It is far more important to base our relationships on biblical principles as a powerful testimony to them and the world.

In addition to the potency of such a testimony, when body members cultivate healthy relationships and continue to do so on a consistent basis, resulting in greater peace and harmony, they will be more likely and willing to share information, time, and energy than when division is the order of the day. They are generally more inclined to be involved in building up, rather than tearing down, thus facilitating body growth and unity.

Body or Church Growth and Development

Paul refers to the organismic nature of the church when he compared it to a living organism. The idea is that just as living organisms grow and develop over time, in like manner, so does the church. He refers to some church members in 1 Corinthians 3:1, 2 (supported in 1 Peter 2:2) as babes requiring spiritual milk and solid food to others who are fully grown or matured in Christ (Heb. 5:14). Organisms require energy in order for them to grow and develop, and the church needs intellectual and spiritual energy for its growth to maturity in Christ. But what is the nature of this growth? How does the body grow? And who is responsible for its growth?

According to Richards and Hoeldtke in *A Theology of Church Leadership*, there are three words related to growth in the New Testament and these are *oikodomeo, auxano, and teleios*.

Oikodomeo means "to build up," to strengthen, or edify as in 1 Peter 2:5 in which Christians are referred to as living stones being built into a spiritual house, the mutual edification benefit of believer to believer ministry in Romans 14:19, and the encouragement given to build up each other in 1 Thessalonians 5:11. This edification concept is extremely critical to the spiritual advancement of the body toward maturity in Christ as well as its numerical growth, and it is one of the primary responsibilities assigned to the New Testament elders, which will be discussed in the chapter on church leadership. Paul wrote about "growing in the knowledge of God" (Col. 1:10, NIV) and Peter admonishes us to "grow in the grace and knowledge or our Lord and Savior Jesus Christ" (2 Peter 3:18, NIV). These admonitions seem to suggest both intellectual and spiritual growth.

Auxano is used in designation with living things; numerical growth as in Acts 7:17 and 2:41, and with God's work in the body as is found in Colossians 2:19, which appears to be the primary theological use in the New Testament. However, too many people in the church, particularly leaders, lay claim to and take credit for both the spiritual and numerical growth of the body of Christ, and programs are instituted to recognize and reward those who are given credit for God's work in the body. Plaques are presented to leaders and evangelists are sent on expensive trips instead of giving God the praise and thanks for His work in the church. How difficult it is for us to discredit our efforts and remember who is responsible for the real growth of the body as Paul wrote: "I planted the seed, Apollos watered it, but God has been making it grow. So neither the one who plants nor the one who waters is anything, but only God, who makes things grow" (1 Cor. 3:6, 7, NIV)

Teleios means that maturing growth in Christ, completeness and full grown as is stated in Hebrews 5:14. This type of growth is inextricably linked to the *oikodomeo* growth that is the edification of or the building up of the body toward maturity in Christ. If this critical component/process is absent in the body, in conjunction with the Holy Spirit, the body is less likely to effectuate its mission or purpose for its existence (Richards and Hoeldtke, *A Theology of Church Leadership.*, pp. 45, 46).

Even though the Adventist Church has instituted some structural components designed for the intellectual and spiritual edification of the body, they appear to be insufficient and not highly effective in achieving the intended outcome. Too many of us neglect the reading, never mind the study of, the Bible; too many are willing to tear down rather than build each other up; there is too much in-fighting, conflicts, animosity, and bitterness created by a number of situations (including the election process and personality clashes) that are left unresolved and are retarding the spiritual development of the body and reducing the impact/influence of the church in its external mission to the world. The significant question here is how do we, as the body of Christ, move from our current status quo to a much better future state in reference to growing to maturity in Christ?

Healthy Body Relations

Changing our current status in order to achieve a better future state is going to require the making of some difficult choices. Many of us have an adverse feeling toward any type of change due to the anxiety that it creates and the uncertainty of the outcome. Change also requires us to modify or totally change our mindset in order to make the necessary behavior modification demands of the change. Like it or not, change is occurring around us daily and for us to grow and develop in Jesus, it is necessary to make changes in our lives as to how we relate to others in and out the body of Christ.

We live in relationships and their healthy maintenance is critical to our success in life because "no man is an island." Christ has called us into loving and redemptive relationships with Him and each other, and any disruption in these relationships may result in conflict, distrust and/or division. Growing in Christ requires warm, loving, intimate, and trustworthy (healthy) relationships that do not occur by osmosis or just by attending church services. These types of relationships are realized through great effort, time, and the grace of God. But in spite of these, the body membership must give priority to the internal cultivation of healthy relationships instead of programs and policy formulations. Paul made it very clear when he wrote in 1 Corinthians 12:25, 26 "that there should be no division in the body, but that its parts should have equal concern for each other. If one part suffers, every part suffers with it; if one part is honored, every part rejoices with it" (NIV). Behaving in such a manner is alien to many of us, but it is a behavioral change that is necessary for good body relationships. Principles, not political alliances, should form the basis or foundation of our relationships; any other guideline can create problems in the body.

Healthy relationships help to create an environment in which Christians can flourish in their spiritual growth toward maturity in Jesus. Just like an athlete focuses on training (taking the time out to do so) in order to build a healthy body because he/she is better able to compete with it than with an unhealthy body, the church needs to zero in on healthy relationship building because God can better use a healthy church than one that is "sick." Much more will be presented in this area later in this book.

Gifts Utilization in the Body

I have often been puzzled by the idea that gifts are distributed by the Holy Spirit to individual members for the common good of the body and that the New Testament elders were appointed to church leadership but that in the modern church, the election process is utilized to select members for certain positions/offices or functional roles. The rationale for the application of this process is understood, particularly in a democratic society, as an attempt to involve as many members as possible in the process. Great good can emerge from such a process if the church, as an integrated whole is functioning/operating on divine principles and every member is given equal selection opportunity, and each is selected on the basis of his/her demonstrated gifts to serve in a corresponding/matching capacity or ministry. Conversely, the election process can have a debilitating effect on a church that is more or less divided into cliques and almost every decision is made along "party line." The process will result in people being given offices for which they are not "qualified" (have no gift), which will in turn stymie church operations when dissatisfaction causes others to withdraw their services from the body. This is a situation that church leaders should do their utmost to prevent while recognizing the importance of keeping the whole body involved..

Member involvement/participation in the work of the church is one of the significant components of church growth. Just as all the parts of an organism need to be functioning in a cooperative manner for it to grow and develop to maturity, in like manner, all church members need to use their imparted gifts for the common good because it is in an organic relationship of gifts utilization that the body will grow to maturity in Christ. Ellen G. White wrote that "every church member should be engaged in some line of service for the Master.... Many would be willing to work if they were taught how to begin. They need to be instructed and encouraged" (*The Ministry of Healing*, p. 149).

The realization of the above is a serious challenge for church leaders and it is one of their major responsibilities. Building up the body of Christ through instruction and encouragement is of great necessity if the church is going to reach maturity in Christ. In addition, members need not only to be instructed for their own development, but they need to be taught how (method) to teach/impart their knowledge/experiences in a manner that is effective in terms of producing changes in the lives of those taught. This is part of the training of a good disciple. Ellen G. White provides confirmation of this idea when she wrote:

> The church of Christ is organized for service. Its watchword is ministry. Its members are soldiers, to be trained for conflict under the Captain of their salvation. Christian ministers, physicians, teachers have a broader work than many have recognized. They are not only to minister to the people, but to teach them to minister. They should not only give instruction in right principles, but educate their hearers to impart these principles. Truth that is not lived, that is not imparted, loses its life-giving power, its healing virtue. Its blessing can be retained only as it is shared. (*The Ministry of Healing*, pp. 148, 149)

Another challenge for church leaders is providing assistance to members in their discovery of their gifts, because if they are unaware of their gifts, how will they be able to apply them in the body for the common good? But what are those gifts? Paul not only delineates the gifts but also admonishes that the opportunity for their utilization should be allowed:

> We have different gifts, according to the grace given to each of us. If your gift is prophesying, then prophesy in accordance with your faith; if it is serving, then serve; if it is teaching, then teach; if it is to encourage, then give encouragement; if it is giving, then give generously; if it is to lead, do it diligently; if it is to show mercy, do it cheerfully. (Rom. 12:6–8, NIV)

The gifts mentioned above are prophesying, serving, teaching, encouraging, giving, leading, and showing mercy. Other gifts are wisdom and knowledge, faith, healing, miraculous powers, prophecy, distinguishing between spirits, speaking in tongues, miracle workers, helpers, administration, and God's appointed apostles, prophets, and teachers (1 Cor. 12:7–10, 28), and in Ephesians 4:11 it says that "Christ himself gave the apostles, the prophets, the evangelists, the pastors and teachers" (NIV).

It is quite obvious that there are some overlapping of gifts in the texts mentioned above and that they are multiple and very different in nature. There is no indication that any gift is of more value or worth that another or should be used for competitive purposes. Equality in terms of value is what Paul intended since the parts of an organism are of equal worth, are interdependent, and need to function cooperatively for the good of the organism. The body of Christ must function in like manner for the realization of its survival, maturity development, and mission or purpose fulfillment. Unfortunately, the modern church has placed greater value on certain offices and has even ranked these in an attempt to accord more authority to the holders of these positions at the expense of the underlying principle of equality of gifts. What is of greater significance is why were the gifts given to the body or church members?

Once again, we turn to the God-given wisdom of Paul who unequivocally stated that the gifts were given "to equip his people for works of service, so that the body of Christ may be built up until we all reach unity in the faith and in the knowledge of the Son of God and become mature, attaining to the whole measure of the fullness of Christ! Then we will no longer be infants, tossed back and forth by the waves, and blown here and there by every wind of teaching and by the cunning and craftiness of people in their deceitful scheming" (Eph. 4:12–14, NIV).

These gifts were given for the intellectual, emotional, and spiritual up-building of the body in preparation for service and maturity in Christ. If there is any negligence on the part of leadership in this body construction area, the church will never reach the level of Christlikeness that is necessary to get out of that rocky, wavering, vulnerable, infant stage in order to escape the crafty and deceitful teachings of others. No wonder Paul placed such great emphasis on this body function in 1 Thessalonians

5:11 where he admonished the church to encourage and build up one another. In Romans 14:19 he links "peace" to "mutual edification" of the body, since the absence of peace in any church is a clear indication of the negation of any mutual building up. In Romans 15:1, 2, he mentions the importance of the strong being patient with the weak and introduces the concept of each Christian pleasing his/her neighbor "... for their good, to build them up" (NIV). Then in Ephesians 4:29 he emphasizes the importance of pure communication in building up others: "Do not let any unwholesome talk come out of your mouths, but only what is helpful for building others up according to their needs, that it may benefit those who listen."

When we consider the destructive work of the tongue and being cognizant of the fact that most of the trouble, ill-will, animosity, and even hatred in the body is caused by the things we say to each other, Paul's advice is both potent and constructive, and if adhered to, it can contribute in significant ways to the cultivation of healthy relationships, a prerequisite of a productive body/church. Unfortunately, the politics of personal destruction is demonstrated in the deliberate untruths told about many and the deep-sea diving for the retrieval of sins, which have been thrown in the depth of the ocean by God, to be used as trophies and blockages (in church board meetings and during election times) of particular members. The application of this type of politics sows the seeds of relationship disintegration that produces disharmony in the operations of the church and diverts its attention from its true mission.

Whatever our talents and gifts are, they should be utilized in humility for the building up/edification of the body. It behooves us, therefore, to align our lives in harmony with the will of God so that He may use us in a fuller sense in service to both the body and the world.

Remember, greater church growth and development are possible when the body members are connected to the Head and each other in a community of loving fellowship and use their gifts for the realization of that Christlikeness in every member.

The Body: God's Family on Earth

Metaphorically speaking, the church is both Christ's body and His family on earth, and also a part of His heavenly family. Paul expressed this idea with great clarity when he wrote: "For this reason I kneel before the Father, from whom every family in heaven and on earth derives its name" (Eph. 3:14, 15, NIV). But why did Paul refer to the body of Christ as a family and part of the totality of the family of God? When I think of a family, the first thing that comes to mind is the biblical perspective of an adult male and female uniting together in holy matrimony with or without children. A sociological or psychological perspective will not be presented here because the biblical point of view is sufficient for what I need to accomplish. The family as is presented in the Bible is not devoid of structure, norms, problems, conflicts, and rivalry because it is made up of imperfect beings. In general, however, if not all, most family members love and care deeply for each other even when disagreements and/or conflicts are present in these families. If you do not believe me, attempt at some point to intrude in the business of a family in conflict and you may be surprised to experience how quickly these same members unite to take care of the intruder.

What is significant for Paul in expressing the idea of the church as being the family of God is the *underlying principle of love*—the in-depth affection and care family members have for each other. Paul advises that such a "love must be sincere" and that body members are to "hate what is evil" and "cling to what is good." They should "be devoted to one another in love. Honor one another above yourselves.... Do not take revenge … but leave room for God's wrath, for it is written: 'It is mine to avenge; I will repay,' says the Lord" (Rom. 12:9, 10, 19, NIV).

Too many church members talk a good game of love. They present themselves in such a convincing manner that they are generally believed. However, when the critical moments arise for them to demonstrate how much they truly love, we realize that love for many is an abstraction with no real-life application. There are members who fundamentally care only about themselves. What is most disturbing about these selfish individuals is that babes in Christ witness such disappointing situations and are so devastated that they leave the body and the name of Christ is dishonored in the process. All young converts should be introduced to Christ and taught to focus on Him and look to Him as the true Head and Example of the body (church). They should also be taught that there are people of all dispositions in the church and that their disingenuous and principle-contradictory conduct in the body should not be allowed to influence their decision to follow Jesus.

Paul also stated that as family members we ought to be loving, loyal, and faithful (devoted) to each other, honoring others above ourselves. This is by far one of the most difficult advice to implement based on our natural proclivity to be selfish or to take care of self first in our dog-eat-dog cultural environment that emphasizes competition and individualism and putting self first. In our weakened human state, it is extremely difficult to achieve such a high and selfless standard of living even in the church, but it is not impossible. His grace is sufficient to achieve anything, and it is the standard for which we should strive, and one that should be kept before the people at all times in order to initiate any kind of change in the church. It is also the kind of cultural change that is urgently needed in the church. Much more will be written about this type of change in the following section.

The Body (Church): His Kingdom Under Construction on Earth

Figuratively speaking, the body of Christ is the church of God under construction on earth. It is, however, not an earthly kingdom but a spiritual one, even though it is located on earth. Whatever it does on earth is done with a heavenly focus and a new world transformation to a sinless state. This is why Jesus said, "My kingdom is not of this world. If it were, my servants would fight to prevent my arrest by the Jewish leaders. But now my kingdom is from another place" (John 18:36, NIV). On the other hand, Paul appears to contradict what Jesus said when he wrote to the Colossians that they, as a church, had been qualified by the Father "to share in the inheritance of his holy people in the kingdom of light. For he has rescued us from the dominion of darkness and brought us into the kingdom of the Son he loves, in whom we have redemption, the forgiveness of sins" (Col. 1:12–14, NIV).

A similar message is communicated to the Thessalonians in which Paul urged them "to live lives worthy of God, who calls you into his kingdom and glory" (1 Thess. 2:12, NIV). But what is this kingdom to which Jesus and Paul are referring and where is it located? Paul wrote to the Roman Christian Church that "the kingdom of God is not a matter of eating and drinking, but of righteousness, peace and joy in the Holy Spirit, because anyone who serves Christ in this way is pleasing to God and receives human approval" (Rom. 14:17, 18, NIV). The implication here seems to suggest that the kingdom is a reality when God's people are living righteous lives and experiencing peace and joy in the Spirit. But the exact location of the kingdom is still somewhat nebulous, and so I turn to Christ's explanation for greater clarification. His response to the Pharisees' question about the coming of the kingdom of God is that "the kingdom of God is not something that can be observed, nor will people say, 'Here it is,' or 'There it is,' because the kingdom of God is in your midst" (Luke 17:20, 21, NIV).

The reference to "the kingdom of God" seems to suggest God's ownership of the kingdom and that wherever He is or dwells is His kingdom. An extension of this logic will lead one to believe that when people accept Jesus as their Lord and Savior, and voluntarily invite the Holy Spirit to dwell in their hearts and control their lives, that the kingdom of grace is present within them and will be clearly demonstrated in the joyful, peaceful, and righteous state of their individual lives. When such people come together as the body of Christ (church), they come with the realization that Jesus, through the Spirit is King, not only in their individual, but collective lives as well, and when this kind of thinking becomes a significant part of the mindset and consciousness of such people, many things will change. When Christ reigns supremely in the lives of body members, including church leaders, the culture will never be the same. Members will align their thinking and conduct with the principles of Christ's teachings. As a result, many of the negative thinking and behaviors will disappear; the struggle to acquire power and authority will be replaced with the spirit of service because Jesus is King and all others are subjects.

Jesus Is King and Head of His Kingdom Church

Jesus is sovereign King of His universal kingdom, and it is to that partial aspect of the kingdom on earth to which He called us, and it is one that is based on a new paradigm which He introduced during His itinerary on earth—His divine laws which are eternal and a different set of principles to those of our secular society or the world. Ellen G. White wrote that "Christ was establishing a kingdom on different principles. He called men, not to authority, but to service" (*The Desire of Ages*, p. 550). Those who think that God's laws were abolished at the cross and replaced by grace are mistaken. Any kingdom that experiences stability, peace, and justice will have laws and principles that are equally applied to its citizens. The absence of these will result in chaos and possibly anomie.

The kingdom of God within us must have some guidelines (laws and principles) upon which we base our decisions (thinking and conduct), and these form the new paradigm advocated by Jesus in His teachings. The old paradigm was based on revenge—an eye for an eye and a tooth for a tooth as was stated by Jesus when He said, "You have heard that it was said, 'Eye for eye, and tooth for tooth'" (Matt. 5:38, NIV). He also mentioned the issue of divorce in the old paradigm when He said, "It has been said, 'Anyone who divorces his wife must give her a certificate of divorce'" (Matt. 5:31, NIV), which was so easy for males to obtain because women were considered to be the property of men and could be dispensed with at men's indiscretion with no serious repercussions. Jesus also addressed the issue of love in its narrowly defined application in the old paradigm, "You have heard that it was said, 'Love your neighbor and hate your enemy'" (Matt. 5:43, NIV). The issue of adultery was also addressed by Him because of the injustice meted out to women in the frequent and harsh punishment for such an offence when it took both men and women for the perpetuation or commission of adultery. Jesus introduced His solution in the new paradigm as follows:

The new paradigm stated that revenge belongs to God and Him only. This means that the eye-for-an-eye principle is obsolete under the new dispensation. As Jesus rightly confirmed, "If anyone slaps you on the right cheek, turn to them the other cheek also" (Matt. 5:39, NIV). If you are asked for your cloak, give not the one only but both. Furthermore, if you are asked to walk a mile, go the second and third. In reference to the adultery issue, He broadened the definition and application when He said, "I tell you that anyone who looks at a woman lustfully has already committed adultery with her in his heart" (Matt. 5:28, NIV). In reference to the divorce issue, Jesus was unequivocal when He said that a certificate of divorce was only granted because of the hardness of the people's hearts since it was God's intention in the beginning that a man should cleave to his wife and love her dearly and sincerely until death intervened and disrupted that relationship.

Jesus also introduced a novel and broad application of the love principle when He made the stunning announcement to "love your enemies and pray for those who persecute you" (Matt. 5:44, NIV), and "do good to those who hate you, bless those who curse you, pray for those who mistreat you" (Luke 6:27, NIV). Then He asked a penetrating question: "If you love those who love you, what reward will you get?" I assume that those who play the political and other games astutely will receive their earthly rewards—economic, relational, and psychological benefits—from loving the people who love them. But for Jesus, the more important reward awaits those who love as He loves, even their enemies, because "then your reward will be great, and you will be children of the Most High" (Luke 6:35, NIV).

In my estimation, these are some of the most difficult, seemingly impractical, psychologically excruciating, emotionally draining, and anxiety producing teachings of Jesus to implement in our lives. Fortunately or unfortunately, these have been included by Jesus as part of the Christian cultural norms. But why are they so tough for us to live by? One very significant factor is that they are antithetical to or run against the grain of our base human nature (they are unnatural). In addition, the norms of our cultural environment that have played such a significant role in shaping the structural pattern of our thinking, mindset, conduct, and/or behavioral expectations are the antithesis of Jesus' teachings, and unlearning these by restructuring our thinking, mindset, and behavioral patterns is by far a difficult task. It seems almost a human impossibility to order one's life by those standards. But these are part of the new paradigm that Jesus expects us to embrace and apply as a guiding framework for our thinking and conduct. Remember, His grace is sufficient for us to make the necessary changes, otherwise why would He ask, "Why do you call me, 'Lord, Lord,' and do not do what I say?" (Luke 6:46, NIV). We must try and do so very hard while we exercise our faith in Him, the One who has the power and authority and the resources we need for conformity with His teachings. These are idealistic standards that are worth striving to achieve, otherwise, what is heaven for?

Laws and Principles of His Kingdom

All civilized countries, nations, and kingdoms need a common set of written (or unwritten) laws and principles, the underpinnings of an orderly and effective society. In other words, these form the basis of practically all citizens' conduct in their interaction with one another. These laws, however, are subject to change as nations and kingdoms become more enlightened. Fortunately, in Jesus' kingdom, laws and principles are eternal in nature and, therefore, changeless. They were given by a perfect, divine God, and they transcend time and space. But what are those laws and principles? They are His ten commandments and their underpinning principles. Foundational to these is the principle of "love" upon which all are founded. These commandments are found in Exodus 20:3–17.

Commandments	**Principles**
1st commandment	Loyalty
2nd commandment	Worship
3rd commandment	Reverence
4th commandment	Sanctification
5th commandment	Respect
6th commandment	Mercy
7th commandment	Purity
8th commandment	Honesty
9th commandment	Truthfulness
10th commandment	Contentment

A short comparison of some other kingdom principles with those generally adhered to in our secular society is in order, since it is important for us as Christians to be cognizant of the distinctive differences for the application of the right principles in our decisions and conduct. Eternal truths rather than being politically expedient. These are as follows:

God's Kingdom Principles	versus	**Kingdom of Sin Principles**
Love		Hate
Kindness/Mercy		Revenge
Grace/Forgiveness		Unforgiving
Holiness		Wickedness
Purity		Impurity

Self-Sacrifice	Self-Love
Self-Denial	Self-Satisfaction
Self-Control	Undisciplined
Benevolence	Selfishness
Faith	Doubt
Humility	Pride
Patience	Impatience
Freedom	Bondage

The above-mentioned Ten Commandments and principles are "God's holy law, the foundation of His government in heaven and on earth" (White, *Steps to Christ*, p. 24). They are eternal and transcend human time and its cultural circumstances. No wonder that when some people thought they were no longer applicable due to the on-going social changes in both pre- and post-modern societies with all their scientific and technological advances that Jesus came and pronounced His divine ratification of His laws and their eternality when He said:

> Do not think that I have come to abolish the Law or the Prophets; I have not come to abolish them but to fulfill them. For truly I tell you, until heaven and earth disappear, not the smallest letter, not the least stroke of a pen, will by any means disappear from the Law until everything is accomplished. Therefore anyone who sets aside one of the least of these commandments and teaches others accordingly will be called least in the kingdom of heaven, but whoever practices and teaches these commands will be called great in the kingdom of heaven" (Matt. 5:17–19, NIV).

These divine commandments and principles are a reflection of who God is, and those whom He called (the *ekklesia*) out of darkness into His marvelous body are called to represent His character to the world. What an awesome, solemn, and humanly impossible responsibility! But His grace is sufficient!

Citizens of the Kingdom of God on Earth

As members of the body of Christ, we have been granted all rights and privileges of the kingdom through adoption. Paul says it quite eloquently when he wrote:

> Remember that at that time you were separate from Christ, excluded from citizenship in Israel and foreigners to the covenants of the promise, without hope and without God in the world. But now in Christ Jesus you who

once were far away have been brought near by the blood of Christ.... Consequently, you are no longer foreigners and strangers, but fellow citizens with God's people and also members of his household. (Eph. 2:12, 13, 19, NIV).

But our citizenship is in heaven. And we eagerly await a Savior from there, the Lord Jesus Christ. (Phil. 3:20, NIV).

As citizens of His kingdom on earth, we are called to perform the sacred roles of (1) ambassadors, (2) saints, and (3) priests.

Ambassadors

Christ was God's Ambassador or Agent of reconciliation to the world as Paul stated "that God was reconciling the world to himself in Christ, not counting people's sins against them" (2 Cor. 5:19, NIV), and in a similar manner, all Christians are commissioned to be Christ's ambassadors or representatives for the continuation of His ministry of reconciliation to the world as was stated by Paul: "And he has committed to us the message of reconciliation. We are therefore Christ's ambassadors, as though God were making his appeal through us" (verses 19, 20, NIV). Paul, in chains, fearlessly declared that he was "an ambassador in bonds [chains]" (Eph. 6:20). The implication here is that, in spite of our circumstances in life, as Christians and disciples of Christ, we are called to represent Him as completely as is humanly possible. According to Ellen G. White,

> We are called to represent to the world the character of God as it was revealed to Moses. In answer to the prayer of Moses, "Show me Thy glory," the Lord promised, "I will make all My goodness pass before thee." "And the Lord passed by before him, and proclaimed, The Lord, The Lord God, merciful and gracious, long-suffering, and abundant in goodness and truth, keeping mercy for thousands, forgiving iniquity and transgression and sin." Exodus 33:18, 19; 34:6, 7. This is the fruit that God desires from His people. In purity of their characters, in the holiness of their lives, in their mercy and loving-kindness and compassion, they are to demonstrate that the "law of the Lord is perfect, converting the soul." Psalm 19:7. (*Testimonies for the Church*, vol. 6, p. 221)

This is by far no small responsibility when one considers the fact that God is omnipresent, omnipotent, omniscient, divine, holy, righteous, and perfect. He is beyond the reach of human comprehension. We are finite, unrighteous, and imperfect; there is nothing omni about us. Yet we have been called to represent His character to the world. The viability of such a representation requires an incomprehensible internal transformation and reproduction of the "very image of God" in us. A human state of this quality—"the perfection of the character of His people" (White, *The Desire of Ages*, p. 671)—requires nothing less than divine intervention and the total dedication, consecration, and determination to let God represent Himself through us or through His empowerment of us for the revelation of His character. The divine empowerment source is available for all, but we must decide to make it happen. It was available to Jesus because "Jesus revealed no qualities, and exercised no powers, that men may not have through faith in Him." Ellen White goes on to assure us that "His perfect humanity is that which all His followers may possess, if they will be in subjection to God as He was" (Ibid., p. 664).

It is very clear that such a spiritual state will not occur by osmosis. There are some Adventists who believe that all we need to do is have faith and wait for God to fulfill His desire in our lives. Ellen White warns against this semi-false theological position when she wrote that "those who are waiting to behold a magical change in their characters without determined effort on their part to overcome sin, will be disappointed" (*Selected Messages*, book 1, p. 336). Christ will not unite with us and make us partakers of His divine nature in which sin will have no dominion over us unless we make the decision to invite Him, through the Holy Spirit, into our hearts and do things that are necessary to maintain His presence in our lives (White, *The Desire of Ages*, p. 664).

As citizens and ambassadors of the kingdom of God, He has given us a very sacred responsibility to reflect His character to the world and the needed resources for its effectuation. The critical question is, are we availing ourselves of this resource He has placed at our disposal?

Saints or Body Members

Members of the kingdom of a king are referred to as subjects, but as Christians or members of God's kingdom on earth, Paul refers to us as "saints" (1 Cor. 1:2; 2 Cor. 1:1; Eph. 1:15, 18; and Phil. 1:1; 4:21). Why does he refer to us as "saints"? The word saint, according to William Barclay, comes from the Greek word *hagios*, which means "Christ's dedicated people" who are fundamentally "holy" (Barclay, *The Mind of St. Paul*, pp. 238, 240). The underpinning idea is that the temple, priest, Sabbath, etc. were holy because they were used or set apart for sacred purposes, and saints are holy because they are set apart from the world to be used by Christ for the continuation of His sacred ministry on earth. This means that saints or Christians are supposed to be different from those of the world in thinking and conduct because "if anyone is in Christ, the new creation has come: The old has gone, the new is here!"

(2 Cor. 5:17, NIV), and "no one who is born of God will continue to sin, because God's seed remains in them; they cannot go on sinning, because they have been born of God" (1 John 3:19, NIV). But what is "God's seed"? It is the enduring word of God (1 Peter 1:23).

The distinctive difference of saints about which Paul wrote is also mentioned in essence in the Spirit of Prophecy. Ellen White wrote that "when the Lord requires us to be distinct and peculiar, how can we crave popularity or seek to imitate the customs and practices of the world" (*Testimonies for the Church*, vol. 6, p. 143). This distinctiveness and peculiarity are to be demonstrated in our none-compromising position on principles because "the world has a right to know what to expect of us" (White, *Evangelism*, p. 179). Saints are followers/disciples who have dedicated and consecrated their lives to Jesus and are determined to live holy lives because they "ought to live holy and godly lives" (2 Peter 3:11, NIV). They have been buried in baptism and raised up to "live a new life" in Christ (Rom. 6:4, NIV); they have a new self, new mindset, and new attitude. They live by God's grace, according to the late William Barclay, as if in the "constant presence of Jesus Christ," and being aware of His presence, they make a "deliberate attempt to listen to the commands of Christ and to carry them out." We are in the world and live "within the affairs of the world, but his whole life is dictated by the standards of Christ, and not by the standards of the world" (*The Mind of St. Paul*, pp. 239, 240).

When this gloriously spiritual state is attained by the grace of God through Jesus Christ our Lord, many things in our lives will change and will be done differently, one of which is communication. This is one critical aspect in the lives of Christians that creates a significant amount of problems and contributes in many ways to the strained and/or disintegration of social and spiritual relationships if not handled with great skill and sensitivity. However, when that spiritual transformation is realized through our consistent connection or unity with the Spirit, political correctness and other forms of political communications will be unnecessary because adhering to the words of Jesus will have greater value or worth and we will simply let our "yes" be "yes" and our "no" be "no," because "anything beyond this comes from the evil one" (Matt. 5:37, NIV). In this ideal state, saints will not be too worried about the impact of truth upon each other because their communication will "be always full of grace," and "seasoned with salt" (Col. 4:6) and the truth will be spoken in love (Eph. 4:15).

Unfortunately, until the saints get to that state of maturity in Christ, conflict as a social phenomenon in the church is ineluctable and should be given diligent and consistent attention. The ethical directions given by Christ in this regard should be followed without question and become a part of the cultural modus operandi of the body of Christ. The general inclination is to ignore or leave conflict unresolved with the false hope that by osmosis it will go away or be forgotten. Remember, victims do not forget and the other reality is that if conflict is not dealt with and brought to some closure or resolution, it will surface in the future and make relatively simple situations appear very complicated. In other words, a simple situation can be easily blown out of proportion when those unresolved feelings resurface and are integrated with the current ones.

In addition, a distinction must be drawn between constructive and destructive conflict. All contrary ideas are not destructive but could be of great value to the advancement of causes and churches. But it depends on the perspective from which issues are viewed. What is destructive for some is constructive for others and visa versa. Our guiding principle should be the Word, not tradition. Let us bear in mind that conflict has played a very significant role in the development of the Christian church. Much truths have come to light because of the persistence and the willingness of some "leaders" to walk in the footsteps of Jesus and challenge the current system based on God's Word, and in spite of the consequences. Jesus did not only "rock the boat," He overturned it.

There are many church members who have excellent ideas but are unwilling to communicate them because of their apparent contradiction to those in the power elite of the church and the church's "666 stamp" that they imprint on trouble makers with very disastrous consequences. We should never be closed minded if truth is progressive, but it should always be measured by biblical principles. If the church is to grow and develop to maturity in Christ, changes will have to be implemented both in the individual and collective lives of the church. Risk will have to be undertaken but not at the expense of principle, and all ideas should be given due consideration before judgmental pronouncement is made. The originators of new ideas may not be as socially astute in their communication; therefore, be patient and/or educate them as to the how to communicate their ideas, but do not ignore and blame the presentation method. Too many excellent ideas are ignored and the church is left impoverished due to the influence and judgment of a few. In all that the saints communicate, let them (us) be mindful of the method we utilize, but let us be more patient, accepting, and tolerant of those who are not as socially skillful as many are.

Another area in which the saints will act differently is reconciliation. Saints are those who are resolute in their dedication to Jesus and exhibit an incredible spirit of forgiveness which is living differently from the general "get even" or revenge standard of the world. As was said earlier, where two or three are gathered, the Spirit is there to bless (Matt. 18:20), but the enemy is also there to upset. It is inevitable for the saints to make mistakes—inadvertent and deliberate. What is critically significant is not that mistakes will be made, but how and when will they be dealt with?

The general inclination is not wanting to be confrontational, which leads to a more serious problem of pushing conflicts under the rug or leaving the "open wound" to putrefy over time and impact current or future situations in a negative manner. In other words, when an apparently simple situation is blown completely out of proportion, remember that past unresolved issues may be contributing in a significant way to the out-of-proportioned reaction of the individual. To avoid these blow ups and the devastating consequences of broken relationships and church disunity, Jesus directed us to live differently as saints through the immediate and/or soon as possible resolution of our conflicts. He said quite unequivocally: "Therefore, if you are offering your gift at the altar and there remember that your brother or sister has something against you, leave your gift there in front of the altar. First go and be reconciled to them; then come and offer your gift" (Matt 5:23, 24, NIV).

The implication in this text is that you, whether the offender or the offended, are conscious of a problem with someone else in the church, and before you enter God's house to worship Him, in part, through your gift presentation, you have a sacred obligation to make right that which went wrong. Christ is directing us (all things being equal) to postpone worshiping Him, go and first reconcile with the brother, and then come back to worship Him. Jesus places an extremely high priority on reconciliation, which should lead to relationship restoration that contributes to church unity, which is a crucial witness to the world that God sent His Son to redeem. Remember, a divided church provides the opposite witness and causes God's name to be dishonored.

Further information on how we should proceed in the reconciliation process is provided by Jesus in the following text: "If your brother or sister sins, go and point out their fault, just between the two of you. If they listen to you, you have won them over. But if they will not listen, take one or two others along, so that 'every matter may be established the testimony of two or three witnesses.' If they still refuse to listen, tell it to the church; and if they refuse to listen even to the church, treat them as you would a pagan or a tax collector" (Matt. 18:15–17, NIV).

The procedural method in the above passage is not in question, but I have some temporary trepidation about the apparent double humiliation of the offended, the injured one, the one who was victimized, being placed in the humiliating position by first going to the victor. Should not the victor be the one to be humbled first, particularly if he/she was the aggressor? Placing the "burden" on the victim appears humanly discomforting, but it is easily understood from the perspective of the offender being unconscious of the offence. In addition, it is that childlike spirit that Christ wants us to develop through practice if we are going to grow and develop to maturity in Him. It may appear very difficult, but it is part of the new paradigm teaching of Jesus, and

He expects His saints to follow through in spite of how humiliating it may be. This teaching does not bar the offender from taking the initiative in terms of approaching the victim first, because the principle of mutual submission is applicable to both victim and victor.

One very important lesson which I think Jesus was trying to teach is that pride (arrogance) is a principle in the kingdom of sin, and humility is the antithetical principle in the kingdom of God. It is the latter that should guide our thinking and conduct in our relationship with each other and secular society. If humility is the guiding principle in matters relating to reconciliation, then saints will be better prepared to effectuate the message in the following: "If your brother or sister sins against you, rebuke them; and if they repent, forgive them. Even if they sin against you seven times in a day and seven times comes back to you saying 'I repent,' you must forgive them" (Luke 17:3, 4, NIV).

The realization of the instructions in that text requires the application of another kingdom principle named "patience," and the implementation of both in conflictive situations requires supernatural intervention. The assistance will come when we decide to do the Master's will in spite of the difficulties we may experience in so doing. The development of a forgiving mindset is an honorable duty, and forgiving one another is a spiritual obligation for all saints because God does not renege on His word. When He said, "For if you forgive other people when they sin against you, your heavenly Father will also forgive you. But if you do not forgive others their sins, your Father will not forgive your sins" (Matt. 6:14, 15, NIV), He meant every word of it.

God is very cognizant of the fact that there are many who are unwilling to forgive. They are more than willing to burn the bridge over which they have passed and to deny the highest need of many—forgiveness. Too many of us, including some saints, have forgotten that all human beings stand in need of forgiveness, but they behave like the unmerciful servant who was forgiven by the king of a large sum of money after much pleading and immediately went after a fellow servant and demanded, choked, and had him thrown into prison for a minor debt. When the king learned of the forgiven servant's behavior, appropriate punishment was applied immediately. The other lesson to be learned is the application of the Golden Rule amongst saints. This is critical to the maintenance of healthy, loving, and redemptive relationships.

We are still talking about how saints should live differently under the new paradigm covenant established by Jesus, and this deals with the fact that saints do not take saints to court. Secular people generally settle their differences in courts of law and, unfortunately, so do many saints. Jesus addressed the issue of lawsuits and the conduct of His followers when they are sued. He said very simply that "if anyone wants to sue you and take your tunic, hand over your coat as well" (Matt. 5:40, NIV). In other words, heap coals on their heads. Material things will last but for a while, the things that are of eternal value are of far greater significance and should be given priority in the lives of the saints.

Paul also addressed the lawsuit issue among Corinthian saints in 1 Corinthian 6:1–9. He wrote, "If any of you has a dispute with another, do you dare to take it before the ungodly for judgment instead of before the Lord's people?" (verse 1, NIV). He asked the question if there was no one amongst them who was competent to judge such cases and pointed out that lawsuits among them was an indication of their defeat. Then he asked a simple yet profound question that is reflective of the new paradigm teachings introduced by Jesus. "Why not rather be wronged? Why not rather be cheated?" (verse 7, NIV). The consciousness of being wronged or cheated and overlooking or ignoring it seems to run against the grain of our nature, appears to condone the sin, and seems to contradict the teaching of Jesus to go and reconcile the situation.

It is my assumption that Paul was much more concerned about the principles of love, forgiveness, unity, and unselfishness with the understanding that earthly property and other such goods are of no real eternal value, so why dishonor the name of Jesus and give the enemy and others any rationale for their rejection of His salvation and mockery of His body or church. This approach by Paul is very consistent with the "turning of the cheek" teachings of Jesus. This is not to suggest that the weightier matters of criminal wrongdoing against the saints or committed by any saint will not be adjudicated in the courts since such legal issues are the responsibility of the state. The point is simply that as saints we must live differently and demonstrate the type of restraint and patience that will show a distinctive difference between saints and the world.

Finally, the saints of God clearly understand that marriage was intended by God to be a lifetime partnership, and that if they lived their lives based on the biblical principles for all conjugal relationships, marriages would last and divorce and adultery would be a thing of the past. The reality is that many are saints in name only and are deficient of those characteristic qualities that disciples of Christ should possess. Under these circumstances, the departure from biblical injunctions is made easier, and adultery and divorce become an exceptionally strong possibility. It is understood, however, that certain marital circumstances should not be tolerated, so even though we are admonished to "take the wrong," situations that threaten a spouse's health or life should be unacceptable. Women are equal partners and deserve much respect.

Two important things should be mentioned here. First, divorce is too easy to legally acquire in our modern-day society and too many of us opt for the easy "solution" too soon. There are also too many of us who have unrealistic expectations and believe that marriage is a continuous honeymoon with no eclipse. Sooner rather than later, there will be difficulties, and we need to deal with them as saints should. In addition, Jesus introduced the no-body-contact marital adultery concept when He said that "anyone who looks at a woman lustfully has already committed adultery with her in his heart" (Matt. 5:27, 28, NIV). This concept is also broadened to include marriage to someone who is divorced for reasons other than "marital unfaithfulness." This is stated in Matthew 5:31, 32, which reads, "anyone who divorces his wife, except for sexual immorality, makes her the victim of adultery, and anyone who marries a divorced woman commits adultery."

Second, in this issue of adultery and divorce, women were the ones subjected to victimization and disenfranchisement by men in biblical times and other cultures, but Jesus introduced a new paradigmatic dispensation for women. It was the prerogative of men to own women as their property, and this gave them the absolute right to abandon or divorce their wives at their discretion. Moses permitted men to ease their consciences by writing certificates of divorce in order to send their wives away. Jesus reminded the Pharisees that this was done because of the hardness of their hearts. What Jesus did was to elevate the status of women to equal partner; He liberated them from the manmade conjugal restrictions. He also restricted the remarriage of men to divorced women by making it an adulterous act with only one exception as is mentioned above. As saints, men and women are equal at the feet of Jesus.

Priests: Saints Are a Priesthood of Believers

Another sweeping paradigm change that was made by Jesus for His body or church was the abolition of the one-tribe priesthood caste system. In the Old Testament, priests were chosen from the Levi tribe only to represent and/or mediate between God and Israel through the use of the sacrificial system. We are, however, very cognizant of the gross corruption of the human element that saturated the system and almost displaced the divine focus of the priests involved. The political struggles for positions and control in the system, as well as for the material benefits of having first rights to the best portions of the sacrificial animal meat, so dominated the minds of the caretakers or priestly functionaries that the system pointing to the future sacrificial Lamb lost its true significance. It was a divine institution that was totally abused by a privileged few and corrupted by human greed and political ambition. But Jesus punctuated history, and through His sacrificial blood on the cross, He eliminated that system and made His body of followers/disciples into "a royal priesthood." He opened up that ministry to all believers.

> As you come to him, the living Stone—rejected by humans but chosen by God and precious to him—you also, like living stones, are being built into a spiritual house to be a holy priesthood, offering spiritual sacrifices acceptable to God through Jesus Christ.... But you are a chosen people, a royal priesthood, a holy nation, God's special possession, that you may declare the praises of him who called you out of darkness into his wonderful light. (1 Peter 2:4–10, NIV)

This all-inclusive nature of the new priesthood seems to suggest at least two things: (1) that the only priest whom the saints need apart from themselves is Jesus, their High Priest. Are we, therefore, still in need of priests, pastors, bishops to intercede with God on our behalf? Any effective intercession on behalf of others will, I assume, be appreciated, but there is no human substitute for each individual approaching the throne of God, and (2) that all believers now stand between the world and Jesus, and this priestly function is no mean responsibility. It is a saintly and awesome spiritual obligation that should be taken extremely seriously because the eternal destiny of many is at stake.

Unfortunately, the divinely instituted all-believers priestly system has been eroding over the last two thousand years, and according to Edwards, "by the time of the Reformation, the biblical concept of the priesthood of all believers had been eroded by a hierarchical and priest-centered church" and that "Luther's reaffirmation of the principle was a protest against clerical powers" (Edwards, *Every Believer A Minister*, p. 82). This particular concept should be studied further to determine the functional limitations of the all-member priests, because in spite of the continued erosion mentioned above and its current institutionalization, it appears that corrective action in the near future is unforeseeable due to the said members being lead to accept the present system as divinely instituted, resulting in the non-alignment of all members to their priestly responsibility.

As a matter of fact, even in the Christian denominations that emerged from the Reformation, all with the exception of a small minority are dominated by the professional clergy (priest, bishop, pastor-centered) that perform those functions being classified as "priestly." There is a ray of hope that is seen in some Christian churches in the Arizona-New Mexico area that have abolished the clergy-pastor system in order to align themselves with the all-member priesthood principle and the biblical elder-leadership pattern of the New Testament. There is also an Adventist church in Illinois, the Richland Bridge SDA Church, that was started by a dentist and does not want a pastor. According to Russell Burrill, director of the North American Division Evangelism Institute in Berrien Springs, Michigan, the church "is not under the control of any one person; it is a church in the safe hand of laity. The church has never had a pastor and does not want one" (*Rekindling a Lost Passion*, p. 75). And as far as he is concerned, "all areas of ministry must be fully restored to the laity—preaching, teaching, evangelism, church boards, committees, etc." (Ibid., p. 25).

The implementation of any change in this area will not be easy and acceptable by those who may be affected by it. Change can be anxiety-producing, and because of its uncertain outcome, many become anxious and remain exceptionally defensive of the current establishment. The church, however, is about change, and we must have the fortitude to make changes particularly when it is needed to correct well-established errors. In addition, there is so much that can be written on this subject, but this is not the central focus of this book. In addition, the biblical leadership pattern mentioned above will be further expanded upon in the church leadership chapter.

The Church Body as the Temple of God

Paul uses another metaphorical expression, the body temple, to describe God's temple. God's temple is His dwelling place and anywhere His presence is in heaven and on earth, of Himself or through the Holy Spirit, that place is made holy. If you recall, it was mentioned earlier in this chapter that the bottom line of the church is that it is the believers who allow the Spirit of God to dwell in and control their minds and actions. It logically follows that those in whom the Spirit is dwelling and controlling are made holy through His presence in them. Paul supports this theological concept when he wrote that we are "God's building" (1 Cor. 3:9, NIV). He then asks the question: "Don't you know that you yourselves are God's temple and that God's Spirit dwells in your midst? If anyone destroys God's temple, God will destroy that person; for God's temple is sacred, and you together are that temple" (verses 16, 17).

The destruction of God's temple is made real when we engage in continuous sin that causes the Spirit to vacate its inner dwelling. When this occurs, sin abounds and the soul becomes polluted. Repentance is critical to avoid Him destroying His temple in us. The bottom line, in this and 1 Corinthian 6:19, for the body of Christ is the underlying principle of holiness. From a pure human perspective, a state of holiness appears to be a total impossibility. This means that a greater power beyond the realm of humanity must be sought and completely surrendered to, and that divine person is none other than Jesus Christ in whom "the whole building is joined together and rises to become a holy temple in the Lord" (Eph. 2:21, NIV). It is, therefore, the responsibility of the saints (body of Christ) to invite Jesus, who is represented by the Holy Spirit, to take up residence in our lives and take full control of our thought processes and actions for the effectuation of that holy state of being.

The challenge for us is to surrender control over our willpower to the Spirit and allow for the effectuation of His will that will empower us to live consistent lives of holiness. The resource is available; we need to tap into it.

The Church Body as the Bride of Christ

One of the most beautiful images Paul paints of the body of Christ in his writings is that of the church being Christ's bride. But why did he refer to the church as His bride? The answer probably lies in the analogy he made between a man and his wife and Christ and His church. The secret is the intimate and profoundly mysterious relationship that exists between a man and his bride, and the "intimate" is not sexual in nature. It points toward an extremely close, warm, and loving relationship that appears so incomprehensible. No wonder Paul refers to it as "a profound mystery" (Eph. 5:32, NIV).

Brides are very special women to their husbands, and those who have remained virtuous and pure from the contamination of other men prior and subsequent to marriage are precious gems and worthy of high honor. Christ is returning for "a radiant church, without stain or wrinkle or any other blemish" because He gave Himself for her to make her "holy and blameless" (Eph. 5:27, NIV). This is the underlying principle of the metaphorical expression of the church being the bride of Christ. It is to be pure, chased, unspotted, or uncontaminated by the world in preparation for her marriage to the Lamb.

Christ expects His body, followers, disciples, and saints, to live pure lives. Sounds too idealistic? Isn't going to heaven also idealistic? Just as we plan to get there by His grace, so can we live pure lives by His grace. In addition, we have a significant role to play in the transformation of our characters. Instead of sitting around and waiting for grace to fall on us, let us remember that without "determined effort" on our part it will not happen because, according to the Spirit of Prophecy, God will not do for us that which we can do for ourselves.

A story is told about a soap maker and a rabbi who went for a walk, and as they were talking, the soap maker asked the rabbi a question about the value of religion because after so many years of prayers and sermons there was still so much violence and hatred. The rabbi was stunned and paused for a while, but as they continued to walk, the rabbi saw a dirty boy playing in a gutter and asked the soap maker about the value of soap when there were so many dirty people in the world in spite of the amount of soap produced yearly. The soap maker was also stunned but eventually responded by saying that soap is useless unless it is applied for cleansing. The rabbi's response was that religion is also of no use unless it is applied to our lives. As saints we need to apply the soap principle to our lives as we surrender to the influence of the Spirit.

The Church: Its Mission

Jesus, through His incarnation, came to planet earth to reconcile the human family back to God. This was accomplished through His life, death, and resurrection. He also came to reveal to us that God, His Father, is not waiting to draw blood from us for every mistake we make, but that He is a kind, loving, merciful, and compassionate God. He came to save sinners and He completed His mission with incomprehensive distinction, was honored by His Father, and is now seated on the right hand of God in His intercessory ministry on our behalf. When He left planet earth, however, the responsibilities for His ministry of reconciliation were delegated to His followers/disciples/saints in the form of His body for the continuation of His work in His absence. It is for this reason that He instructed His disciples to "go into all the world and preach the gospel to all creation" (Mark 16:15, NIV). The preaching of the gospel to the whole world becomes a "testimony to all nations" and will be an indication of the end of the age (Matt. 24:14, NIV).

It appears to me, however, that too much focus has been placed on preaching at the neglect of the great commission in Matthew 28:19, 20: "Therefore go and make disciples of all nations ... teaching them to obey everything I have commanded you" (NIV). There are times when I wonder if the emphasis was placed on *making* disciples if there would be a global gospel explosion and a radical transformation of the world for Jesus. In the multiplication of disciples lies the germinating mustard seed that will take root and spread its gospel branches throughout the world. There are too many of us who are willing and ready to simply accept the Christian label without genuinely sensing the responsibility of making disciples. When we surrender ourselves to Jesus and accept Him as our Lord and Savior, the process of making disciples ought to begin there, and it is not an end in itself. The building up of the body of Christ is for the purpose of our individual salvation and the making of disciples. We fortify that we may share for the redemption of others.

The body of Christ is not a social club where members go to be entertained for their own personal satisfaction. There are too many of us who spend time in church on Sabbaths and do little or nothing on that day or any other day. I fully understand the fact that modernity has brought with it incredible stresses and we live such busy lives that there is little or no time to contribute in a significant way to discipling others during the work week. Why not then follow the example of Jesus who went to church and then left in reasonable time to share the gospel with others. It may be that the Sabbath should be utilized more to share the gospel and contribute to the effectuation of the great commission

A More Balanced View of the Church

There are many saints who may be thinking after reading this chapter that it is too idealistic and, therefore, impossible to achieve. My question to those is, "What is heaven for?" There is no question that heaven and eternal life are ideals worth striving after by the grace of God, and so is an ideal church. Jesus painted a realistic and balanced view of the church when He said that in His church are located "wheat" and "tares," "goats" and "sheep," bad and good. But does this mean by implication that an ideal state of the church is unattainable? If this was the case, I wonder why Jesus did not accept the situation facing Him as factual and too idealistic instead of asking, "Why do you call me, 'Lord, Lord,' and do not do what I say?" (Luke 6:46, NIV). It appears to me that He was implying the possibility of an ideal church if all members call upon Him and then do that which are required of us by Him. The point is that the evil in the church should not diminish our efforts to achieve an ideal state by His grace. Remember, the ideal is the standard to achieve and every effort should be made to reach this state. It is by His grace and His grace only that His bride will become a pure church in preparation to meet the Groom at His coming.

Conclusion

God's church (He is its Originator, Owner, CEO, and President) on earth is the local and global body of followers who have been called out of a spiritually dark world of sin into a community of redemptive love and fellowship. No generic man can usurp His status and the church is not for sale. God has called the church body to live their lives in redeeming relationships with Jesus and each other as though in His constant presence. These people (saints, ambassadors, citizens of the kingdom) have dedicated their lives to Him and allow the Holy Spirit to control their minds, hearts, and conduct. This is reflected in the different spiritual and cultural lifestyles they live from those of the world. But such lifestyles do not occur by osmosis. They demand a resolute decision by both the individual and collective body to walk with the Master, as well as purposeful and determined/sustained efforts to do His will with much prayer, study, constant soul searching, or what Paul refers to as "dying daily." When these things are made operational or become the modus operandi, both in the individual and corporate lives, changes of a reformational or revolutionary nature will be experienced by those directly involved with Him as well as those who witness the changes.

The church is about change and changing lives for Jesus. Therefore, it should contribute in significant and positive ways to the maturing of the saints. The usual sermons, Sabbath School lesson studies, youth programs (some churches have none of the latter, which is so unfortunate), and some sporadic outreaches seem insufficient to produce the needed revolutionary changes for Jesus. Church leaders must be informed and convinced of the body's destiny (that is probably axiomatic) and the processes (including the process and direction) involved in getting it there and be able to apply the needed biblical principles to affect the necessary changes.

The structures and programs needed by the church to inculcate the godly attributes that the church needs to develop and sustain in its members for their reflection or mirroring to each other as examples for one another and the natural emanation of the same from the members to the world must be thoughtfully and skillfully designed and implemented to accomplish that specific goal. It will not be easy, because getting members to fully understand and practice what it means to genuinely love one another in thoughts, words, and actions will be a challenge of great magnitude. It may require a comprehensive focus of the church for a whole year or more in reference to preaching, teaching, seminars, workshops, small groups sessions, and individual/collective commitment to attend the planned programs in order to change mindsets through this educational process and achieve the necessary behavioral changes for members to genuinely love one another. Similar structures and programs may be needed to encourage or teach members how to be kind, respectful, merciful, compassionate, humble, and all the other attributes that members are expected to naturally exude in their daily walk with Jesus. However, such structures and programs will not succeed without a lot of prayer and fasting. Divine intervention is a necessity for the effectuation of such grand but needed changes in God's church.

If church leaders are uninformed and unprepared (lacks knowledge, skills, and experience) for this type of leadership role, the churches that they lead are probably doomed because it is virtually impossible for us to become what we need to be (mature Christians) in Christ by remaining what we are, and leaders play a very significant role in this regard. If we are not growing and changing, becoming more Christlike as individuals, in preparation for a more important contribution to the spiritual advancement of the corporate body, we are wasting our time. The following African American church prayer is a reflection of the change idea Christians need to pursue on a sustained basis until we get to *teleois* (Christian maturity) in Jesus.

> Lord, we're not what we want to be; we're not what we need to be, but thank God almighty, we're not what we used to be.

Now that we have increased our understanding of the church (limited in the sense that it is not comprehensive but sufficient for the purposes of this book), its nature, function, structure, and mission; the fundamental kingdom principles on which it ought to operate and by which we ought to order our lives; and the type of relationships we ought to develop both with Jesus and one another, it is time to determine, based on the Word of God, what type of followers ought we to be and, more importantly, what type of leaders best fit into this biblically principled-oriented body of Christ.

This understanding of the church is critical to all followers and, more so, its leaders, due to the fact that spiritual/church leadership takes place within the context of the church and with members/saints. Leaders must have a comprehensive understanding of the nature, structure, mission, function, and how to operate in it through the application of right leadership philosophy based on the correct interpretation of our theology, style, and principles in order to move the church in the right direction toward its destination.

Those members who have worked in the secular world and experienced the success of a specific type or a combination of types of secular leadership styles and believe in the full-scale application of such leadership styles to the church must come to grips with the idea that any secular form/type of leadership is irrelevant or is a misfit for the unconventional body of Christ. Therefore, the remaining portion of this book will focus mainly, with the exception of two chapters, on the type of followers and leaders needed in the church for it to fulfill its sacred obligations/responsibilities and become a serious witness to the world that God sent His Son to this world to save it from eternal destruction. I want to believe, however, that you, the reader, has begun to make some good assumptions about the type of leaders who will function best within the church. Read on!

Remember that His grace is more than sufficient to get us where we need to be if we reach out by faith and take hold of the promises offered in His Word.

Chapter 2

Followership

Followership, like leadership, is an exceptionally critical aspect of organizational life, and leaders cannot afford to take it for granted. It is so important that many authors believe it is of greater importance than that of leadership, because without good to excellent followers, very little or nothing gets done and leaders are discredited for such results. Leaders, therefore, should take into account or sense the criticality of good followership, maximize the importance of its function, and provide the kind of leadership that resonates with followers for a sustained high level of productivity. This means that leaders should do their utmost to discover the wants, needs, dreams and aspirations of their followers and work very closely with them for the fulfillment of those dreams because fulfilled followers are generally more supportive and productive.

In addition, if leaders are going to be successful in the creation of a productive working environment and sustain a high motivational level over time, they need to clearly understand both the formal and informal structural dynamics of their organizations, including the church. This knowledge is needed due to the influential follower-leaders who can sufficiently impact the work processes for good or ill, and leaders need not only to know who those people are but how to work with them for the good of the whole.

There is definitely a need in every organization/institution for good leaders, people who clearly understand not only how to lead but also how to follow; leaders who know how to light a spark and keep it burning in the hearts and minds of those whom they lead. There is even a greater need for good followers who comprehend the art of followership and how to do so intelligently in order to avoid the mistakes and conflicts that can potentially undermine the progress of the organization of which they are a part and for which they are responsible. Good followers are a significant key to the success of any institution because in spite of how good a leader may be very little will be accomplished without good followers (and the reverse is also probably true). But what is followership? Why is followership so important? Why do people follow leaders? Things that followers should know and avoid and what type of followers should people be are some of the areas I will attempt to address/answer, inclusive of the Christian perspective, in this chapter.

Following is an art that all people should learn because in life, most will function in both leadership and followership roles. It is a type of self-mastery, the mastering of one's egos and/or willpower, something that demands significant effort, especially from those who consider themselves to be independent (Donnithorne, *The West Point Way of Leadership*, p. 20).

An excellent example of teaching people how to follow is that which is practiced at the United States Military Academy, West Point. Its approach is based on the philosophy that learning to follow is just the beginning of leadership. All cadets (generally young recruits) entering the college spend their first year learning self-discipline and stress and time management. Initially, they are "asked" to surrender their independence in exchange for the values of the military institution of which they have become a part. The heads of male cadets are shaved while the hair of the female cadets is cut short, and they are given uniforms to wear that make them look alike. They are taught how to sit, stand, eat, speak, and make their beds. And they are told when to go to bed, when to wake up, what to do, and when to do it. What the military attempts to do is to erase their past and begin to "write" on the minds of the cadets its way of thinking and behaving. This is a very rigid and disciplinary approach that facilitates the inculcation of the military's culture and some erosion (unlearning) of the cadets' history, and there is no doubt that it is very successful (Ibid.).

It is the author's belief that another significant reason for this rigid approach by the military is to rid itself of what Koestanbaum refers to as "the greatest danger in the world," which is " unthinking people—people who feel passionately but do not think, people who have no education, people who have nothing to lose" (Koestenbaum, *Leadership*, p. 310), because those who fail to measure up to the military's standards are expelled.

It appears to me that there are some implicative parallels in the military's accomplishments for that of Christian discipleship making. Or one may perform some extrapolation from the same with the intent of applying some military principles to the self in reference to the making of oneself into a disciple since Christianity does not have the power of imposition as does the military. However, two important parallels for discipleship making are apparent: (1) surrendering our independence in exchange for the values and principles of our Lord Jesus Christ and (2) learning to follow Him through the empowerment of the Holy Spirit. Self mastery of our ego will produce a new paradigmatic and cultural experience, a completely different life in Jesus.

Surrendering One's Independence

The ultimate example of surrendering one's willpower to that of another, which resulted in an excellent following was that exercised by Jesus during His itinerary on earth. He became the second Adam, divinity clothed in humanity, and had the choice, as all humans do, to assert His independence and follow the first Adam. Instead, Christ made a conscientious decision to do that which His Father sent Him to accomplish, the grand mission to reveal who the Father is and sacrifice His life for the redemption of the human family. This is clearly evidenced by His words, which were in complete harmony with His actions, that "my meat is to do the will of him that sent me, and to finish his work" (John 4:34) and "I came down from heaven, not to do mine own will, but the will of him that sent me" (John 6:38). In the final analysis, Jesus humbly admitted that "I have finished the work which thou gavest me to do" (John 17:4), an act that He accomplished on the cross as was further expressed by Him prior to His last breath when He proclaimed "It is finished" (John 19:30).

Another example is that of numerous young people joining the military institution. It is not very surprising to understand how citizens of a country will subject themselves to life-threatening situations by becoming members of the military establishment. They do because they believe in the principles and values that form the foundation of their government/country and will fight in defense of those principles/values and country. They are more than willing to give up a great deal of their independence to become a part of a prestigious institution in spite of the potential dangers. How many of us as Christians are willing to sacrifice our independence in exchange for Jesus' system of values and principles that will significantly improve our lives here on earth in preparation for a life of eternal bliss with Him? The center of Christianity is Jesus Christ, and accepting Him as our Lord and Commander in Chief is a pledge of allegiance to Him, as well as a decision to join His "army" to fight in the spiritual warfare that will have some physical consequences of many having to make the ultimate sacrifice of literally dying for Him.

I heard of an incident that occurred in New York on a Sabbath morning in which several masked men with guns walked into one of our churches and asked how many of the members were willing to die for Jesus? The response was not surprising. Almost all of the members got up and walked out the church without knowing that it was staged.

How often we forget that when we accept Jesus as our Lord and Savior it transforms our way of thinking, speaking, and behaving to that of the secular society in which we live. Sometimes I wonder what is it that is preventing or making us so reluctant to make the kinds of sacrifices needed to conform to the principles of our newfound faith culture in Jesus. Why is it that members of the military seem to adhere more closely to the values of their newfound culture and respond more readily to their commander-in-chief, even when required to place themselves in life-sacrificing circumstances, than Christians do? Accepting Jesus is tantamount to surrendering our independence in exchange for our dependence on Him, which is far more potent and life saving than anything on earth.

Self-mastery of the Ego/Will

Learning to master one's ego and/or will, and changing to a new cultural lifestyle in Jesus are two very different processes. We are all born with some amount of ego, and I assume that some aspects of it are acquired from our environmental conditioning. It is a natural thing for individuals to be concerned about their self-interests and needs over those of the broader society, but when people come together and live in civilized/organized groups, there is a greater need to become more concerned with the collective good by submerging much of our egocentric needs and controlling our willpower when the need arises.

It is probably even more difficult when we accept Jesus as our Savior in that we are expected to surrender our total self to Him and give the Holy Spirit supreme control over our lives, something that is problematic for the egocentric and self-willed person. However, in spite of the size of the ego or the strength of the will of any individual, the military has an established program that is designed to effectuate the acculturation of all new members/recruits. On the other hand, the church does not seem to have a specific program designed to make "recruits" or new church members into disciples for Christ. If this is the case, and it appears to be, because only a small percentage of Adventists are involved in sharing their faith, who is to blame? Is this the result of a lack of a discipleship training program in the church or is it because redemptive decisions are made on an individual basis and not collectively? The time is now for the development of a discipleship training program and implementation throughout the church. This would bring the church into alignment with its true mission of not only preaching the gospel but also making disciples for Christ that would

Chapter 2 Followership

plug the hemorrhaging of new and relatively new members through the churches' back doors. Such a program would help in a significant way to facilitate the change over to the new cultural lifestyle in Jesus.

Nothing is a more potent witness than experiencing Christians living the teachings of Jesus and mentoring others to do the same. People are more likely to follow the example of others than just their teachings.

The Significance of Good Followers

The importance of good to excellent leadership in organizations cannot be underestimated because leaders provide directions and generate the necessary energy to move the organization forward and accompany or lead the way. Followership, although not placed in the same value category as leadership, cannot be underestimated because good to excellent followers play extremely critical roles in organizations. Without followers there is no need for leaders. Followers are the most important resource of both leaders and organizations because organizational plans are devised and implemented through them as well as problems are identified and solved with their cooperation.

The bottom line is that followers are the producers, the ones who do the "dirty work"; it is at their level where the organizational rubber meets the road and very little gets done without their involvement. Organizations are, therefore, very dependent upon the services of followers for their success, and the church is not an exception.

Why Do People Follow Leaders?

There are too many leaders who take great offense to followers providing them with either constructive or destructive criticism. They fail to realize that they are living in a fish bowl and that followers are evaluating them in totality and drawing conclusions about them on a consistent basis. They do so because they are not passive but active participants and they will choose to or not to follow on the basis of their conclusions.

There are quite a number of reasons why followers are attracted to, connect with, and follow leaders. According to the literature, the following are the most significant reasons, although not limited to, why people follow leaders.

Trust

The first law of followership is trust. Larry Donnithorne refers to this as the glue that holds a team together and any leader who forgets this does so at his/her peril (*The West Point Way of Leadership*, p. 75). If followers do not trust the messenger/leader, they will not trust the message, and if both message and messenger have no credibility with followers, they will not follow the leader. But what is trust? It is an assured reliance or confident dependence on the character, integrity, credibility, ability, strength, or truth of someone or something; confidence that is placed in someone (*Webster's Third New International Dictionary*).

Trust is probably the most important component in almost all relationships. Even con artists want to know that those with whom they are dealing can be trusted in order for them to con them. It is very difficult for relationships to remain healthy and survive exclusive of trust. If husbands and wives do not trust each other, at some point in time the relationship will disintegrate. Trust is, therefore, a key ingredient in the initial development and growth of a leader and follower relationship.

If trust is so critical to human relationships, why does the Bible paint such a bleak picture of trust between people? It reads:

- "Put not your trust in princes" (Ps. 146:3).

- "Trust ye not in a friend, … keep the doors of thy mouth from her that lieth in thy bosom" (Micah 7:5).

- "Beware of your friends; do not trust anyone in your clan. For every one of them is a deceiver and every friend a slanderer. Friend deceives friend" (Jer. 9:4, 5, NIV).

- We are unequivocally admonished not to put our trust in family members and friends who are potential deceivers, but there is One who will never deceive us and that is Jesus Christ (Ps. 118:8; Job 13:15).

Two things are of importance here: (1) trust comes in degrees and (2) all relationships should be handled with great intelligence. As gregarious human beings, many of us have experienced serious problems in relationships and have learned to invest varying amounts of trust in each of them. For example, someone whom we know very well and have had a healthy relationship with is trusted much more than someone with whom we have had a rocky relationship over the same time period. In addition, because all human beings have been deceived by family members or friends at some point in their lives, they have decided to be cautious and behave in more intelligent ways by doling out trust in increments. As a person proves himself/herself to be trustworthy in one situation, he/she is given more trust, but absolute trust is reserved for God alone.

Why is mutual trust so important in relationships? When mutual trust is present in a relationship, this allows for the opening of the communication doors through which information flows freely and people are much more willing to collaborate their efforts for the good of each other than work in their self-interest. In addition, feeling safe with others is very important for all of us, and when we feel secure and confident in the presence and absence of those whom we trust, we are much more inclined to open up and make ourselves vulnerable. Finally, we are much more inclined to remain a part of the group or organization instead of voting with our feet if we trust the group. There are people who withhold their contributions and eventually withdraw if there is no change in the trust factor. We should bear in mind the words of John Gardner who wrote that "trust is not only the glue that holds a human group together, but when it dissolves, the capacity of the group to function effectively is seriously impaired " (*The Heart of the Matter*, p. 18).

The impairment of an organization to function effectively because of diminished or lost trust is due to the fact that its members are more inclined to be suspicious of each other; are very unreceptive to any proposal or suggestion; and will resist any influence exerted by leaders or other suspects. Under such circumstances, members tend to misinterpret ideas or conclusions and twist the motives behind what is put forth. At the same time, members are more inclined to multiply their defenses and pretenses, which results in the loss of time and energy, and little or no time or energy is spent in the constructive expression of real feelings for genuine resolution. Until the suspicion is removed through the rebuilding of the trust factor, little or no forward movement will be accomplished.

Leaders should be cognizant of such crossroads and realize that it is time to begin talking about feelings in constructive ways to start the rebuilding process with the goal of repairing the breach and restoring some sense of trust among members of the organization or church. In other words, leaders and followers should sense when group relationships are deteriorating, and every effort should be employed to stop the "bleeding" before the group goes into "shock" or total disintegration. Before the latter is experienced, followers will cease following.

James Kouzes and Barry Posner, in their landmark international leadership study, which was published in 1995, *The Leadership Challenge,* stated that when followers perceive their leaders to be honest, forward-looking, competent, and inspiring they are more inclined to follow them because they are seen as credible.

Honesty

As was stated earlier, followers consistently assess their leaders' every move and action based on their stated principles, values, ethics, truthfulness, etc., and if they conclude that they are honest, people of integrity, they are generally more inclined to follow. Leaders should be aware of this reality and align their words and conduct in order to create the right perception and gain the trust of their followers if they desire to continue the journey with them.

Vision/Forward-Looking

The Bible states unequivocally that "where there is no vision, the people perish" (Prov. 29:18), and because people have no interest in perishing, they will either jump ship or get off at the nearest stop. Followers need to know that their leaders have dreams, goals, and a road map for their group or organization. Followers need to know where they are going and how to get to a destination with the shared input of everyone. Followers have little interest in the same hum drum beat, the old routine of organizations and churches. They believe in progress, not stagnation, and they want to know that they will not be at the same place tomorrow where they are today.

The reality is that many leaders enjoy the status quo because they are the beneficiaries of the current system, and changing it creates great uncertainty and involves too much work. However, today's educated, enlightened and empowered followers are seeking greater involvement and/or participation, so leaders need to be cognizant of this fact and make the necessary infrastructural adjustment for greater inclusion and the development of a shared vision for their organizations or churches. This is one factor that creates much attraction for followers that generally leads to an even deeper involvement and the desire to stay with the organization/church.

Competent/Knowledgeable

Followers are generally inclined to follow leaders who are not only aware of what is to be done but possess effective implementation skills. They want to be proud of their leaders; they want to know that their leaders know what they are doing. Imagine that one day you boarded a plane and it was rumored that both the pilot and co-pilot got ill suddenly and were replaced by two incompetent pilots who, in the past, made some near-death decisions and experienced some minor crashes. Would you have boarded that flight? Or how about a surgeon who has a record of consistent failures when operating on patients. Would you subject yourself to such a doctor for any operation? Why do we, therefore, subject ourselves to and follow leaders who are incompetent and have no vision for the group or organization/church, no plan, no agenda, no road map and who have no idea where they are going and how to get there?

Unfortunately, church members are notorious for following leaders of this caliber. The vast majority of members seem not to know what it means to follow intelligently. Many seem to be caught up, not in the realization of the church's mission, but in the appeasement of the leaders, feeling vicariously powerful by doing that which is necessary to be friendly with church leaders, and sometimes at any cost. The reality is that many follow for selfish reasons, to see what is available for them to acquire rather than what they need to contribute for the benefit of the whole. Remember, church is about serving; it is better to give than to receive.

Inspiring/Motivating

Followers in general expect their leaders to be inspiring, energetic, enthusiastic, and positive about the future. They want leaders who are full of energy and are skillful at transferring that energy to them by lighting a spark or setting ablaze a fire that burns deep down within their souls for God and His church and the fulfillment of the great commission. On the other hand, it is difficult to follow leaders who are dull, uninspiring, lack energy, and are hopeless. Remember, leaders, you cannot light a fire in the hearts and minds of followers with a wet match, and followers are waiting to be lit up (Kouzes and Posner, *The Leadership Challenge*, pp. 22–25).

Purpose/Mission

Every group, organization, and/or institution comes into existence for a specific purpose(s), and both leaders and followers should fully understand the purpose or reason for the existence of their organization of which they are a part. For example, Ford, General Motors, and Chrysler exist to manufacture motor vehicles, so if these companies are producing computers, they are not fulfilling the true purpose for their existence. If these organizations have not changed their mission or purpose and are not working toward the realization of their existing purpose, there is no real reason why they should continue to exist.

Leaders, therefore, have an exceptionally serious obligation to both explain to and keep the mission of their organizations before all members/followers and design the necessary infrastructure for the effectuation of the purpose(s). In general, when this reality exists in groups or organizations, followers become more inclined to act in ways that contribute to the realization of the mission because they understand how they fit into the larger purpose, which leads to a greater recognition of their interdependence and the level of collaboration necessary for the accomplishment of the purpose.

In addition, the latter situation helps to moderate the competitively individualistic spirit to win self-credit and discredit others as well as lift followers above the provincial and liberate them from the belief that they should protect themselves from the corporate predators who are lurking at every corner and quietly competing to win the next available position at any cost. There is no doubt that an understanding of the purpose of the organization and where each follower fits into that picture leads to a sense of interdependence and greater collaboration, which in turn leads to higher productivity and followers' satisfaction, and this increases their inclination to follow leaders.

Vicarious Power

There are many followers who attach themselves to leaders whom they perceive to be powerful and follow them blindly. These are people who will not attempt to "rock the boat" but will go along with any and every suggestion/proposal in order to get along and demonstrate their support for leaders whom they think will empower them with important positions and assignments that will make them feel powerful. Unfortunately, these are followers who "suck up" and get sucked in. This particular situation can produce serious consequences in the future.

Manfred Kets de Vries describes a certain psychological phenomenon that occurs in organizations called transference, inherent in which are two modes: idealizing and mirroring. These two concepts, to a large extent, explain the mysterious effect or magic spell that so many leaders have on followers and why many followers are attracted to them. Idealizing is the concept in which followers attempt to endow leaders with powers and attributes that are unrealistic in and absent from them. Mirroring is the concept of a mirroring screen in which followers look for what they want to see and avoid seeing what they are fearful of seeing. This mirroring is performed by both followers and leaders, and it can be an instrument for truth and distortion, fantasy or reality. In distorted mirroring, the components of power, authority, hero worship, flattery, ambition, and attention seeking are used, and leaders at times feel the need to act out the fantasy of followers, the consequences of which can be disastrous (*Leaders, Fools, and Impostors*, pp. 10, 13). Jim Jones is a classic example of the acting out of his followers perception of him.

Some time ago I saw a documentary of Jim Jones in which he was preaching to his followers, and at a particular point in the process, he took a Bible, threw it on the floor, stomped on it, and declared that he was Jesus. The documentary was limited, but I got the impression that Jones had done such a great work for his followers that they began to attribute to him powers of a super human nature. He then sensed the attribution and acted out on that distorted fantasy. This resulted in him leading a few hundred followers to their untimely death. It is regrettable that both leader and followers did not wake up from their make-believe world before the catastrophe occurred, leaving others behind to grieve and pick up the pieces (Ibid.).

When and where we find ourselves in a followership role, it is critically significant that we avoid the pursuit of vicarious power and follow leaders as intelligent human beings. The Jim Jones situation may appear to be an extreme case, but a glance into history reveals that there have been many other cases in which millions of lives were lost due to blind followership.

Charisma

There are many who follow leaders due to their personalities. They like them because they possess attributes that some followers are attracted to in leaders. The leader may be tall, good looking, winsome, dynamic, or inspiring, and so followers identify with those characteristics. In addition, leaders may also possess certain abilities, qualities, strategic insights, and/or an extraordinary ability to motivate and light fires in the hearts and minds of their followers, and people follow because one or some of these may be of significance to them (Conger, *Building Leaders: How Successful Companies Develop the Next Generation*, p. 133).

Extraordinary Concern for Followers

Many follow leaders who demonstrate not only competence, commitment, and consistency over time, but a significant concern for their followers. They love their followers and they show it. These are leaders who are cognizant of their position and role as servant leaders and use their position and what power they possess for the benefit/good of their organization or followers rather than for their own personal gain (Weems, *Church Leadership: Vision, Team, Culture and Integrity*, p. 118). Followers are far more inclined to follow such leaders when they experience such concern for them.

Things Followers Should Know and Avoid

There are at least three things that followers should know and avoid in their followership role.

Linking Your Self-worth to Leaders

There are many followers who identify so closely with leaders that they develop a dependency and an emotional bond, with the latter being so strong that their self-worth is defined by their association with their leaders. This could be both a negative or a positive in that a leader's rejection may result in low self-worth and a leader's acceptance in high self-worth (Ibid., p. 133).

To base one's self-worth on one's association with any person, leader or not, is a dangerous situation in which to find oneself, and unfortunately, it is not an uncommon circumstance. It is one that provides for manipulation and abuse by indiscreet leaders, and followers are at times pressured to and violate their consciences in the interest of their leaders.

I have known and experienced followers who, because of their strong attachment to a leader, have lied, turned a blind eye to wrongdoing, and defended the leader in question in spite of gross violation of law and organizational policies. There are also some followers whose self-worth took a steep decline due to the disintegration of their relationship with their leaders. Ellen G. White affirms that "we have an individuality and an identity that is our own." She advises that "no one can submerge his identity in that of any other. All must act for themselves, according to the dictates of their own conscience" (*Testimonies to Ministers and Gospel Workers*, p. 422). Why? Because all people "are individually accountable to God, and each must act as God moves upon him, not as he is moved by the mind of another" (White, *Testimonies for the Church*, vol. 5, p. 725).

The Denial Trap

According to Kets de Vries, there are many followers who fall into the denial trap through their self-deceptive perception of their leader(s). They believe that their leader(s) is a gifted individual even when the leader clearly demonstrates his/her leadership incompetence. This failure to recognize the reality of the situation leads followers into a false hope of believing that through some magical spell or by osmosis, their leader will develop the needed leadership skills (*Leaders, Fools and Impostors*, p. 19).

This is a situation that occurs over and over again in some organizations and the church in particular. Many church members seem to believe that there are halos suspended over the heads of their leaders, and in spite of what they do, they are always right and will find sufficient support to maintain themselves in office. I have experienced many church leaders who have no idea of what it means to lead in God's church. They employ pure dictatorial and manipulative tactics to achieve their objectives, and many members think they are the greatest of leaders. Even under adverse circumstances in which leaders are discovered to be involved in unethical and immoral situations, many deny the reality of the situation and proclaim the leaders innocent in spite of the overwhelming evidence. This is certainly a denial trap that should be avoided, and members should listen at all times to the voice of the Holy Spirit.

Leaders Are Human Beings

Whatever our positions in life are, we should be conscious at all times that there is none righteous, no not one, and this includes leaders (ministers, pastors, elders, etc.). All human beings are subject to life's frailties; all are sinners saved by grace; all have Achilles heels (vulnerable points); and no one is more righteous than any other. There are many leaders who have vowed to do the right thing under all circumstances until given the conducive opportunity for wrong. There are also those who appear to be well adjusted—morally and ethically—but will change for the worst when given positions of power. Unfortunately, these are some of the leaders to whom we look for leadership, but caution must be exercised and not thrown to the wind because "it is often the case that those who are looked up to are not what they are supposed to be. Often sin lurks in the heart, and wrong habits and deceptive practices are woven into the character" (White, *Testimonies to Ministers and Gospel Workers*, p. 385).

Therefore, it behooves us not to overlook these critical factors and the potential for abuse of power due to the nature of human beings. Kets de Vries warns that if we "choose to ignore the essence of human nature, and the historical evidence of against the abuse of power, [we] do so at [our] ... own peril" (*Leaders, Fools and Impostors*, p. 182).

Due consideration should be given to all these critical factors (human nature, the potential for the abuse of power, and the historical evidence) in order to avoid entrusting unlimited power to anyone because of its intoxicating nature. All groups, organizations, and institutions should strive to maintain an equilibrium of power and authority in these entities and other relationships. People in positions of power should not only be accountable to those higher up in the bureaucratic structure, but also those whom they lead. When we understand the politics of power in organizations, there is no guarantee that justice will be forthcoming when an injustice is inflicted on a rank-and-file member. Some members of organizations, including the church, are of lesser value to those with organizational power, and they will be sacrificed for the protection of some bureaucrat and the general interest of the group. There is a greater chance for justice when leaders are also accountable to their followers.

I recall a certain clergyman telling the members of his congregation that if they needed to contact the president of the administrative branch of the organization he would give them the dime for the phone call. This to me was not only the epitome of arrogance but a clear demonstration of the clergyman's political connection with the president. Under those circumstances, it would take probably only a monumental mistake for justice to be achieved, and unfortunately, it happened.

Followers, and Christians in particular, should never follow any leader blindly. As they follow, one eye should be on the leader and the other on the Master. If the leader is not guided by the Master, place both eyes on the Master. Remember, "leaning upon men, and trusting in their wisdom, is dangerous to the spiritual life of any Christian" (White, *Testimonies to Ministers and Gospel Workers*, p. 385).

What Type of Followers Ought We To Be?

The contents of chapter one and what has been written so far about followership should provide some clues as to the type of followers we ought to be as Christians. The following enumerated types have been deduced from the previous written information of this book and should be given serious consideration by all Christian followers.

God-Fearing/Trusting Followers

The church is in need of good to excellent followers who love God supremely and others sincerely—people who study His Word, understand it, and bring their lives into conformity with its principles. Followers and leaders who recognize the importance of human leadership (both groups operate in leadership and followership functions) and follow intelligently with the understanding that God is the perfect and ultimate Leader, know that leaders are to be respected, not feared. Followers should be treated the same way, with mutual respect.

Too many followers are inclined to cross that abstract and philosophical boundary between respect and fear and become more fearful rather than respectful of leaders. The proclivity (willingness) is also present to place too much trust in leaders and end up being disappointed through the discovery of repeated confidential information, or when certain decisions do not favor the expectations of certain followers. Love God with all your heart and soul, and trust Him alone completely.

Intelligent Followers

These are followers who daily seek godly understanding and wisdom. They comprehend the principles inherent in God's word and are able to apply them to all aspects of their lives. They are constantly growing and stretching their minds through prayer, meditation, and the reading of the Word and other literature. As a result, they know the direction in which God wants His church to go, and when human leaders depart from His path, they (followers) are courageous enough to inform leaders of their diversion and, when necessary, depart from following human leaders into the path of God.

Intelligent followers are Christians who make wise decisions based on biblical principles and not on friendships and other political considerations. They are wise but not politically correct. Their yes is yes and their no is no in love. They are independent thinkers who do not group think unless what the group is thinking is principled centered. They do not go along just to get along even though they are peacemakers. They realize that there are times when it is necessary to "rock the boat" and sometimes to turn it over when people or members have strayed from God's predetermined will as is outlined in His Word. The greatest enemy to the human family and other groups, including organizations and institutions (the church also), is unintelligent thinkers who are unaware that, according to the Bible, God has not given to us the spirit of fear but of love and a sound mind for utilization in the advancement of His work on earth. Pray for understanding and wisdom.

Courageous Followers

Courage is that human quality of being brave; it is a mental or moral strength that propels people to venture, persevere, and withstand danger, fear, or difficulties; it is a firmness of mind, a temperament that enables anyone to hold fast to one's position in the face of opposition when one knows one is right.

This attribute is one that is developed over time and is necessary for godly independent thinkers/followers who know the Word of God and are willing to become righteously indignant when evil is perpetuated by both leaders and followers. Godly courage provides the backbone and fortification from being brow beaten and strengthens one to stand firmly on principles and prevents one from wallowing in the politically polluted mud for some personal gain or to pay back a favor. These are followers who, in the face of evil and injustice, are willing to make waves lovingly, gracefully, and/or otherwise in spite of the glaring consequences of social isolation, office denial, invitation exclusion, or communication of misinformation intended for character assassination. Christians with this quality will not buckle or cringe in the presence of leaders or other "power elites" in the church. They are strong and brave in the name of Jesus, and if it means that they have to stand alone for that which is right, just, and pure, they will.

Such followers understand the need to follow leaders under the right circumstances. According to Paul in his reference to himself as a father of the Corinthians, he urged them to "... be ye followers of me" (1 Cor. 4:16). However, he clarifies the statement in chapter eleven, verse one when he stated that the said Corinthians should "be ... followers of me, even as I also am of Christ." Then he informed the Ephesians: "Be ye therefore followers of God, as dear children" (Eph. 5:1). That which is so important in these statements is the acknowledgement that leaders should be followed only to the point that they are following Christ. Paul was very aware of the enormous influence of leaders and provided excellent advice to church members to be intelligent in their following. If spiritual shepherd-servant leaders are following Christ, they should be followed, but if they are not being led by Christ, then followers should follow God. This places the onus or responsibility on followers to become knowledgeable of God's will for both leaders and followers so that they will be in a state of spiritual discernment to distinguish when leaders are following and not following God, and to follow them when they are and not follow when they are not following God. It takes courage to so respond in not following, but each person is responsible for his/her salvation and needs to make that critical decision to follow God and Him alone when leaders make themselves like gods.

This kind of courage has its foundation in our connection with the Master and is not one of foolish and reckless daring. It is a controlled and balanced inner strength that is divinely inspired and will not compromise even in the face of death. The church is in need of courageous followers.

Equality of Followers and Leaders

The church is in need of followers who believe in the concepts of equality and the priesthood of all believers. We seem to pay more lip service to these theological concepts since the church has not provided any type of infrastructure for an unequivocally clear application of an egalitarian system and the practice of all believers as priests. There are still in place the structural and functional roles that inherently create an artificial division amongst God's people. I have never read in the Word where there is any divine or manmade social class division amongst God's people, never clergy/pastor and laity. Such a class system was undeniably dealt with by Jesus when He told His disciples that "one is your Master, even Christ; and all ye are brethren" (Matt. 23:8). This classless church/society is supported by Paul when he wrote that even our ethnic and biological distinctions are wiped away in our baptism in Christ because "there is neither Jew nor Greek, ... bond nor free, there is neither male nor female: for ye are all one in Christ Jesus" (Gal. 3:27, 28).

The current two-tier system of clergy/pastor and laity leads to what I refer to as the "halo effect" or the touch-not the Lord's anointed, which inevitably causes many church members to experience injustice and see evil practices perpetuated by some leaders and say nothing for fear of invoking the wrath of God on them. We should remember that in the Old Testament the whole of Israel was the Lord's anointed also (1 Chron. 16:16–22).

It is time for us to get back to our biblical roots and clearly understand that the body of Christ, the church, is not a bureaucracy with all its implications, but the family of God, a priesthood of all believers, and one in which members have different functional roles to play in the maturing of the body but that there is no inherent superiority in any of the roles or offices. The church needs intelligent followers who understand the equality of all brothers and sisters and can interact, function, and collaborate their efforts on that basis. But how do we get to the point of the priesthood-of-all-believers implementation when there are so many administrative/structural blocks that prevent most believers from performing certain priesthood roles. Jesus, our great Example, performed His priestly role on the basis of His baptism—as far as I know, He was never ordained by any man. Some may venture to say that He was ordained by God, but I would say that He was baptized by a man, John the Baptist. Think on this for a moment. Followers are needed to walk in the footsteps of Jesus.

Principle-Centered Followers

In light of the infiltration and proliferation of politics into the decision-making processes of the church, and particularly when it appears to be part of its cultural fabric, I can understand the difficulties involved in being a principle-centered follower. God and His system of operation, based on His principles, should be our number one priority and foundation on which we base every decision in life. Unfortunately, this is not the case.

Let us consider for a moment the concept of principle. It appears to me, based on my decades of experience in the church, that if a simple survey is conducted in the local church as to the definition of a principle, the results would be startling. Sufficient time is not spent in the education of our church members with the goal being a clear understanding of doctrine, objective, or concepts taught and how to teach them to others. The latter process creates reinforcement in the minds of the teacher and things are fortified in the mind for a much longer time. In addition, one's spirituality tends to enhance in the process of sharing. Leaders ought to follow the example of Jesus and do more teaching and less preaching for the edification of the body in preparation for the making of other disciples. It does appear to me that when followers are not taught or are kept in ignorance, and when the church culture does not reflect the significance of principle-centered decision-making, members will continue to make politically based decisions. The consequence of such a reality is that the church heads down a slippery slope into a more social club status.

The God whom we serve is not politically correct, but is a principled-centered Being, and if we are called to reflect His character to all people, this attribute is to be demonstrated in every decision we make in the church. This is not just a principle to be implemented by leaders, followers also have an obligation to do the same in spite of who may or may not be in compliance with the application of this principle. Remember, if the church (all members) does not stand for something (principles), followers will soon stand for nothing.

"Submissive" Followers

As members of the body of Christ, we are called to submit to one another. Irrespective of the position or "office" and/or function/role one plays in the church, all are expected to submit to one another according to Paul. This all-member submission role can be an exceptionally difficult one, especially for those with egoistic personalities and for leaders in general. There are too many leaders and others who are inclined to believe their own press and are too willing to exclude contrary ideas (contrary to theirs) for fear that those with better ideas will be given greater credibility and that of the leader will be diminished. Such exclusions are based also on tunnel vision and the perception that inherent in their "position" is a natural propensity for the production of the best ideas. What is even more troubling is that so many leaders use their "positions/offices" as conduits for the imposition of their will/ideas on followers in spite of the high quality of followers ideas. Are these the type of leaders to whom followers should submit in the body of Christ?

From a biblical perspective, leaders are to be respected and followers should "submit" to their leading. Conversely, followers should be respected and leaders ought to "submit" to them also. Submitting to leaders is to be done with much intelligence and concern for the direction of the body of Christ or the church. Intelligent followers should know the nature of church leadership and its role in the church. This knowledge should place them in a position to distinguish between when leaders are led by the Spirit and when they are not. This means that such followers should also have the courage not to submit to leaders when they are heading in a direction that is contrary to that of the Master. Under such circumstances, followers must take off the blinders and allow the Spirit to guide their consciences in the making of the right decision for Jesus rather than just following the dictates of man. Intelligent followers do not allow their respect for any person to be a justification for the contravention of any biblical principle and the disappointment of their Lord. Remember, God is no respecter of persons (Rom. 2:11). When leaders and others are going contrary, Christian followers are to stay the course in the Master's footsteps.

What should Christian followers do when their adherence to the mutual submission principle violates their individual rights? It is understandable that each individual has rights that should be protected for the safety/protection of the individual/minority from the imposition of the will of the majority. Individuals' rights are deeply rooted in the Bible and constitutions of many nations, and when they are violated, people will take legal action for their rectification. Christians on a whole, however, are advised to seek reconciliation when such rights are violated or when other difficulties arise. Jesus established a structural procedure to rectify problems among body members. He directed members to go to the offender and/or the victim upon recognition of an offence. If that does not work, take two or three witnesses and try again. If that also does not work out, take it to the church as a last resort. Finally, if all avenues have failed to bring about a resolution, let the guilty party be as an outcast. If this is the end of the process, there is that possibility that there may be no redress to the individual's victimization and other problems in God's church. This actually means taking the wrong or "licking your wounds" and moving on under such circumstances, difficult as it may be.

What if church leaders are leaning in a certain direction that appears to be unjust and are able to influence sufficient non-independent thinking followers to fall in line for the victimization of another member? This is not a hypothetical question, it is a realistic one.

Many members have been made to be victims by the political decisions of the body or majority of the body, and Jesus seems to have sanctioned the authority of the church in terms of making finite decisions. (I assume with the exception of those legally mandatory ones that must be resolved by a court of law.) Should the church's decisions be submitted to by all members in spite of the obvious flaws and their unjust nature? I am convinced that Jesus never intended to imprint His imprimatur on such decisions but expected the body to do the right thing and base its decisions on nothing else but biblical principle.

It does appear that even when the church's decisions are flawed and/or unjust that a certain type of "submission" is still required. Paul, in his counsel to the Corinthians concerning lawsuits among them, advised that in so doing, they have been defeated already. Then he asked two significant questions: "Why not rather be wronged? Why not rather be cheated?" (1 Cor. 6:7, NIV). Implied in these is the idea that accepting the church's decisions when it means taking the wrong is the epitome of submission and a bitter-sweet pill to swallow, but it is part of the new cultural paradigm introduced by Jesus and supported by Paul as one of the foundation pillars of Christianity. My conclusion is that the submission to such decisions helps to bring members to Christian maturity and that Christ will eventually execute justice for all.

The concept of mutual submission is an excellent one when viewed from the perspective of consensus building. The willing submission of Christian leaders to followers and vice versa provides for a grand opportunity to dialogue (not impose), find common ground, reach consensus from shared information in the spirit of fairness, and do that which is best for the body or the church. This means that followers should be thinking people with ideas to share and a willingness to participate in the decision-making processes that move the church toward the effectuation of its mission. Impossible? Church members must follow and lead in ways that are designed to change the prevailing mindset and cultural impediments that are road blocks to changing the way the body functions for greater efficiency and improvement. If Christians want to change and do things differently, they have to make it happen, and both leaders and followers play an extremely important role in this regard.

Conclusion

Following leaders is relatively easy for some people who are dependent oriented, but for those with large egos who sincerely value their independence, it is a task that is performed with much reluctance, difficulty, and/or not done at all. Following is an art and should be learned by all since all are involved in both leadership and followership roles at different times in their lives. In part, it is learning to master self, ego,

Chapter 2 Followership

and will and developing sufficient wisdom to follow intelligently and not blindingly as many do. It is learning to put oneself in the place of a leader with the understanding of certain expectations of followers and behaving in positive ways for the realization of those expectations.

Leaders must understand why people follow them in order to know what drives, motivates, or makes them click. This information will enable leaders to reach and keep followers inspired for their continuous contribution to the good of the group. It is a complicated issue for leaders due to the wide variety of factors that motivate people to follow. Some of these are leader-oriented and others are follower-oriented, and they include, but are not limited to the following: trust, honesty, vision, competence, inspiring, purpose, charisma, deep concern for followers, and vicarious power.

As followers journey with leaders, they should keep things in perspective. They should be careful not to define their self-worth by their association with leaders, should be realistic and objective in how they perceive both the strength and weaknesses of leaders, and should not elevate leaders beyond the human realm. They should exercise as much intelligence as is possible to avoid present and future problems for both leaders and followers.

Christian followers should seek divine understanding and wisdom and a knowledge of the direction and path to the kingdom of God in the event that leaders advertently or inadvertently divert from that way. These followers should be intelligent enough to discern right from wrong; courageous enough to stand on principles irrespective of the cost, even if it means doing it alone; and mature enough to act on the principle of mutual submission for a positive contribution to the unity of the body of Christ, which is a powerful witness to the world that God sent His Son to this world as a complete revelation of who He is. This may mean giving up your individual rights and taking the wrong (difficult as it may be) with the understanding that it is a more honorable way to conduct oneself in Jesus.

There is no doubt that Jesus was an exceptional leader, but He was also an exemplary follower, the One after whom we should pattern our followership. As a follower, He stated in no uncertain terms that His "meat is to do the will of him that sent me, and to finish his work" (John 4:34; see also John 6:38–40). And even under the most difficult of circumstances when He claimed that His soul was "exceeding sorrowful, even unto death" (Matt. 26:38), He fell on His face and prayed, "O my Father, if it be possible, let this cup pass from me: nevertheless not as I will, but as thou wilt" (verse 39). Finally, upon completion of the work He was assigned to do, He exclaimed, "I have glorified thee on the earth: I have finished the work which thou gavest me to do" (John 17:4). Difficult as it may have been to imagine, Jesus followed His Father's instructions perfectly, even to the grave. What a courageous, exceptionally intelligent, and sacrificial follower He was. His footsteps are worth retracing and remembering when things appear to be unbearable—His grace is always sufficient!

The following chapter will emphasize the type of leader Jesus was during His itinerary on earth because even though He came to fulfill the will of His Father, He also came to lead us out of our sin-sick state to a more blessed life in Him.

Chapter 3

Jesus' Leadership

When people talk about great biblical leaders, some of the first names that are generally mentioned are Moses, David, and Solomon, but rarely is the name of Jesus suggested. The former names are those of prophets and kings who led relatively large groups and nations and were very successful. They wielded significant power and authority, and organized their people/kingdoms in ways that are similar to our modern-day bureaucratic structures for organizational leadership. A vivid example of this was the one suggested by Jethro to Moses in Exodus 18 when he realized the tremendous burden Moses was bearing in his unilateral adjudication of the problems of all the Israelites. The suggested model of leadership is classified today as the command-and-control in which leaders take charge, make decisions, and give commands. It is also the type of model that some modern-day Christians deem acceptable for church leadership in our advanced age of participation.

The first three leaders mentioned above and others are still admired today, but none of them instituted the type of system of morality and ethics and a horizontal leadership structure for transition purposes that Jesus introduced, which revolutionized the world. He was by far the greatest, most powerful, and successful leader, not because of His position as Creator, but from the perspective of the foundation He established with His disciples (and those to follow) for the continuation of His mission, the success of which is reflected in the current share size of the Christian church and the transforming power of His gospel. He was a charismatic leader and well respected teacher/healer who commanded the attention of people, yet He did not exercise the kind of monarchial powers and authority, as other biblical leaders, while He was here on earth. What He also did that was of great significance was the introduction of a seismic shift in the leadership paradigm from a command-and-control model to that of the shepherd-servant model. He broke the mold by breaking away from the leadership practices of His day and setting a new standard for the commencement of His own "revolutionary" movement for God in which He led His followers to places beyond the horizon where they had never visited before—a totally new direction for all.

This chapter is not an exhaustive study about the leadership style of Jesus; it is intended to provide an overview of some of the major leadership attributes, qualities, and actions that contributed in significant ways to His success as the greatest of leaders. We will be studying the Gospels, which is a major source from which deductions about His leadership will be made.

A Shepherd-Servant Leader

Jesus proclaimed himself in John 10:14 to be "the good shepherd" and declared that "I know my sheep and my sheep know me" (NIV). In addition, He stated in verse 11 that "the good shepherd lays down his life for the sheep," and as a leader, the shepherd goes into the sheep pen and "when he has brought out all his own, he goes on ahead of them, and his sheep follow him because they know his voice" (verse 4).

Jesus used the metaphorical expression of a "good shepherd" to describe Himself because it was not only an appropriate description of who He was and His mission, but it was also a figure of speech that people understood due to the fact that shepherd and sheep were a common sight in biblical times and the shepherd relationship with his sheep was well known. Sheep were a significantly prized possession of shepherds, and they paid special attention to them through loving care and nurturing while providing human protection. Shepherds cared so deeply for their sheep, according to Dr. Lynn Anderson, that they went to almost any distance to ascertain fresh green pastures for feeding and pure water for drinking. It is said that at night shepherds who were great distances away from home would gather their sheep in a pen and sleep at the entrance to protect their sheep from wild beasts. In other words, such ferocious predators would have to pass through the shepherd first before getting to his sheep, and many made the ultimate sacrifice in an attempt to protect their prized possession. It is to this situation that Jesus referred when He said that the shepherd lays down his life for the sheep (*They Smell Like Sheep*, pp. 20–23).

This special shepherd-sheep relationship also involved helping his sheep that had birthing problems to save their lives. He was their obstetrician. When sheep went astray, or fell over cliffs and injured themselves, the shepherd was their rescuer who went out of his way to find them, mend their broken bones, and bandage their wounds. When the shepherd was away from home, he did not find a hotel or inn in which to sleep. He slept with or among the sheep, and at the end of the day, because of his close association with them, he smelled like and was liked by his sheep, and was known by them.

One of the significant features of the relationship between the shepherd and his sheep was that the sheep did little or nothing for the shepherd except when they were sold or slaughtered for food. Apart from this, the shepherd was the ultimate human servant of the sheep. He waited hand and foot on them, and where he led, the sheep followed because they trusted him. The shepherd did not drive nor command the sheep, but to a large extent, he depended on that unique (very caring) relationship with his sheep to lead them. Hirelings drove, shoved, commanded, and when convenient to save their lives in difficult circumstances, ran away. This was the difference between shepherds and hirelings (Ibid.)

Jesus came to this world to be our Shepherd because He loves and cares so deeply for us. His unconditional love for His "sheep" who went astray was demonstrated on the cross where He, on His own volition, made the ultimate sacrifice for our rescue and redemption. He has called us, therefore, not into a command-and-control relationship, but into a loving, caring and redemptive relationship with Him. Even though He has the power and authority to command and control, He is a God of love. He prefers to know that our response to His call and relationship with Him is based on our love for Him. Jesus did not call His disciples into a command-and-control relationship (if He did, the case of Judas would be considered a failure). Instead, He called them into one of a redemptive nature. This is the type of relationship that Jesus expects the elder leaders in His church to demonstrate. No wonder Paul admonished the elders from Miletus in Acts 20 to shepherd, not rule, God's flock. Jesus' shepherd-servant leadership is the method to be implemented in His church. He is our Example and is worthy of imitation.

A Praying Shepherd-Servant Leader

When shepherds were away from home with their sheep in places where animal predators roamed, they needed protection for their sheep and themselves that only God could provide. Jesus gave up the serenity of His majestic kingdom in heaven to dwell for a time in Satan's evil territory that was filled with spirit and human predators who were willing and ready to devour Him at a moment's notice. He also laid aside His divine power in order to experience what it meant to be fully human and completely dependent on the Father, the Source of His spiritual, mental, and physical strength, for His survival on earth.

Staying connected with the Father was of ultimate significance to Jesus, so He took the time out of His daily schedule on a frequent basis to commune with God. Imagine a fish without water from which it is able to extract oxygen for its survival; a new car without gas; and a refrigerator and computer without electricity. Without water, gas, and electricity, these things lose their utility or usefulness. Without that source of energy for the latter three, their functionality and productivity (those functions for which they were created and manufactured) would be extremely limited and/or made null and void. In order to avoid any limitation and unproductiveness, Christ stayed connected with the Source of His daily energy. To keep His "battery" well charged, Jesus would leave His disciples and go up on "a mountain to pray" (Mark 6:46), and other times, He would get up very early "in the morning, rising up a great while before day" and would go off "into a solitary place" to pray (Mark 1:35). There are other times when He "went out into a mountainside to pray, and continued all night in prayer to God" (Luke 6:12).

Three things are of great importance here in reference to Jesus' prayer life: (1) He prayed quite frequently, (2) He did much of His praying while it was dark, and (3) He spent all night at times praying. The frequency of praying and doing so alone on many occasions is understandable for the purpose of consistent communication with God in a solitary place that eliminated any interruption of His focus on the Source of His prayer. But what is difficult for me to understand (and this may have been a significant part of His successful prayer life) is what does anyone find to say to God all night? I can only assume that one would have to be at a certain level of spiritual maturity and love God supremely enough to spend all night in His presence. This is probably one of the most glorious and spiritually rewarding experiences, knowing that time does not matter when one is in the presence of and communicating with God.

As Christians, and particularly church leaders, we must come to a full understanding of the critical importance of prayer and implement it in our daily lives for our spiritual growth and development. Jesus is the Example to be followed, and we must do our best by His grace to walk in His footsteps.

A Visionary Shepherd-Servant Leader

When shepherds in biblical times moved out with their sheep (and there are times when they went beyond the horizon), they had a vision of where they were taking their sheep to feed and drink, and they knew how to get there. Wandering in the desert or across large areas of land with no grass or food for their sheep and not knowing where the water holes were would have been disastrous. They had to know where the green pastures and water holes were prior to commencing the journey.

"In the beginning God created the heavens and the earth" (Gen. 1:1, NIV), and what a splendid realization of a magnificent vision. Nothing on a grand and relatively orderly scale as that of the universe coming into existence happened by chance. It requires greater faith to believe that out of some humongous explosion or the Big Bang emerged such an exquisite universe. The point is that God had a vision and Jesus made it happen (John 1:1–3). He created a universe of such grandeur and complexity for man to enjoy. "Then God said, 'Let us make mankind in our image, in our likeness'" (Gen. 1:26, NIV), and He made a perfect man and woman with his own hands, the first being from the dust of the ground. Fortunately or unfortunately, He created generic man with great intellectual abilities to think and reason, with the freedom of choice and decision capacity to remain or not to remain loyal to the Creator. Unfortunately, man did not remain loyal, and to this day, we are experiencing the devastating consequences of man's disloyalty/disobedience.

Fortunately for us we serve a visionary God and with the disloyalty came another vision to salvage man from the sting of sin, which is death (Gen. 3:15). This prophetic judgment and promise of a Savior fulfilled in Jesus is a vision of great complexity and one not fully understood by many of us. This vision is what brought Jesus on a mission to this earth.

During His relatively short itinerary on earth, Jesus spoke about the church but never established a physical structure in this regard. But this should not diminish or undermine the significance of those kingdom principles that He preached and taught and that are a reflection of His character or the essence of who He is and form the foundation upon which His church is built. As was mentioned in chapter one, the church is not the physical structure but the people who have accepted Jesus as Lord and Savior. Therefore, Jesus was the One who initiated, started, established, installed, and built His church. His vision was to lay the framework by calling, training, and empowering twelve men (Judas being the exception) for the continuation of the building process in His absence, and what a magnificent job they allowed the Holy Spirit to perform through them, the effectuation of the magnificent vision of Jesus for His church. He was truly a visionary.

A Mission-Centered Shepherd-Servant Leader

One of the critical components of leadership in any organization is the complete understanding of the mission or purpose for the existence of the entity and the establishment of an infrastructure for its realization. Jesus' mission to the earth was at least twofold: (1) to reveal to the world the character of God. As He said, "Anyone who has seen me has seen the Father" (John 14:9). And (2) to sacrifice His life as a ransom for the redemption of the human family (see Matt. 5:17; 9:12; 18:11; John 3:17; 12:47). Through His incarnation and perfect life, He demonstrated to the world how loving, caring, kind, merciful, and compassionate God is. According to Him, "God so loved the world that he gave his one and only Son, that whoever believes in him shall not perish but have eternal life" (John 3:16, NIV).

His mission was an exceptionally difficult one. The degree of difficulty was revealed when Jesus went to Gethsemane on the Mount of Olives to pray. Before He prayed, He said to His disciples, "'My soul is overwhelmed with sorrow to the point of death'" and soon after, He prayed to the Father and said, "'My Father, if it is possible, may this cup be taken from me. Yet not as I will, but as you will'" (Matt. 26:38, 39, NIV). This psychological/mental anguish is further strengthened by Luke's addition that as Jesus prayed more earnestly, "his sweat was like drops of blood falling to the ground" (Luke 22:44, NIV). This was a clear demonstration of the high level of stress that Jesus experienced days before He made the ultimate sacrifice for humanity. Yet, He stayed the course and completed the mission because He was not only totally committed and focused, but He was determined to see it through. To God be the glory!

Jesus, in His redemptive role, can be classified as the first missionary from heaven to earth. As leaders and followers in His church, we are required to know and implement the necessary infrastructure for its realization. God is depending on us to carry on His work in Jesus' absence, and He, through the Holy Spirit, will be with us to the end.

A Revolutionary Shepherd-Servant Leader

Jesus was the most successful non-violent and godly revolutionary in the history of the world. His words and actions were His swords and guns, and He was wise enough to educate and empower men for the continuation of His revolutionary movement that continues to impact our world today. He did three exceptional things, which we will discuss more fully: (1) He challenged the religious system; (2) He turned conventional leadership on its head or upside down; and (3) He broke down racial/ethnic and other social barriers.

He Challenged the System

Jesus could have chosen to become a part of the religio-political system and conform to the principles and practices in order to get along and initiate a clandestine revolution from within. But just as we are currently cognizant of organizational inertia and the fact that the wheels of any organization/institution grinds slowly, and that the bureaucratic beneficiaries of the system will erect any number of road blocks to protect their self interests, Jesus was also aware of the dynamics of His time. Jesus was aware of His limited time on earth and chose to begin a separate movement. In so doing He also chose to disassociate Himself in order to expose the corruption and hypocritical pretenses of the religious leaders. He paid little or no attention to political correctness or the "touching of the Lord's anointed." Furthermore, He reserved some of His most unpleasant criticism for the said system beneficiaries who enjoyed lording it over God's people.

Here are several examples of what Jesus did. A Pharisee invited Jesus to dinner and became very impolite to Him. He questioned Jesus about not adhering to the traditional practice of washing His hands before a meal, and the unexpected response was, "'Now then, you Pharisees clean the outside of the cup and dish, but inside you are full of greed and wickedness'" (Luke 11:39, NIV). To our modern-day minds and culturally defined ethical standards, Jesus would appear to have been very impolite. On the other hand, the Pharisee did not truly comprehend who Jesus was, otherwise he would have withheld his critical question and been more polite, considering his own weaknesses and the distance he had strayed by placing a higher priority on traditional practices over kingdom principles.

However, this was a glorious opportunity for Jesus in a one-on-one setting behind closed doors and He was unrelenting. "'Woe to you Pharisees, because you love the most important seats in the synagogues and respectful greetings in the marketplaces'" (Luke 11:49, NIV). By now, the Pharisee was probably wondering who this man was? He may have thought, "He is not one of us, so why is He so knowledgeable about my motives. He does not sit in our private meetings where we flippantly talk about our pretensions, self-importance, and the need to maintain an untarnished public image to cover up our greed and other vices." In other words, these were very pretentious men of religious orientation who cared very little about God's people and pleasing God. They seemed to have enjoyed the high visibility of the seats of power and the greetings of the people who perceived them to be honorable and highly religious leaders.

Such a confrontation did not leave a pleasant taste in the Pharisee's mouth, but Jesus had only touched the surface. Matthew records the inexorable (unrelenting) attacks of Jesus on the religious system and leaders in which He referred to them (Pharisees and Scribes) as "hypocrites" (Matt. 23:23, 27); Pharisees and Sadducees as "blind leaders" leading blind people (Matt. 15:14); as "whited sepulchers" being beautiful on the outside but unclean with dead men's bones on the inside (Matt. 23:27); as "vipers" or snakes that should not be trusted (Matt. 23:33). Imagine for a moment the indignation of these "respectable" men for Jesus and the seed sown in their hearts for His destruction.

Jesus not only "rocked the boat," but He sent seismic shock waves through the religious system by His confrontation with the chief priests and elders when He upset the temple economic activities. When the chief priests and elders questioned the teachings of Jesus, His response was that "Truly I tell you, the tax collectors and the prostitutes are entering the kingdom of God ahead of you" (Matt. 21:31, NIV). A response of this nature today would be considered insulting, insensitive, and unsophisticated. But because Jesus knew what the people did not; He spoke the undiluted truth without any apology. He was aware of the prevalence and depth of corruption, and the selfishness that existed in the priestly order, and the conscious effort to keep these things from the public. Even the meat of the sacrificial offerings that went to the priest for food was called into question. Not only was the meat unequally distributed, but the priests jostled among themselves for the best portions.

However, the commercialization of the offerings on temple grounds for personal gain was the last straw for Jesus. During His visit on the Jewish Passover, He witnessed this economic activity in the outer court of the temple where the Gentiles went to pray and realized that such a business activity should be conducted off the temple grounds. Why? Because the temple and grounds were set aside for holy purposes, and it had been turned into a marketplace. Jesus became righteously indignant and turned over their tables, scattered their money, and drove out both men and beasts. He made a cord or whip but did not actually strike the people. "The whip was symbolic of His authority, and a flourish in the air would suffice to make His intention clear" (*Seventh-day Adventist Bible Commentary*, vol. 5, p. 923).

This very bold act of Jesus did not go unnoticed by the beneficiaries of the economic activities of the temple and may have been "the straw that broke the camel's back" as these leaders laid plans to capture and kill Jesus. Not only did He touch the pocket books of these people, He interrupted the traditional operations of the well oiled temple system over which He had been given no authority by those in charge. But Jesus knew of the radically imminent change that His death (the real sacrificial Lamb) was going to produce, and He issued a wake-up call in preparation for that change. There is no doubt that from that day Jesus was a marked man.

Chapter 3 Jesus' Leadership

Anyone who challenges any system today should be prepared to suffer the serious consequences, particularly if it is a religious system that embodies certain fundamental values held dearly by its members. There are times when even such a system needs cleansing due to the infiltration of many secular practices that have been embraced by its members over the years and accepted as legitimate components of the religious and cultural milieu. There are many current religious practices that need to be weeded out. Sometimes I wonder what things Jesus would overturn in His church if He was here with us today. Would He overturn the head table at a church potluck? Do you think He would scatter the tithes and offerings being counted on the Sabbath? One of those things is addressed in the next section of this chapter.

He Turned Conventional Leadership Upside Down

The annual salmon run is one of the natural wonders of the world and is very fascinating to watch. It is a very difficult journey for the fish due to the fact that they have to swim upstream, and this is made worse by all the manmade barriers (hydroelectric plants, damns, etc.) they encounter along the way. But their destination must be reached if the goal of spawning is to be realized for the species continuation. So with determined focus and effort a sufficient number reach and achieve their goal.

While conventional leadership is "swimming" downstream with the river flow, Jesus introduced, as part of a new paradigm, a new theology of leadership that is still swimming upstream today. In other words, He did not compare, but made bold contrast "between aggressive, competitive, controlling, worldly leadership and spiritual leadership" (Anderson, *They Smell Like Sheep*, p. 52). Jesus made it unequivocally clear that shepherd-servant church leadership is *not* based on power and authority but on service and humility with kingdom principles being its foundation. He changed the Old Testament command-and-control model of leadership in which leaders were organized in a hierarchical structure of an institutional nature with enormous powers and authority to that of the shepherd-servant model.

James and John, two of Jesus' disciples, were vying for political power in God's kingdom with the help of an agent—their mother. These two men had some inclination as to what it meant to have some power and authority, and they wanted to secure a powerful seat on the right and left hands of Jesus in His kingdom. In our modern-day society such seats may not have the same value as they did in the Jewish culture in which the two individuals who sat on both the right and left hands of any leader were the second and third in command respectively. Imagine, therefore, how indignantly displeased the other ten disciples were when they discovered James and John's political ambitions. The result of the disclosure of these men's intentions brings to remembrance the situation of Joseph and his brothers in which they became infuriated about his dreams of them bowing down to him, symbolic of his rule over them, and we know what eventually happened to Joseph. People today still take great offense to those who are fiercely competing for positions that will give them power over others, and the church is no exception given the misguided understanding of members in reference to the power and authority attached to offices.

This misunderstanding was cleared up by Jesus in His response to James and John. If the body of Christ is the family of God on earth, then we are all brothers and sisters, not rulers and subjects. And the offices to which we are elected annually or otherwise are not positions of power but opportunities to serve the body (members) in different capacities. But read thoughtfully His response:

> "You know that those who are regarded as rulers of the Gentiles lord it over them, and their high officials exercise authority over them. Not so with you. Instead, whoever wants to become great among you must be your servant, and whoever wants to be first must be slave of all. For even the Son of Man did not come to be served, but to serve, and to give his life as a ransom for many." (Mark 10:42–45, NIV)

The contrasting message between worldly and church leadership in the above passage or statement is exceptionally clear. There are secular leaders who are in high positions of enormous power and authority and who lord it over those in their jurisdiction and receive tremendous psychological satisfaction from what they do. Many are very egotistic leaders who are intoxicated by the power and authority inherent in their positions. They are at the top of the corporate ladder and their game, and they cherish all the perks, attention, influence, and service that come with the position. These elevated statuses create a thirst and hunger that drive/motivate those competitors who are on their way up in the pipeline to do almost anything in the process to reach the top of the corporate ladder. (We read in the media some of the immoral and unethical things people do.)

Fortunately, the body of Christ has one Head, and there is no ladder leading to that position. There is one Sovereign Chief Executive Officer who is in that position for eternity, so attempting to knock Him off and taking over the top spot in His kingdom is futile. In addition, all members (shepherds and sheep) are under His authority and accountable to Him. So whatever role is played by any member in His kingdom under construction on earth is done not for self or self-glorification but in the spirit of service and for the glorification of God. Any member who has his/her eyes on a "high position/office" or wants to be considered great in His church should realize that the requirement is "slavery" or being a slave/servant to all. Officers and all others are there to serve, not to be served.

People (leaders, etc.) who are recognized as great in the church should be those who are converted and humble as a child (Matt. 18:1–5) and are servants (Matt. 23:11). The emphases in the church should be conversion, service, and humility because there is no ladder to climb. The way up is really down, and Jesus left a very distinguished example for us to follow in John 13:14–17:

> "Now that I, your Lord and Teacher, have washed your feet, you also should wash one another's feet. I have set you an example that you should do as I have done for you. Very truly I tell you, no servant is greater than his master ... Now that you know these things, you will be blessed if you do them." (NIV)

This example does not exclusively apply to leaders in the temporary setting of foot washing, a part of the Communion service, but in the totality of their lives. If members of the body of Christ (including leaders) are converted, the byproducts of humility and service, and many other Christian attributes will be clearly demonstrated in the lives of such members. Remember what Jesus said that by their fruits you shall know them. Jesus was also intimating that leadership may be a significant gift or role in the church but it was imparted for the edification of the body or church and not for the elevation of any member to a number one position or special status such as first elder or pastor. Irrespective of how exclusive we think or conduct ourselves, we are brothers and sisters in the family of God—sinners saved by grace. God is no respecter of persons or positions; He is primarily concerned about each individual's character, the only important aspect of our being that we will take to heaven.

The Jewish religio-political/sacrificial system and its leadership badly needed reforming, and Jesus sent shock waves through it from an external position. Although He went to the synagogue to worship, He kept His distance from its corrupt leadership.

There are times when God uses individuals to accomplish great things for Him. If He calls, will you be courageous enough to stand, even alone, with Him in the struggle against evil? Are you courageous enough to continue the unconventional (upside down) approach of Jesus in order to maintain the distinction between secular and church leadership? His grace is sufficient!

Furthermore, Jesus was fearless in His attempt to break all racial and ethnic barriers. He is the God of all people regardless of the structure of their faces or the color of their skin—He could not discriminate against anyone.

An Exemplary Shepherd-Servant Leader

Jesus is the most honorable role model and exemplary leader the world has ever known. When He proclaimed He is the way, the truth, and the life, it was not a political statement to draw attention to Himself in His bid for a political office. It was an accurate reflection of who He is and His character. His talk and walk were congruent. In other words, what He preached and taught and what He lived were in harmony. There was no contradiction between what He said and lived. He walked the talk and talked the walk. As a result, He was perceived as a person of impeccable credibility and character, someone in whom anyone could place complete confidence. Imagine the Roman governor Pilate, upon interrogating Jesus, concluded, "I find no fault in this man" (Luke 23:4).

It can be said with great accuracy that Jesus was a person of perfect integrity because He lived the life that He taught the people to live. He did not preach and teach one thing and live another. He never thought of telling the people to "do as I say and not as I do." His philosophy was that the people should live as He lived. His morality and ethics were beyond question. When He taught about the shepherd-servant model of leadership, He did not become caught up in the religious leadership elitism of His day by expecting those He led to serve Him; instead He took a basin and towel, got down on His knees (the Creator, Sustainer, and Redeemer of the world), and washed His disciples dusty feet. That act meant something in His day. It was probably the epitome of humility except for the cross. When He said that "I came not to call the righteous, but sinners to repentance" (Luke 15:32), He truly associated with those whom He came to call, not the elite and self-righteous chief priests, elders, Pharisees, and Scribes. (Of course, He came to save all, even them). He was always accused of associating with the lowest class of people. He was classified as one who "welcomes sinners and eats with them" (Luke 15:1, 2, NIV).

Jesus was exemplary in His communication. Understanding the process of and how to communicate to followers is a critically significant component of leadership. If a leader is desirous of having followers go along with him/her on a "journey" to some untested destination, it is imperative for him/her to transmit information (ideas, facts) to followers in ways that are convincing. It is not sufficient just to transmit information, the manner/method is very important. Being able to interpret one's communication from the receiver's perspective is an art that leaders need to develop. This means that leaders should be aware of the prevailing cultural meaning of words if one is to be an effective communicator. Jesus was the Master of this approach. He also knew when it was appropriate to be direct, indirect, and compassionate. He knew how to appeal to the intellect, emotion, and heart, and people gathered around Him constantly to hear His preaching and teachings. No wonder the soldiers who were sent to arrest Him reported back to their superiors that "never man spake like this man" (John 7:46).

He was exemplary in demonstrating the equality of the human race by breaking down national, racial, and ethnic prejudicial barriers. For those who are not aware, the Jews and Samaritans were neighbors (cousins), but they lived as though they were millions of miles apart. The Samaritans (half breeds) were hated and even referred to as dogs, and in turn, the Jews were hated by the Samaritans. So when the Jewish lawyer asked Jesus "who is my neighbor?", He dealt with the question in an indirect way with the parable of the good Samaritan. The Jewish victim on the road between Jerusalem and Jericho was passed by a priest and Levite, but was helped only by a Samaritan traveler. The lawyer was "forced" to admit that the person who was most neighborly to the wounded Jew was the hated Samaritan. Then he was advised to go and do likewise (Luke 10:25–37).

In Luke 17:16 ten lepers were healed but only one returned to express his gratitude, and he was a Samaritan. In John 4:4-42 Jesus revealed His divinity in some miraculous way to the Samaritan woman at Jacob's well in Sychar. She told her story of the Man she met at the well and many believed that "this man really is the Savior of the world" (verse 42, NIV). The vision given to Peter in Acts 10:9–23 convinced him that Jesus came to save everyone regardless of nationality. "I now realize how true it is that God does not show favoritism but accepts from every nation the one who fears him and do what is right" (verse 34, 35, NIV).

Why would Jesus reveal His true identity to a non-Jewish person (the above-mentioned Samaritan woman) and inform prejudicial Peter of His status as the world's Redeemer? Because regardless of people's national origin, race, color, creed, or ethnicity, Jesus accepts all who believe in Him and do that which is right. Jesus could have conducted Himself based on the culturally prejudicial practices of the Jews, but as the Leader of leaders, He exemplified in His decision and conduct that which was right even if it meant that He had to stand alone, which He did. Jesus mixed freely with all peoples and demonstrated His contempt for ethnocentric attitudes and other culturally prejudicial practices that were out of alignment with the principles of His teachings. He was truly exemplary in every way. He broke down racial, ethnic, economic, professional (clergy-laity), and other social barriers to show us how to live as His followers. He was the greatest exemplary Leader of all times.

A Shepherd-Servant Educator

One of the identifying marks of a great leader is that of being an excellent teacher. You may be asking "why?" The answer is that great leaders have ideas, vision, values, and beliefs that must be transmitted to followers, and teaching, not preaching, has been proven to be the most effective method when leaders desire followers to remember those things communicated to them. I remember quite vividly many things taught to me decades ago, but ask me about a sermon that was preached two days or a week ago, and I will not be able to fully inform you of its contents. One of the differences between teaching and preaching is the opportunity for repetition and reinforcement and a systematic approach in the presentation of a concept. On the other hand, preachers are more inclined to be nonsystematic in their approach. They preach one sermon today and something of an entirely different nature tomorrow. There is a disconnect between sermons, and therefore, the lack of opportunity for reinforcement. In addition, excellent leaders, not only are good teachers, but they reinforce their ideas, beliefs, and values through their conduct because they are cognizant of the fact that followers "hear" what they do more loudly than what they say.

Jesus was very aware of the products or end results of teaching and preaching, and so He invested an enormous amount of His time in teaching (Matt. 4:23; 9:35; 11:1; Luke 4:15, 31; 5:3). Two things of eminent distinction about His teaching were (1) He "taught them as one who had authority, not as the teachers of the law" (Mark 1:22, NIV) and (2) His methodology and content were of such a nature that "the people were amazed at his teaching" (Ibid.). I am convinced that when Jesus spoke He did so with great passion, confidence, and without any hesitation. With absolute certainty, He was the Author of the ideas, beliefs, and values He taught. And the thing that fascinated the people of His day, as well as us today, was His use of the examples within the cultural milieu (including plants, springs, wells, water, animals, sickness, and human deformities) with which the people were familiar to teach very significant lessons about the kingdom of God. His exclusion of the popular philosophical approach and inclusion of the simple everyday things such as stories and parables had a profound effect upon the people that no one ever expected. Even the hard to swallow but simple theological lessons of "love your enemies, do good to them which hate you" (Luke 6:27) were unforgettable, and who would really forget these ideas that ran against the grain of the culturally acceptable standards of "an eye for an eye and a tooth for a tooth"?

Something of great significance that Jesus did as a distinguished educator was the multiplication of His leadership. (1) He called and equipped twelve men; (2) He inspired them with courage; (3) He empowered them with the Holy Ghost; and (4) He provided them the opportunity to lead (sent them out two by two).

Called and Equipped

Many leaders are very reluctant to educate and train potential leaders for fear of being prematurely replaced by one of the trainees who demonstrates leadership development beyond that of the trainers. This was not a concern of Jesus because He was more focused on the continuation of His ministry after His departure from the earth. So He called twelve men and provided the best possible education for them (theory and practice), not in isolation from the people but in the context of rubbing shoulders with those whom they were going to lead and thus avoided the development of a superior attitude in these future leaders. According to Russell Burrill who quoted another author, "Christ trained His leaders in the midst of their own people, so that the intimacy of their relation to their own people was not marred," and they felt at home to "move freely among them as one of themselves." He went on to write that "we train our leaders in a hothouse, and their intimacy with their own people is so marred that they can never thereafter live as one of them, or share their thought" (*Radical Disciples for Revolutionary Churches*, pp. 62, 63). What Jesus did was to shepherd, mentor, equip, and reveal the secret of His success to His future leaders, the disciples, and upon His departure, they turned the world upside down.

Excellent leaders educate and train others, not reluctantly nor out of fear, but with the understanding that the work must go on and cannot be accomplished by one leader, and that no leader is in a leadership position for eternity. Replacement is inevitable. The only exception is the position of Jesus. He is there for eternity, and as the most distinguished Educator, He cannot be replaced.

Inspired Them With Courage

There are times in our lives when we become tired and discouraged and make mistakes in the pursuit of paid or voluntary work. The discouragement is further multiplied and becomes more psychologically devastating when beginning a new job or assignment because of our vulnerability and eagerness to justify our selection for the job or assignment. But what will go wrong will. When this occurs, it is a crucial time when leaders are needed to provide some encouragement to weather the storm. Jesus, being in the form of human flesh, clearly understood the reality of such moments. He was also cognizant that His new paradigmatic teachings would result in hatred, arrests, and even death for the disseminators involved in the propagation of His teachings. He warned His disciples of these serious consequences, but as the wise leader, He encouraged (provided the needed courage and confidence) them to look beyond the hardship to the opportunity to witness for Jesus with the power of the Holy Spirit who would tell them what to say (Matt. 10:19); that eternal salvation is the reward for those who endure to the end (Matt. 10:27); and that they should not be afraid of those who can destroy the body because they cannot destroy the soul (Matt. 10:28).

Of more importance was the encouragement He gave when He commissioned them to go and make disciples of all nations, teaching them to observe all things He taught them because He will be with them to the end of time (Matt. 28:19, 20). The epitome of encouragement came in the promise of His return in John 14:1–3 and the place He has gone to prepare for them. It is a promise that applies to all those who accept Him as Lord and Savior. Be not afraid!

He Empowered Them

If not all, many leaders realize that they cannot provide all the leadership their organizations need to accomplish their mission. However, there are also too many who are willing to delegate leadership responsibilities while hoarding the power and authority needed to get things done. These are leaders who are obsessed with the spotlight and have no interest in sharing it. However, when failure is a result of this hoarding, it provides a justification for leaders to do less delegating and say, "See, I told you so." This also gives the leaders a reason to continue to hoard power.

Jesus had real power and authority, and He had no reservation of sharing it for use in the redemption of people. He called His disciples and sent them out to practice what they had learned and He "gave them power over unclean spirits" (Mark 6:7). Matthew records that He gave them "authority to drive out impure spirits and to heal every disease and sickness" (Matt. 10:1, NIV), while Luke reports Him giving them "power and authority" (Luke 9:1, NIV), which they utilized in their ministry to others.

After His resurrection, He appeared to the eleven and in the "commission service," He told them that as the Father sent Him, He was sending them and "he breathed on them and said, 'Receive the Holy Spirit'" (John 20:22, NIV). This appears to be a prelude or preliminary event that preceded the empowerment of the disciples on the Day of Pentecost. Jesus said to them in Acts 1:8, "But you will receive power when the Holy Spirit comes on you; and you will be my witnesses in Jerusalem, and in all Judea and Samaria, and to the ends of the earth" (NIV).

The evidential occurrence of the empowering of the disciples through the outpouring of the Holy Spirit was apparent in their witnessing/preaching/speaking simultaneously in numerous languages, which resulted in the baptism of three thousand souls (Acts 2:1–41). They also performed miracles by healing many sick people, even the shadow of Peter passing over them resulted in healing (Acts 3:1–5; 12:12), and the handkerchiefs and aprons that touched Paul cured many sick people and drove out evil spirits from many (Acts 19:11, 12). It was the power of God working through these men. This is real power and one worth having in the ministration of God's work. But why do we not witness such outpouring today?

He Provided Opportunities to Lead (Practicum)

The reality of any job is that after a certain length of education/training, employees are expected to apply the things they learned in the workplace under proper supervision. In other words, they are given the opportunity to practice the skills they acquired in the classroom. Jesus educated/trained His disciples and then sent them to put into practice that which He taught them. He provided them with the power and authority to make other disciples that they in turn may make other disciples. This approach creates the exponential multiplicity of disciples necessary for the continuation of the work of reconciliation in His absence (Mark 6:7; 16:15; Matt. 28:19).

It is significant to educate and train God's people for the responsibilities delegated to them for the effectuation of both internal and external ministries in and out of the body of Christ respectively. Too many body members are appointed to offices and given tasks to perform for which they have no training or education, and when they fail, they are blamed for the failure. It is also important to give people the opportunity to practice those skills they have acquired in training sessions such as seminars. As far as I am concerned, responsibilities minus education/training equal failure in general.

A Compassionate Shepherd-Servant Leader

No one should be a leader who lacks compassion for the people whom he/she leads. This may contradict the type of self-centered leadership of the world in which we live and which is filled with selfish and self-centered leaders who care very little or not at all for others. I remember a male student at the high school where I work who said in no uncertain terms that everything centered around him and that he cared for no one except himself. Leaders who lead themselves only can adapt this student's philosophy, but if they lead others, it is imperative for them to be compassionate if they will be accepted and appreciated by those who follow them. Why do I write this? For leaders, compassion is like their credit card and they cannot afford to leave home without it or they will be discredited.

Jesus came into this "I" world and set about changing the selfish, self-centered, and compassionless world of leaders and followers. He set an example by demonstrating to His disciples and others what it meant/means to be compassionate. He preached and healed the sick because He had compassion on them. In the feeding of the 5,000, the disciples encouraged Jesus to send the people away because it was late and they had no food in that remote place. But Jesus could not, and we know the outcome of that situation in that they were all fed (Matt. 14:13–21). Prior to feeding the 4,000, Jesus said to His disciples, "I have compassion for these people; they have already been with me three days and have nothing to eat. I do not want to send them away hungry, or they may collapse on the way" (Matt. 15:32, NIV). When He met the leper in Mark 1:40–45, Jesus was "moved with compassion, put forth his hand, and touched him" (verse 41). And when He saw the funeral of the widow of Nain's son, "his heart went out to her and he said, 'Don't cry'" (Luke 7:13), and He restored her son. There are numerous other situations in which Jesus demonstrated His great compassion to many who needed His help.

Compassion moves leaders to action. How would a shepherd genuinely care for his sheep by ignoring those with broken bones and those with birthing problems? A real shepherd would not, but a hireling would. Jesus exemplified this significant attribute (compassion) that all members of the body of Christ should possess. They may not be able to heal people of their physical and mental illnesses as Jesus did, but they can follow His example in terms of showing real concern for body members and others in both words and actions.

A Principle-Centered Shepherd-Servant Leader

There are too many leaders who neglect to take a critical look or observation, never mind conduct an objective evaluation, of their organization, and this is probably much more pervasive in the church than any other organization. In my few decades of membership as an Adventist, I have never experienced any leader or leaders conducting a church, department, program, or individual evaluation. Everything is done on a very subjective basis, and things continue as they always were without any critical understanding of whether the church is fulfilling its mission or purpose for its existence and if it is not, what direction to take in order to effectuate that purpose. There are times that it is said, "This is the way we have always done things around here and we would like to keep it that way."

In addition, when questions are directed to leadership about this and many other issues, many leaders take offense to such questioning and perceive it as an undermining of their leadership. The reality is that many church leaders are more concerned

Chapter 3 Jesus' Leadership

about form over substance and politics over principles. Their moral and ethical standard is not getting caught for doing the wrong thing. They spend a great deal of their time becoming very proficient at the political game and less so at the principle-centered game. As body leaders we ought to take a careful look at the life of Jesus and pattern our approach to decision-making after Him.

Jesus demonstrated unambiguously the value and importance of basing everything we do and say on principle rather than on tradition or politics. When the traditional hand-washing accusation was made against Him, He could have chosen to appease His host by being politically correct and washing His hands. But because Jesus knew the enormous significance religious leaders placed on traditional matters and the outward facade of correctness, He chose to address the issue head on. There is no doubt that hand washing is conducive to good health, but Jesus chose to emphasize to His host that the internal cleansing of the heart was of far greater importance from a spiritual perspective than external cleansing and that priority should be given to ridding himself of the pollutants of greed, power grabbing, jealousy, and other sinful thoughts lodged in the heart.

Another excellent example occurred on the occasion when Jesus and His disciples were passing through a cornfield on the Sabbath and His disciples broke ears of corn and ate them. Some Pharisees saw what they did and accused them of committing an unlawful act on the Sabbath. Jesus' response was that David and his men were justified when they entered the temple and ate the consecrated shewbread that was set aside for the priests because they were hungry. Once again, Jesus provided a principle-centered answer. The primary point in His response was that the implementation of the principles of life preservation and mercy in our daily walk are of greater value than tradition in the sight of God, and so also is His Lordship over the Sabbath (Matt. 12:1–8).

Not long after the above encounter, Jesus met a man with a withered hand in the synagogue. Immediately, the Pharisees assumed that Jesus was about to heal him on the Sabbath, so they tried to preempt Jesus by asking Him the question if it is lawful to heal on the Sabbath. Once again, Jesus provided an indirect but very shrewd answer through a possible scenario of an animal falling into a pit on the Sabbath. He asked the Pharisees if they would rescue it on that Sabbath. Then He informed them that people are more valuable than animals, and "it is lawful to do good on the Sabbath" (Matt. 12:12, NIV; see also Mark 3:1–6; Luke 13:10–17).

In actuality, Jesus told them that the Sabbath was instituted for the benefit of generic man and not for his destruction. It is more acceptable to God to do good and save lives than to do evil and see suffering and ignore it on the sacred day. My question to you is, what do you think Jesus would say about going to a restaurant and spending money on the Sabbath? Or going to the cafeteria at camp meeting and alumni events and paying for our Sabbath lunches? Would you equate such an action with going to Burger King or McDonalds on the Sabbath? Do you think that Jesus would give an all inclusive answer of "yes, it is okay to go" or "no, it is not okay to go"? Whichever one you choose, why do you think He would give such an answer? Or do you think that Jesus would apply the same principles in this situation and probably say that it is alright to go on certain occasions and not alright to go on other occasions? Would you do as Jesus would have done as to reserve judgment when you see some members going to a Burger King on the Sabbath because you do not know the circumstance? Think about it!

Jesus said in no uncertain terms that He did not come to abolish the law but to fulfill it by emphasizing in word and conduct the deep underlying principles (see chapter 1) and His total commitment to it rather than just external acknowledgement and public obedience for show. The religious leaders were in it for the show, and Jesus was very cognizant of this. He called them hypocrites because they lived by the superficial letter of the law by giving, for example, a tithe of the smallest things such as mint, dill, and cumin but neglected the more significant things such as justice, mercy, and faithfulness (Matt. 23:23).

There are numerous other examples where Jesus exemplified the importance of thinking and conducting oneself on the basis of principle over situations and politics. This was His emphasis because He was a principle-centered person and so should we. Anyone who claims to be a follower, never mind a disciple, is obligated to walk His talk and talk His walk. His grace is sufficient.

Additional Shepherd-Servant Leadership Qualities

I have associated with a number of religious leaders in a variety of situations, and almost without exception, the spotlight is always focused on them as a result of their conscious or unconscious domination of dialogues and/or conversations in which they participate. It appears that leaders have that natural or unnatural inclination to believe that because of their position in a group or organization they should have the most "say" or be more verbal due to the perception that they are more well informed on the issues than any other. Many of us enjoy the spotlight and, if given the opportunity, will do our utmost to outshine all others or dominate those conversations in which we are involved. We generally fail to realize the ratio between our mouth and ears which is two to one (one mouth and two ears). If this is any indication of how much we should talk versus how much we should listen, let us take careful note.

Listening is an art that we, in general, need to learn. It is a potent tool that if properly utilized can have a significantly positive impact in the building and sustaining of relationships. Particularly when people are hurting or experiencing problematic situations and need a sounding board to bounce off ideas or just to express their hurt, it is necessary to find someone who is a good listener and not someone who dominates the process. It is also important for the one listening to do so intently with a focus and intense interest in the speaker. This will clearly indicate to the one hurting that the one listening is genuinely concerned about the person and the process. It is very unfortunate that many tend to listen with a blank stare and have no real interest in that which is communicated to them.

A Good Listener

Jesus preached and taught frequently, but He was a well balanced individual in that He was a great listener. When people came to Him, it appears that if they spoke first or after He asked how He could help them, He listened with great intensity on an intellectual and emotional level at what was requested, said, and/or felt by the individual speaking. It seems to me that He treated each person as though he/she was the only person in the world. He also gave each individual the opportunity to fully express what he/she needed before He responded. An excellent example is that of the woman with the issue of blood in Luke 8:43–48. She had heard about Jesus, and realizing that no one else could help her, she decided to touch the hem of His garment, believing that He had the power to heal her. After she successfully touched His robe, Jesus asked, "Who touched me?" (verse 45, NIV). She shyly came forward and "told why she had touched him and how she had been instantly healed" (verse 47). Jesus listened to her whole story and then said to her, "'Daughter, your faith has healed you. Go in peace'" (verse 48).,

Other examples are found in, but not limited to, Matthew 8:1–4 in which the leprous man came to Jesus and He listened to his request before responding with a healing hand. Matthew 8:5–13 documents the story of the centurion with the paralyzed servant who told his problem to Jesus. He listened to the man before responding and healing the servant. It appears that those who came to Jesus felt very comfortable around Him because He was an excellent listener.

He Was Patient

Some leaders are so far ahead of their followers in terms of their comprehension of their organization's mission/purpose for existence and/or vision and how followers fit into the larger organizational picture in terms of their contributions to the effectuation of its mission that they are inclined to become very frustrated when followers appear to lack an understanding of that mission and function in ways that create a negative impact on the achievement of the vision and/or goals. There are times when leaders must take responsibility for not fully informing followers of the mission and how it is to be achieved, and there are times when followers should take responsibility for not trying hard enough to understand and implement those processes necessary for the achievement of their organization's vision. Leaders, however, must be patient enough to engage their followers in conversation, dialogue, and whatever other teaching methods are available to ascertain their comprehension of that vision, and when all these are exhausted, good leaders should sit and wait for them to catch up. As difficult as this may appear, particularly for Christian leaders, it is a challenge that they must face and conquer for their own credibility and involving all members for the good of the body of Christ.

Jesus was the exemplary model of patience for all to imitate. He called twelve men of Jewish and non-Jewish heritage but from varied socio-economic background, and I can only wonder about all the unrecorded problematic situations He encountered with them. The difficult challenge for Jesus, I assume, was to teach these men concepts and ideas they had never heard before and which ran contrary to their cultural norms and beliefs—the principles of God's kingdom by which His adherents are expected to live their lives. This process involved, and still does, the difficult task of unlearning all the theological, philosophical, ideological, and cultural values and beliefs one has learned since childhood before embracing the new paradigmatic teachings of Jesus. This is a very significant reason why, as Christians, we need to understand the time consuming element of unlearning all these things before potential candidates are willing to accept the new teachings of Jesus. It takes time and much patience for this process to work.

Repetition is not the object here, but it is necessary to say the above in a different way as a confirmation of the difficulty involved. It is so much easier for children to unlearn certain ways of thinking and behaving than for adults. An adult's mindset is a reflection of all things learned from the institutions of life over an extended period of time. These things have passed through a mental filtration system and those values and beliefs embraced by that person and thought to be significant to his/her survival form a type of mental fixation that is very hard to erase. This is the kind of mentality that Jesus was up against. After three and a half years the disciples still did not fully grasp His teachings until after His resurrection. Too many modern-day Christians are expecting people to change their way of thinking and living "overnight" without the realization of the difficulties involved in unlearning or invalidating things learned from birth.

Without a significant amount of patience, Jesus would have probably failed to reeducate His disciples. He did a lot of "sitting and waiting" for them to catch up. The apparent patient frustration surfaced from time to time as in Mark 4:35–41 when Jesus calmed the storm that terrified His disciples and then asked: "Why are you so afraid? Do you still have no faith?" Another example is that of the boy with the evil spirit whom His disciples could not heal. Jesus again asked them, "How long shall I stay with you? How long shall I put up with you?" And then He said, "Bring the boy to me," and He healed him (Mark 9:19, NIV).

There are numerous other occasions where Jesus demonstrated great patience beyond human expectation. Think of His arrest, interrogation, and crucifixion, all of which He endured with incomprehensible patience. May He grant to us, His followers, that type of patience!

He Was Dependent, Not Independent

In our western industrialized societies, and particularly in the United States, adults are clearly expected to demonstrate independence as a personal quality. It should be noted here, however, that "no man is an island." No person is truly independent. All people depend on others to supply them with goods and services for their survival. Dependence was a very transparent quality in the life of Jesus. He depended on the generosity and good heartedness of many as He traveled far from home. He often enjoyed a good meal and a place to rest at the home of Mary, Martha, and Lazarus. However, His dependence on God the Father clearly transcended that on any human being. He said in John 5:19, "The Son can do nothing by himself," and just before the resurrection miracle of Lazarus, He turned to God and said, "Father, I thank you that you have heard. I knew that you always hear me" (John 11:41, 42, NIV).

The implication is apparent in that Jesus was confirming His total dependence on God the Father who was the Source of His divine power. Based on this fact, one can only assume that Jesus prayed silently on many occasions prior to some of His miraculous healings and other activities—calming the storm is one example. On other occasions He prayed audibly for people to understand that it was the Father working through Him that allowed Him to produce such wondrous things for the glorification of God's name and the strengthening of people's faith in Jesus as the One sent from God.

A Wise Communicator

The unequivocal preeminence of wisdom above most human qualities is confirmed in the Bible. At the royal inauguration of King Solomon in 2 Chronicles 1:1–12, he sensed the enormity of and the overwhelming leadership responsibilities of being installed king of Israel, and when God appeared to him one night, Solomon was given the opportunity to request whatever he wanted. Instead of asking for riches or revenge on his enemies, he requested "wisdom and knowledge, that I may lead this people, for who is able to govern this great people of yours?" (verse 10, NIV). Due to his unselfish request, God gave him not only wisdom, but "wealth, possessions and honor, such as no king who was before you ever had and none after you will have" (verse 12, NIV). Later in his reign, Solomon advised that "wisdom is more precious than rubies" so desire it above all else (Prov. 8:11, NIV). But what is wisdom? Solomon wrote, "The fear of the LORD is the beginning of wisdom, and knowledge of the Holy One is understanding" (Prov. 9:10, NIV).

Jesus was not an earthly king as was Solomon, but the wisdom and understanding He manifested in His interaction with members of the human family during His earthly itinerary appeared to surpass that of any king, ruler, or ordinary person. He was and is the Source of true wisdom and understanding, and there are times when, in His discourse, He sounded like the wise philosopher but was wise enough to provide explication needed for understanding. In His theological discourse with a Pharisee named Nicodemus, He presented His "born again" theological concept as a prerequisite for entrance into God's kingdom. He further expounded on being "born of water and the Spirit." He also said, "The wind blows wherever it pleases. You hear its sound, but you cannot tell where it comes from or where it is going. So it is with everyone born of the Spirit" (John 3:5, 8, NIV). This probably created greater confusion in Nicodemus' mind, but Jesus came back and explained what God did by sending His Son to redeem the world and that those who live by the truth come into the light in order to demonstrate that whatever is done, is done through God—there is no self-exaltation (John 3:1–21).

Another outstanding example is Jesus' encounter with the Samaritan woman at Jacob's well. The Jews hated the Samaritans and vice versa. Jesus could have easily walked away or ignored the woman, but as a loving Savior, leader, and wise communicator, He demonstrated the interdependence of the human family and dispelled the long-standing traditional bigotry of a Jew becoming "unclean" by handling a vessel used by a Samaritan. He acted as a true leader of the whole human family. There was a serious social problem, and Jesus intervened to change it. He asked her, "Will you give me a drink?" (John 4:7, NIV). The record does not reveal if she did, but based on the cordiality of the conversational exchange, it can be assumed that

He took and drank water from her and remained clean. Then Jesus got into a theological/philosophical conversation when He told her about living water that would cause her to never thirst again. It appears that she did not understand this idea, but He revealed Himself as the Living Water Messiah to her when He said, "I, the one speaking to you—I am he" (verse 26, NIV).

Other distinguished examples of Jesus' wise communication were exemplified in His response to the trick questions, "Is it right to pay imperial tax to Caesar or not?" (Matt. 22:17, NIV) and "Who is my neighbor?" (Luke 10:29, NIV). He had an uncanny manner of answering questions by use of symbols, things in nature, stories, parables, and sayings of a culturally identifiable nature and appropriate for the immediate situation to, not only answer the questions, but to teach unforgettable lessons. No wonder the guards who were sent to arrest Him returned without Him and reported, "'No one ever spoke the way this man does'" (John 7:46, NIV).

Conclusion

Wisdom and understanding are of great significance to leaders if they are going to lead people in a manner that will encourage and motivate followers to stay on board. Jesus was the greatest of all leaders and is the one Model worthy of imitation particularly by Christian leaders. All the leadership attributes and methods of handling situations are worthy of in-depth study and implementation in the process of leading others. Christian leaders should, by the grace of God, do everything humanly possible to develop those qualities and lead in the manner as Jesus did. By far, the most important thing to be considered by Christian leaders is their personal connection with Jesus, the Source of their everything and the only legitimate Head of the church.

We now turn our attention to the voluminous secular leadership literature (types, styles, attributes, and practices) to determine if there are significant discoveries that may have some application to the church.

Chapter 4

Secular Leadership

Leadership! Leadership! Leadership! It is the most critical component cited in the leadership literature and elsewhere in the determination of the failure or success of any group, organization, institution, or nation. Poor leadership, if maintained, will lead ineluctably to ineffective organizational performance with failure as its end product. Conversely, credible/exemplary leadership will produce positive and effective organizational performance with success as the end result. This chapter will focus primarily on the following aspects of leadership: (1) the critical shortage of exemplary leadership; (2) the criticality of leadership in organizations; (3) the different definitional perspectives on leadership; (4) the determination of who is a leader; (5) the forces that contribute in significant ways to the development of leaders; and (6) the signs of effective/credible/exemplary leaders. The leadership information presented in this chapter is from a non-biblical and non-ecclesiastical perspective and is intended for comparative and contrasting purposes with that of biblical/church leadership in the following chapter.

The Critical Shortage of Exemplary Leadership

I believe it to be a truism that no group, organization, nor institution can function effectively without some type of leadership and, according to Harry Levinson, "No organization can endure without leadership" (*Executive*, p. 227). If this leadership is so pervasive and such a critical function then why does a glance at the daily newspapers and the leadership literature reveal an unequivocal message of an unprecedented need for credible/exemplary/effective leaders worldwide. It is this kind of leadership that is in short supply according to Jay Conger and Beth Benjamin in *Building Leaders: How Successful Companies Develop the Next Generation* (pp. 1, 6).

One of the most significant aspects of this problem lies in the fact that there are too many people in leadership positions who cannot be classified as exemplary because they lack the critical leadership skills, a sound practical and workable philosophy of leadership, and the culturally acceptable ethical and moral values needed to lead themselves and others. Two current and classical cases of leadership failure are those of the Enron Corporation collapse and the very unfortunate ongoing child sexual abuse cases by priests in the Roman Catholic Church. It was of great interest to hear the CEO of Enron testify before the United States Congress that he was not aware of some very significant business operations of his company when, as is reported, some of the top officials sold their stocks in the company and made millions prior to the announced collapse of the company in which investors lost millions of dollars. It is the responsibility of leaders to know what is going on in the companies they lead. Conversely, Cardinal Law, the head of the Archdiocese of Boston, knew of the numerous abuses, according to released documents, and acted in a manner that was contrary to credible leadership by transferring those priests to other parishes. All that was fundamentally done was the transfer of the problem priests to other parishes for the continuation of the same problem. When there are problems in organizations, exemplary leaders take credibly corrective actions.

One very important reason for the shortage of credible leadership alluded to above is the lack of leadership education. In a study conducted by the International Consortium of Executive Development Research, as reported by Conger and Benjamin, "leadership again emerged as the number one content area for future executive education" (Ibid., p. 6). The two authors reported about a business student from Duke University who surveyed the top twenty-three business schools in the United States and concluded that in all of the programs students were taught to crunch numbers to death, but not how to manage, motivate, or lead people. Leadership cannot and should not be taken for granted as many people and corporations think and do. Too many people are placed in leadership positions based on their years of work experience in fundamentally non-leadership positions with little or no consideration for their leadership education/training. Many business schools offer MBAs to potential future leaders in business with little or no leadership information in their curricula. People are the most important resource of an organization, and if leaders are misinformed in this and other relevant areas, leading people will become problematic for both leaders and the organization for which they work.

The Criticality of Leadership to Organizations

There is a very interesting Pilot pen commercial that was shot in what appears to be the fake body of a plane with "passengers." Suddenly, someone asked about a pilot (meaning a Pilot pen) but another responded based on the assumption that either something was wrong with the pilot of the plane or that there was no pilot on the plane, and the other "passengers" began to panic. An organization is like the passengers in a plane and its leader is like a pilot. Passengers assume that pilots are well educated and/or trained to pilot the plane on which they are flying from point A to point B. If passengers know that a pilot is incompetent (lack the knowledge and skills) to perform his/her functions proficiently, even after boarding the plane, I can say with much certainty that before that plane moves all passengers will evacuate or get off.

Imagine for a moment boarding a cruise ship for a two-week vacation only to be informed that the captain is very incompetent and has a record of accidents at sea, resulting in serious injuries to passengers. Would you stay on board for even one day and jeopardize your own safety? Just as ships and planes need competent captains and pilots, respectively, to guide their crafts safely from point A to B, in like manner, organizations need credible, effective, proficient leaders to take their organizations from where they are to where they need to be. Without credible leaders, organizations become like ships adrift in turbulent seas with no compass, no map, no navigational instruments, no direction, and no hope. There is a Chinese proverb that states that "if we do not change our direction, we are likely to end up where we are headed." This is one more reason why organizations need competent, exemplary leaders who know their organization.

In addition, organizations look to leaders for direction, guidance, and energy as they journey together to a shared destination, and if the leader cannot provide relevant information and needed support for the safe passage, then such leaders are not worthy of their positions as leaders. According to Lovett Weems Jr., who quoted Robert R. Blake and Jane S. Mouton from their book *Executive Achievement*, "In the final analysis, leadership is everything. The best message, opportunity, resources, facilities and people will count for little if leadership falters and is ineffective" (*Church Leadership: Vision, Team, Culture and Integrity*, p. 17).

What Is Leadership?

There are more than 150 definitions of leadership in literature. It is a concept that seems to elude those who study it and attempt to arrive at some definitional position. Some claim that it is mysterious in nature due to the fact that it is most studied yet least understood. Others claim that it is like beauty, when you see it, you will recognize it. It appears that researchers in this area have relatively failed, from a consensus perspective, to arrive at a conclusive definition of leadership.

One author purports that "Leadership is Action Not Position" and it is a relationship founded on trust and confidence as well as "a form of service" (Adair, *Not Bosses But Leaders*, pp. 24, 140). Kouzes and Posner define leadership as the art of mobilizing others to want to struggle for shared aspirations. This means that leadership can be learned by almost anyone because it is a set of skills that can be acquired and practiced. They described it as a performing art with self being the instrument and that the "mastery of the art of leadership comes with the mastery of the self" (*The Leadership Challenge*, p. 336).

Another author quotes Dwight Eisenhower's definition of leadership as "the art of getting someone to do something that you want done because he wants to do it" (Tan, *Encyclopedia of 15,000 Illustrations*, #6851). Professors Tichy and Cohen from the University of Michigan reflect the core idea as well as expand upon Eisenhower's statement in their definition of leadership. It is "the capacity to get things done through others by changing people's mindsets and energizing them to action." Next, they explain in a nutshell how it can be accomplished. "Successful leadership," they claim, "must accomplish this through ideas and values, not through coercion or Machiavellian manipulation" (*The Leadership Engine*, p. 44).

The above definitions reflect a cross section of the definitions in the literature. However, when I refer to leadership in this chapter, the conceptual definition will include a combination of that of Kouzes and Posner and Tichy and Cohen because that definition reflects the essence or core of what leadership is about.

Who Is a Leader?

Talbot Adair claims that "leader" is a general word that is about one thousand years old and comes from the word for path, road, or course of a ship at sea, and that it is "one who accompanies you and guides you on a journey" (*Not Bosses But Leaders*, pp. 65, 66). This coincides with Webster's New World Dictionary's definition of a leader as one who shows the way by going before, meaning, before those being led. The assumption here is that a leader knows the path or where he/she is going and is able to safely take followers to their destination. The leader is the one who goes ahead of and is in a position to see obstacles and dangers and can provide guidance around and/or away from these in a different direction. Changing course to avoid danger is a significant function of a leader (remember the Titanic).

A person is not a leader unless he/she has followers and not until those being led ratify in their minds and hearts the appointment of that leader (Ibid., p. 163). This ratification is of extreme importance since leaders cannot force followers to do anything, so they must or should be able to light "fires" in the hearts and minds of followers as a means of motivating them to follow on their own volition. Even if leaders use the "carrot" of important assignments, offices, promotion, and raises and the power of the "stick" to demote, transfer, or fire, followers always have the option not to follow, even if that means leaving their positions and the company, withdrawing their support by pretenses, sabotage, and/or undermining the leader's vision or orders. Leaders, therefore, need to be relationship builders (much more will be mentioned about this idea in the next chapter).

Leaders are people who not only know where they are going and how to get there but also are physically, emotionally, and mentally strong enough to face and overcome obstacles, read the danger signs and change direction when necessary, and endure the journey with those whom they lead—they do not quit. Included in the strengths of leaders mentioned here is that which is captured in the Chinese proverb written by Loa-Tzu that states, "He who overcomes others is powerful. He who overcomes himself is strong." This is significant because leaders should be able to lead themselves first before leading others. Through the conquering of one's self (the ego and will), a person becomes a stronger and better leader because self-control is a critical attribute for any credible leader. It is a strength that allows leaders to control internal messages and not allow certain thoughts to be reflected in their speech and action, including their body language.

In addition to all of the above, leaders must be credible if followers are going to stay on board with them. What is it to have credibility? In two intercontinental studies conducted by Kouzes and Posner in 1987 and 1995 concerning effective leaders, certain significant characteristics consistently surfaced as the top attributes of credible leaders. These are honesty, forward-looking, inspiring, competence, and fair-mindedness. The first four are very interconnected and I venture to say interlocking. If a leader is in possession of all four, he/she is perceived to be credible and people are much more inclined to follow that person. On the other hand, if only one of these is lacking, it causes the leader to lose credibility. When credibility is lost, people become unwilling to follow and will even attempt to get rid of the leader. Credibility is the foundation of leadership, and any other foundation is like shifting sand (*The Leadership Challenge*, pp. 21–25).

Much more will be said about credible leaders and particularly about what they do; however, before we get to that point, I will attempt to succinctly discuss the question of whether leaders are born or made.

Are Leaders Born or Made? The Forces that Contribute to Effective Leadership Development

A very important philosophical question about leaders is whether they are born or made. In other words, is genetics by far the determining factor in the making of leaders or is the environment the determining factor? In generic man's attempt to answer objectively the question, many myths have surfaced in the process that have cast a dark shadow over leadership. Some of these myths are: (1) Leadership is a rare skill; (2) leadership exists only at the top of organizations; (3) leaders are charismatic; (4) leaders control, direct, prod, and manipulate; and (5) leaders are born, not made (Beausay, *The Leadership Genius of Jesus*, pp. 3, 4). It is this last myth on which I seek to shed some light.

The literature on leadership clearly indicates that leaders are not born but made. The following is a limited sample but reflects a cross-sectional view of the essence of leadership in the literature. Tichy and Cohen concluded that "all people have untapped leadership potential, just as all people have untapped athletic potential" and that "There are clear differences due to nature and nurture, that is, genes and development, as to how much untapped potential there may be" (*The Leadership Engine*, p. 6).

If all people have leadership potential and if leadership by definition is a "performing art" and "a set of skills and knowledge that can be acquired," then all potential leaders are born, but effective, credible, and exemplary leaders are made intellectually and probably emotionally. This notion of the making of effective leaders is confirmed by Warren Bennis who also introduced the idea that such leaders are not necessarily made by others but by themselves (*Why Leaders Can't Lead*, p. 23). What he means by "by themselves" is unclear, but I make the assumption that in spite of the education and training made available, and to which people may be exposed, if they have no desire to be a leader, it would be virtually impossible to make such people into any kind of leader. If on the other hand he meant that people can develop as credible leaders independently of others, when the complexity of leadership is considered, I question the possibility of such an undertaking.

One very respectable institution that places supreme priority, not on the selection of excellent leaders, but on the making of good leaders, is the military. As was mentioned earlier, it spends an enormous amount of money on the leadership education and skills training for its personnel. Beginning at West Point and continuing after, leadership is taught by teaching all new recruits how to follow commands. This may appear to be an oxymoron, but it is a part of the military philosophy of leadership that credible leaders are also good followers because in the final analysis, all military personnel function as leaders and followers. Leaders must, therefore, understand how to follow intelligently and do so when called upon. So the military begins its leadership education by teaching all recruits how to follow from a military perspective.

Based on that which I have read of military leadership, I am extremely impressed, as are Donnithorne, Conger, and Benjamin, with the length to which that institution goes to instill the leadership spirit and ethos in its personnel; the depth to which its leadership program contributes to its leaders' thinking and conduct through the inculcation of its vision, values, duties, and expectations; the common understanding of the quality character, attributes, and skills of which its leaders ought to be in possession; and the shared dedication to its culture, value, ethics, and operation (*The West Point Way of Leadership*, pp. 40, 115, 165, 166; *Building Leaders,* pp. 81–83).

It cannot be overstated that the bureaucratic nature of the military plays a significant role in, and is no doubt linked to, its success in this area. I would also want to assume that if leaders were born and not made, the military and/or some other institutions would have developed an objective instrument to select all such leaders and save millions of dollars that are now spent in leadership education. This discussion will continue into the next section due to its nature. If leaders are not born but made, what are the environmental factors that contribute to the development of credible leaders?

Leadership Developmental Forces

There are environmental forces that go far beyond genes and family to education, work experiences, opportunities to lead, role models, mentors, and hardships. However, it appears that the three most powerful forces that contribute in significant ways to the development of leaders are genes and personality, education (acquired knowledge and skills), and life/work experiences.

Genes and Personality

There is no guarantee that any transfer of natural potential (genes) for leadership will occur from parents to children, but the probability of children inheriting a higher level of leadership potential significantly increases if born to parents who are professional leaders. This position is very difficult to substantiate from a scientific perspective because such children would be environmentally influenced by their parents from birth, which makes it extremely difficult to distinguish that which was inherited versus that which was learned. Being born to such parents is still no guarantee that those children will become better leaders than those with the same or less potential born in families without professional leaders. It should be understood, however, that those born in families with professional parent leaders stand a greater chance of developing their leadership skills earlier in life due to earlier exposure of such skills and knowledge from their parents (Conger and Benjamin, *Building Leaders*, pp. 21–28).

In addition, people who are born with naturally likeable personalities and develop their leadership skills are more likely to succeed as leaders because of the combination factor and the likelihood of followers liking such leaders. Remember, however, that natural leadership potential and general likeability do not play an overriding role in leadership.

Education: Acquired Knowledge and Skills

Education in terms of formal and informal instruction in and out of the classroom plays a significant role in developing leaders. Instruction should include knowledge about leadership, not only from the perspective of theoreticians and researchers, but also from practitioners who live and work in the real world of leading people and probably have written about it. Written/spoken information from all three perspectives (theoreticians, researchers, and practitioners) should provide a theoretical framework from which to launch a leadership career. The knowledge and skills gained from instruction is only a good start; it is insufficient for the total development of well-rounded leaders (Ibid., pp. 53, 176, 177). Life-work experiences must be added.

Life-Work Experiences

In a study conducted by Morgan McCall and others of 191 successful executives to determine the forces that positively contributed to their success, they discovered that experience was a common factor. But what was the quality of the common experience? According to them, what happened to them on their jobs mattered in reference to experiential knowledge of the business operations; demonstrated ability to work with senior executives; handling tense political situations; firing people; demanding assignments from both good and bad bosses; managing difficult relationships; dealing with complex situations; handling mistakes; setbacks and misfortunes; making tough life changes/transitions, e.g. getting derailed (Conger, *Learning to Lead* , pp. 29, 30). And according to Conger and Benjamin, many of the research subjects pointed "to experiences taking place much later in life, often during periods of intense challenge, or derailment" (*Building Leaders*, p. 11).

John Kotter of Harvard University conducted a similar study to the one mentioned above in which he studied 200 executives of very successful companies. He interviewed twelve of the executives who demonstrated highly effective leadership skills and concluded that experience played a significant role in their development; that the said leaders had opportunities to lead early in their careers, to take risks, and to learn from their successes and failures. The following opportunities were identified as developmental in nature: (1) challenging assignments early in their career; (2) visible quality role model leaders, good or bad; (3) assignments that enhanced and broadened their knowledge and experiences; (4) task force assignments; (5) senior executive coaching and mentoring; (6) attending meetings outside their core responsibilities; (7) executive assistance job engagement; (8) work on special projects; and (9) formal training programs (Conger, *Learning to Lead* , p. 30).

Being given the opportunity to lead and taking risks are very important. However, making mistakes is inevitable in the process. What is really significant here is to learn critical lessons from mistakes made and avoid repeating them in the future. This process is not as easy as anyone may think. There are too many people and leaders who make the mistake of believing that they know more about leadership than those they are leading and that they are always right, at which point they become very opinionated and, therefore, feel there is no reason to change their way of thinking and approach in dealing with followers. When this situation exists with leaders, here is what may happen.

I read a story written by Alvin Lindgren, which was published in 1965, about a clergyman who spent forty years in the ministry and felt very dissatisfied with his performance after that length of time. He felt that he was running back and forth, doing many things while accomplishing little or nothing, and he decided to see a counselor (also a former minister). After a lengthy interview, the counselor concluded that the clergyman had about one year's experience repeated forty times. In other words, what he basically did in his first year of ministry he repeated for the next thirty-nine years.

Before people can learn from their mistakes, they must recognize that they exist. Admitting to mistakes for many is not an easy decision. It can be very difficult and embarrassing, but before leaders can learn from their mistakes, they must first admit and then remember not to repeat them, and they need to select credible alternatives to be utilized the next time. Admitting to mistakes and changing involves losing a bit of one's ego and upsetting one's mindset in terms of how certain situations ought to be dealt with. It involves the unlearning of certain methods or perceived ways of acting (unlearning is always hard) and substituting or learning new methods or ways of performing or handling certain situations. The important point is to remember to learn from your mistakes and not to ignore them, for if the latter is embraced, the mistakes will be repeated, professional growth will be lacking, and one's credibility as an effective leader will be brought into question.

What Effective/Credible Leaders Do

If there is anything worth doing, it is worth doing poorly or incompetently! Correct or incorrect? I cannot be sure of your position or response to this statement, but it appears to be outrageous from a superficial perspective. Think for a moment of all the worthwhile things you have undertaken and performed poorly. Think of your first day on a new job and all the mistakes you made in your profession from day one. Whether we like it or not, the human factor is the reality highway on which the inevitabilities of mistakes and failures travel, but credible leaders emerge from collisions unscathed. These are people who admit their mistakes and failures and take corrective action to avoid repeating them. Credible leaders perform an intellectual transcendence that causes them to take an objective view of those things and perceive them as "steppingstones" to a new beginning and more risk taking.

Effective leaders take charge of themselves first and situations after; they continue to dream new dreams and translate them into new realities by making things happen because they are the architects of their organizations (Nanus, *Visionary Leadership*, p. 10). These are leaders who do not cover up their mistakes. They do not blame, manipulate, or dictate; they deal objectively with the situation and continue to lead by making things happen because yesterday's good performance is insufficient to satisfy today's obligations. They continue to make things happen.

A story is told about a boy who was very bored on a hot summer day because he had nothing to do. He went to his father to complain about his boredom and mentioned that nothing was happening. His father looked at him and said very straightforwardly, make something happen. Credible leaders do not wait around for things to happen; they take the lead in making things happen. What are some of the important things that these leaders do?

In a study that was conducted by Kouzes and Posner, they discovered some commonalities of practices that effective leaders do. The top five characteristics from the above-mentioned authors will be enumerated/outlined in conjunction with those significant ones described by other authors:

They Challenge the Status Quo

Credible leaders do not believe in the old cliché "if it ain't broke, don't fix it." They are cognizant of the importance of innovation for the improvement of the system/organization in order to stay ahead in their competitive environment while recognizing that the enemy of innovation is routine work. Therefore, they search for every opportunity to change the process (how things are done); to do things smarter and better; and to change things that need changing. They look for new ideas, venturing into the unknown, taking risks, and finding creative ways to improve their organizations (Kouzes and Posner, *The Leadership Challenge*, pp. 35–86). These leaders understand that in the process of transition, mistakes and failures will be made and encountered respectively, so instead of punishing followers, they encourage them to learn from their mistakes and failures.

A story is told about an employee of a certain company who made a very serious mistake that cost that company ten million dollars. Upon the discovery of the mistake, the employee offered his resignation, which was immediately refused, and he was promptly informed that the company had just invested ten million dollars in him and that he could not leave. If there are smart and credible employees who are worthy of employment within your organization, why get rid of them because of a relatively simple legitimate mistake. Effective leaders take responsibility for mistakes and work closely with employees to avoid repeating the same and/or other mistakes where possible.

Credible leaders also understand that once the system/process/status quo is challenged, some positive/negative consequences, such as uncertainty and hope, sadness and elation, will be created, as well as fear, anxiety, and apprehension, which are barriers to organizational success. Therefore, effective leaders consciously set about dealing with these mixed emotions for the stabilization of their organization in recognition that the "key for leaders is to ultimately deal with emotional energy in a positive way while recognizing the reality of the struggle" (Tichy and Cohen, *The Leadership Engine*, pp. 243, 244). The bottom line is that credible leaders are always seeking to improve the status quo of the organizations they lead.

They Develop/Formulate a Shared Vision

All organizations, institutions, and social movements begin with a purpose/dream/vision. Without either one of these, organizations would be like ships without rudders, adrift in an ocean and tossed about by the wind and waves. This is the reason why, according to Kouzes and Posner (*The Leadership Challenge,* p. 11), effective leaders dream dreams and picture images in their minds of great things that can become realities. They look beyond the horizon and over mountain tops and see things that others do not see; they see images of opportunities for their followers and themselves and set about developing a plan to achieve the shared vision. Such leaders live their lives backward because, in principle, they begin with the end in mind and work their way backward. In other words, they begin with the completed imaginary product and decide how to make it a reality.

Credible leaders realize that in order to achieve their dreams or shared visions they need the energy and commitment of their followers (stakeholders who have a stake in the vision); the ownership of the vision is critical and may be transformed through sharing and input, so they try to "shape people's opinions and win their enthusiasm, using every available opportunity to send their message and win supporters" (Tichy and Cohen, *The Leadership Engine*, p. 36); and the shared vision is like a magnet that draws energetic people to it and unites them in their quest to achieve the vision. Credible leaders also realize that they cannot journey alone, so they are inclined to integrate followers' input into their vision even if it amounts to a transformation of the original vision. They realize that making demands and dictating to followers are counterproductive, so they do their best to motivate by lighting flames in the minds and hearts of followers, which cannot be accomplished with a wet match. Such leaders are hopeful, optimistic, and energetic, and they lead the way in the areas of self and followers' motivation (Kouzes and Posner, *The Leadership Challenge*, pp. 91–146).

They Empower Followers to Act

One of the functional realities of leaders is that they cannot do all the work by themselves. Effective leaders are aware of this fact and set out to solicit support and assistance from followers through the cultivation of trusting relationships, the assignment of responsibilities, and the sharing of their power (not hoarding it) for the realization of the vision.

Credible leaders cultivate trusting relationships because trust lies at the heart of human relationships and produces greater collaboration among followers. It is a critical element in organizational effectiveness. When leaders become arrogant or aloof or show no sensitivity to the needs and interests of their followers, distrust develops. And where there is distrust, fear and uncertainty are created, and the consequences of these are less cooperation and collaboration and more organizational ineffectiveness. Leaders with credibility work hard to dispel any distrust, fear, and/or uncertainty in order for followers to feel safe and secure, a climate that creates greater collaboration and effectiveness.

In addition to building trust, credible leaders educate and train followers (employees) and then share their power with them for three fundamental reasons: (1) decision-making purposes that contribute to getting the work done; (2) because educated and/or well trained followers are less reluctant to use power to accomplish the goal or vision; and (3) such followers (employees) are more likely to embrace the paradox that they become more powerful when they share power (Ibid., pp. 180–204).

They Model the Way

Kouzes and Posner wrote about a WWII story of great fascination that exemplifies and epitomizes how effective leaders model the way. An American platoon was pursuing some renegade German soldiers over a mountain pass. When the platoon got to the top of the mountain, which opened up into a wide field, the Germans were nowhere to be seen and the Americans decided to retire in the woods for the night. When they awoke the next morning, the wide open field through which they had to cross was covered with snow, and not knowing whether the field was mined, the commanding officer told his platoon that they had to create a single path through the field for everyone to follow, and he would be the one to go first. If he died crossing, then another one would become the leader until a clear path was made for the others to follow. His assistant vigorously objected to him going first and asked, "If you die, who will lead us?" The response was, "You would!" The commanding officer went first and made a safe path for the platoon to follow. Here was a truly credible leader who led the way by making a safe path in which his followers walked. He had the authority to endanger the life of any other ranking soldier in the platoon by sending him first, but instead, he placed his own life on the line and modeled the way for others to follow.

Exemplary leaders are credible people who embrace deep-seated societal standards of ethics and morality. They conduct themselves on the basis of principles and values with broad social appeal. They understand that followers are constantly watching and evaluating their every move. Therefore, they model their principles, values, and beliefs in their talk and conduct. They not only talk a good talk, but they walk their talk; they not only do things right, but they do what is right on a consistent basis and encourage others to do the same, thus setting the right tone in their organization. Principles of ethics and morality; values, beliefs, and integrity (character) are extremely important to effective leaders because they are cognizant of the power of and influence of character on others. In the final analysis, those who choose to walk in the path created by them are walking on solid ground. Credible leaders model the way! (Ibid., p. 209– 240).

They Give Courage

Many years ago during my childhood, I was fortunate to witness the last half mile of a thirteen-mile race in what was referred to as the Recreation Ground on the Island of Antigua. As the runners filtered into the "arena" for the last, either half or quarter mile, one particular competitor made an exceptional impression on the people in the "stadium." (I think his name was Tim Hector.) He appeared as though he had consumed every ounce of energy in his body and was about to buckle and fall. He did and stayed down for a short while. He got up and began to run again, and very soon after, he buckled and fell again. By this time, the people were on their feet cheering for him, and amazingly enough, he got up again, and as the crowd continued to cheer very loudly for him, he stayed on his feet and completed the race. The courage from the crowd seemed to energize him enough for him to struggle across the finish line. There are times when I wondered if he would have finished the race without the support of the crowd.

Credible leaders understand the nature of human beings. They know that certain circumstances, events and/or challenges can produce discouragement, fear, anxiety, and trepidation, which must be faced head on and conquered. There are times when everything in people's lives seems to be out of balance; there are times when everything seems to go wrong in spite of how hard one tries. These are times when people or followers need courage from their leaders to continue the journey. Effective leaders, however, must have courage enough to conquer themselves and take charge of their lives and become strong, confident, and courageous in order to share their courage because to lead is also "to help others be courageous in their own lives" (Koestenbaum, *Leadership*, p. 154).

Effective leaders are aware of their role of setting high expectations for their followers due to the fact that followers generally behave in ways that are in harmony with leaders' expectations. And they know that followers who feel secure, competent, empowered, and well connected are the ones who are generally most productive. Leaders should, therefore, provide courage in great abundance to their followers, and they do so by providing them with the knowledge and skills needed for high expectation performance; they motivate, support, and bring the best out of followers by making them feel self-confident and rewarding them based on performance (Kouzes and Posner, *The Leadership Challenge*, pp. 271–273).

They Teach

This notion was alluded to under the subtopic of empowering others to act, but because teaching is such a significantly fundamental component of leadership, it has to be dealt with separately. It is so important that many distinguished authors on leadership believe that if a leader is not teaching, he/she is not leading. This means that a leader has to be a good learner, for he/she who does not learn has little or nothing to teach. Great leaders are great learners. Tichy and Cohen believe that teaching for effective leaders is not an off-and-on, now-and-again activity, it is at the heart of what they do and is demonstrated in the structural designs of their organizations, decision-making, and meetings (Tichy and Cohen, *The Leadership Engine*, p. 191).

Credible leaders teach for three fundamental reasons: (1) to transmit their ideas, values, beliefs, and direction to their followers; (2) for the multiplication of leadership in their organization; and (3) for the empowerment of their followers.

Followers need direction and guidance as they travel the organization's shared path. They need clear, realistic, and shared understanding as to their contribution to the big organizational picture, and it is the leader's responsibility to provide such information. Credible leaders have ideas, values, principles, vision, goals, and objectives that need to be communicated to followers/workers, and they do so by teaching them in an atmosphere of openness and with the intention of receiving feedback from followers. In other words, they teach to ascertain that followers and leaders are on the same page and that there is no misunderstanding in reference to the direction and goal(s) to be achieved. This is what distinguished leaders like Jack Welch, former CEO of General Electric (he went to the extent of establishing an institute of leadership in Connecticut for the education of GE's leaders), Roger Smith of Pepsico, Bob Knowling of U.S. West Airline, Larry Bossidy of Allied Signal, and many others who significantly contribute to the success of their companies. These men invest an enormous amount of time and energy in teaching for the advancement of their organizations. Teaching is a way of life for them, and they expect the other leaders in their companies to do the same (Tichy and Cohen, *The Leadership Engine*).

Effective leaders teach not only to transmit information, but for a higher and more important purpose of creating leaders at all levels of their organizations. These are leaders who comprehend the significant fact that they cannot provide all the leadership their organizations need for the successful effectuation of their mission. Therefore, they teach to ascertain that all levels of their companies receive the needed leadership for the realization of their contribution to the success of the whole.

These leaders also teach for the important reason of educating, motivating, building up, and making competent followers for greater productivity. In essence, they teach to empower their followers to make decisions and take action and to be less dependent on the leader. What they really teach is "how to attain a different, uncommon, but highly specific form of intelligence: the Leadership Diamond method of thinking and acting" (Koestenbaum, *Leadership*, p. 8).

Credible/effective leaders understand that there is a deeper aspect to their methodology of teaching. They know that who they are is far more effective in having a positive impact on followers than what they say. They are aware that if followers perceive them to be competent but lack integrity they will lose credibility, which is foundational to leadership and something that could lead to their downfall. These leaders fully understand that without credibility their teaching would have little of no impact.

They Share Power

I remember my undergraduate sociology professor, Dr. Earl Gooding (someone whom I still admire to this day), saying to us in one of his classes that anyone who can get another to do something he/she does not want to do has influence over that person. However, if someone sticks a gun to your head and compels you to do something you do not want to do, that person has power and control over you. In very simplistic terms, power is influence and control over things and people. It has its roots in and is divided into economic, positional, and personality, and positional power is supported by authority. Leaders have power based primarily on their position and personality. It is ironic, however, to know that leaders get their power from their followers' ratification of them as their leaders. This idea was confirmed by a bureaucrat of the U.S. Armed Forces, Major General John Stanford, who said, "We don't get our power from our stars and our bars. We get power from the people we lead" (Kouzes and Posner, *The Leadership Challenge*, p. 186). There is no doubt that leaders have positional power, and whether it is ratified by followers or not, they are still in possession of it. However, when positional power is given the green light through the confirmation of followers' consent, it becomes a more potent force in the realization of organizational goals.

The notion mentioned by the general seems to suggest that power is a two-way street; that both leaders and followers have it; that they both empower each other; that leaders give responsibility and authority and followers give their consent. Credible leaders understand the qualitative difference between both powers and the impact of their power over followers, so they use it intelligently. They also realize that hoarding their power is counterproductive to what they want to achieve, and so they share their power. They do so because it ironically makes them more powerful. General Stanford once said that "we become the most powerful when we give our own power away" (Ibid., p. 185). If the power given to followers is utilized intelligently and in the interest of the organization, it comes right back to the leader in terms of the accomplished work; their image enhances; and they look and feel "good" and receive the credit.

The implementation of this concept—the leader sharing his/her power and the irony of becoming more powerful by so doing—is an extremely difficult task for many leaders. The difficulty lies in the belief that as one gives power away, one becomes less powerful and loses control over certain aspects of the organization. In addition, many leaders are fearful of losing the spotlight and having it shine on others and their accomplishments, and/or being outperformed by a subordinate, which may lead to the elevation of that person's status and the diminution of that of the leader. A situation of this nature makes leaders feel vulnerable and could threaten a leader's position. Leaders must understand that they cannot provide all the leadership needed for their organization, and even though sharing power means letting go and allowing others take the lead and confronting the reality of their vulnerability in the process, they recognize that it is a necessary condition for the effective operation of the organization. Leaders should also be cognizant of the fact that they have weaknesses where others are strong and that they should be courageous enough to do what Max DePree refers to as "abandoning oneself to the strength of others" (*Leadership Is an Art*, p. xvi).

Credible leaders are secure enough to allow others to take the lead, particularly when it is in the best interest of their organizations. These leaders operate in a spirit of openness, and they know how best to respond in unselfish ways to the needs of their companies by not allowing themselves to be intoxicated by their power. There is no doubt that power corrupts, and absolute power corrupts absolutely. Power is very intoxicating, and there is something about it that even those who say they have no interest in it as well as those who have never experienced it, if given a "sip," will become drunk by it. Given the intoxicating nature of power and the potential for its abuse, effective leaders structure their operations for the equilibrium of power. They make themselves accountable to those whom they lead apart from those in the upper echelon to whom they are organizationally accountable.

This power equilibrium (balance) should be mandatory in all organizations as a counter to its abuse. Such power balancing is clearly demonstrated in the three-tier government established in the Constitution of the United States. This concept was made unequivocally clear to me in the Republican impeachment and very humiliating trial of the most powerful man in the world, President Clinton. Many were probably asking, how could this happen? But it was a clear demonstration that all people, including the most powerful, are accountable to someone or some body of people. This is wise in that abusers of power have an excellent example to refer to and to heed for fear of being discovered and brought to justice. (This is not a statement of justification for what was done to President Clinton.)

Given the potential for abuse of power and the nature of human beings, all should consider the warning provided by Kets de Vries in the following statement. "Given the psychological make up of human beings, one of the major aims of society should be the maintenance of a certain balance of power." Why? Because many "seemingly well-adjusted people change for the worse when put in a position of power." And he goes on to assert that "it is easy to become a sorcerer's apprentice when playing with power." Therefore, "people who choose to ignore the essence of human nature and the historical evidence against the abuse of power, do so at their own peril" (*Leaders, Fools, and Imposters*, pp. 181, 182).

They Embrace Dissent and Contrary Ideas

One of the ineluctabilities of life is that people will think about things and issues differently and have contrary perspectives for a wide variety of reasons (educational level, socio-economic background, philosophical, ideological, etc.). A story is told about two prisoners who looked out of their cell window one morning after a rainstorm, and one saw the sun in all its brilliance and declared it to be a beautiful day! The other looked on the ground and saw the wet, muddy surface and concluded that it was not a good day. The story demonstrates quite clearly how two or more people can look through the same lens and see things from a different point of view. For the objective person, looking at things and issues from all possible perspectives is a necessity, but for the subjective individual, one perspective (his or hers) is sufficient.

Unfortunately, too many leaders are inclined to believe their own press (that their point of view is always right) and use whatever means possible to stamp out all contrary ideas, irrespective of their benefits to the organization just because the ideas did not originate with them. Too many leaders are inclined to perceive views that are contrary and challenging to the establishment as negative, unproductive, conflict-producing and relationship destroying, and engage in mini-emperors' behaviors that are repressive to the open expression of such ideas, which is the norm in bureaucratic structures—zero tolerance for dissenters (Bennis, *Why Leaders Can't Lead*, pp. 73, 124). Under such circumstances, followers are inclined to preserve their investment in the organization by withholding the expression of any new idea or opinion, and the company suffers from the infusion of new and excellent ideas that may have the potential for growth and prosperity.

Credible leaders, however, not only embrace contrary ideas but also those that challenge and/or question the current status of their organizations because neither leader nor organization is perfect, and they recognize that "unanimity leads rather quickly to stagnation" (Ibid., p. 124). They also encourage divergent thinking and the expression of dissenting notions, which may lead to creative confrontation. Contrary and dissenting ideas enable leaders to see beyond their blind spots and narrow way of thinking. Such leaders (credible ones) have no interest in shadows or people who mirror them, but those who can augment them.

In a world driven by creative ideas and change, effective leaders understand that for their organizations to survive and thrive they need people who are smart and courageous enough to know and express the "truth" or their perspective on any issue without reservation. This is what companies like Intel and Johnson and Johnson do. They engage their workers in "creative confrontation" in which they not only encourage but demand dissent in the executive suite, and "they surround themselves with people smart enough to know the truth and independent enough to speak it" (Ibid., p. 91).

When people/followers/workers know that they are operating in an atmosphere of openness in which they are allowed to contribute their opinions and ideas without reservation, irrespective of how contrary they may be, and particularly when there is future compensation for successful ideas contribution, they are generally more inclined to submit them. There is no doubt either that companies for which such people work will be better off in the long run because it contributes to relationship building and greater productivity. Credible leaders welcome contrary ideas.

They Change Organizational Cultures

There are many leaders who enter organizations and begin making random and superficial changes without a comprehensive knowledge of that which they lead. Some fail to comprehend that certain changes should not be made in isolation due to the integrative nature of certain structural and programmatic components of organizations. The history and culture of an organization are critical for leaders to know prior to making changes in any aspect of their companies.

A story is told of a young Presbyterian minister who accepted his first assigned pastorate upon graduation. Upon arrival he visited his new church on the first day, during which time he saw a large cherry tree blocking the back door, which was one of two entrances. Deciding that it was not safe, he cut down the tree without consulting any member, not realizing that the tree was planted by John Wesley on his visit to the church some years before and that it was highly cherished by the membership.

Word of his action got around, and he was reassigned two days later, resulting in the shortest pastoral assignment in the history of the church.

Credible leaders endeavor to understand the culture of the group or organization they lead, and when they thoroughly do, they are still cautious about the process and speed applied to making cultural changes. Why? Because culture defines how people think and behave in organizations, and their conduct, which is a reflection of their thoughts, is based on the beliefs, expectations, norms, rituals, communication patterns, symbols, and reward systems of their organizations (Nanus, *Visionary Leadership*, p. 51). But what is culture? It is defined by Edgar Schein as "a pattern of shared assumptions that the group learned as it solved its problems of external adaptation and internal integration, that has worked well enough" for it "to be considered valid and, therefore, to be taught to new members as the correct way to perceive, think, and feel in relation to those problems" (*Organizational Culture and Leadership*, p. 12). The essence of culture, in other words, "is the shared patterns of thought, belief, feelings, and values that result from shared experience and common learning," from which emerges a "pattern of shared assumption" that he refers to as the culture of a group. (Ibid., p. 52). One can, therefore, assume that organizational culture develops over time and plays a significant role in the development of the group or organizational identity and stability, thus providing the moral and ethical standards on which members base their interaction.

Schein divides culture into the following three sections: (1) artifacts, (2) espoused values, and (3) basic assumptions. The artifacts level is the most superficial and reflects what people see, hear, and feel when they encounter people in a group or organization. It has to do with the physical environment, language, technology products, artistic creations, dress, manners of address, emotional display, or myths.

The espoused values level is about the world view and beliefs about how things are done. They predict what people of the organization will do and say in a variety of situations. These beliefs and world view go through cognitive transformation to shared values, beliefs, and ultimately to shared assumptions.

The basic assumptions level is a set of shared basic assumptions that defines what things mean, what to pay attention to, and how to behave in certain situations. It is critical, therefore, to understand all aspects of organizational culture, but it is even more crucial to know the latter basic assumptive level if leaders want to decipher the pattern and predict the behavior correctly. It is also when the basic assumptions are questioned that anxiety and defensiveness are produced (Ibid., pp. 17–27). Cultural assumptions reflect the deeper issues about the nature of truth, time, space, human nature, and human relationships (Ibid., p. 49).

Culture can also be thought of as interlocking sets of assumptions. This is another significant reason why credible leaders spend sufficient time in their attempts to understand organizational culture by getting to the deeper level in order to comprehend the function of assumptions in their organizations. It provides for a deeper understanding of the cultural issues that are critical to deciphering what is occurring in the organization; the anxieties that may be created by challenging the assumptions; and whether suggested changes will be embraced, reluctantly accepted, or totally rejected.

Effective leaders are aware that changes which will impact the cultural assumptions are difficult, time consuming, and may produce high anxiety and hostility. Here in lies the power of culture which "comes about through the fact that the assumptions are shared and therefore mutually reinforced" (Ibid., p. 25). Such leaders also understand that if such changes are necessary to achieve the mission of the organization, certain strategies must be established and utilized in educating the members/followers in order to reduce the anxiety, stress, and possible hostility for the support and eventual acceptance of those who are so invaluable to making the changes into a success. These leaders understand that they do not walk alone and that there are times when it is necessary to educate, then when appropriate or necessary, sit and wait for followers to catch up before moving forward.

They Cultivate Healthy Relationships and Get Results

Any leader who thinks that he/she can use the power of his/her office or position to demand effective performance is playing a losing game. People in general respond much more favorably to those with whom they have a healthy relationship than to someone who is attempting to impose his/her ideas on them because of their position or office. Therefore, credible leaders strive to cultivate healthy relationships with followers due to the positive correlation between good relationships and effective performance/excellent results. These leaders seek to understand human nature and what makes followers tick, and they use information to motivate, woo, and encourage, as well as create systems and social functions that are conducive to building good relationships that will result in high productivity. They also understand that monologues produce negativity and isolation from the decision-making process, so leaders dialogue with followers to arrive at shared values and goals that help to shape the beliefs and assumptions of their organizations. They are proactive and involve the followers in conflict resolution prior to the escalation of things that may lead to the destruction of relationships. They work cooperatively with their followers to achieve predetermined results.

Effective leaders know that positive relationships are good not only in and of themselves but that they are a means to effectuating good results, which is the language of followers and stakeholders because it makes sense to them. People have high expectations of leaders, and when there is a disconnect between those expectations and results produced, leaders are doomed. As Adair correctly wrote, "Do Not Tell Me How Hard You Work, Tell me How Much You Get Done" (*Not Bosses But Leaders*, p. 52).

Credible leaders hover over their organizations to get an aerial view in order to ascertain the smooth functioning of each and all systems and make the needed changes for the improvement of the entire system and the achievement of their mission and shared goals.

Application/Implications for Church Leadership

When the above information, the enormous amount of research and significant findings that have contributed in important ways to the advancement/improvement of secular leadership, and the commonalities discovered among credible leaders, is seriously considered, one is tempted to think about the applicability of these critical findings to church leadership on a wholesale basis, particularly the immediately aforementioned eleven functional qualities of challenging the status quo, developing a shared vision, empowering followers to act, modeling the way, giving courage, teaching, sharing power, embracing dissent or contrary ideas, changing organizational culture, cultivating healthy relationships, and getting positive results; and the five individual qualities of honesty, forward thinking, competence, knowledge, and inspiration, which work so well for secular leaders.

A superficial examination of these functional qualities and personal attributes seems to suggest that they are relevant, appropriate, and applicable to the church, if for no other reason than human leaders lead people, and people are people in spite of their organizational circumstances. They have certain fundamentally common needs and aspirations and are seeking ways through which to meet or fulfill those needs. This, however, is true only to a certain degree, because when one delves below the superficial and comprehends the unseen philosophical assumptions underpinning secular leadership practices, which are deeply rooted in the bureaucratic nature of institutions with ranked positional power and authority, which highly influences their selective leadership principles and methods of implementation (practices), only then does one begin to question the wholesale applicability of these in light of the conversed nature of the church.

If one's philosophical assumptions about the nature of the organization and its leadership in which one leads are incongruent to the existing realities in these two areas, then one's principles, beliefs, values, and actions/behaviors, which are based on the said assumptions, would be in disharmony with the expected organizational practices. In other words, our philosophical assumptions influence our thinking, words (speech), actions, policies, and relationships with others in almost any organizational setting/context. For example, in institutional bureaucracies, there is one fundamental two-tier structure consisting of leaders and followers or bosses and subordinates. Superordinates or leader-CEOs are endowed with positional power and authority that are not accorded subordinates. In that context, relationships are generally based on the superordinate-subordinate principle with the former having institutional authority over the latter. This is a very pervasive principle that is generally applied across the institutional/organizational spectra.

In addition, there are two other broad principles that are applied inter-organizationally as well as intra-institutionally. These are the principles of *competition* and *hard work*, which are acceptable on an interpersonal level and utilized by people or employees to get ahead of each other on the promotional ladder. Leaders also use these two critical principles in their decision about who should be promoted and to what level. And last but not least is that very pervasive organizational/business *black-ink* principle that undergirds some of the most serious decisions made by practically all organizations. Things are generally considered to be well when the balance sheet summation figures are written in black ink rather than in red, which is a negative symbol indicating that the organization is beginning to be or is in financial trouble.

It appears that the eleven broad functional practices and the five successful leadership attributes have some relevant application to the church at the exclusion of the philosophical assumptions and principles of operation. These concepts, though important, must be reconfigured and/or redefined on the basis of a Christian philosophy and principles because Christian philosophy is deeply rooted in Christian theology, and any leadership model or practices that have no theological roots should not be transferred to nor practiced in the church. They are not appropriate and will not work well on a sustained basis due also to the nature, structure, principles, beliefs, and end results to be achieved in the church.

As was mentioned previously in chapter 1 (and this cannot be overemphasized), the church is *not* an institution with a bureaucratic structure consisting of bosses and employees, or CEO leaders and subordinate followers, with those in certain positions in the hierarchy possessing power and authority over those in the lower echelon. It is the metaphoric body of Christ, a community of believers living in a fellowship of redemptive love with one another and in a redeeming relationship with Jesus. It is a brotherhood and a sisterhood; it is God's people who have submitted themselves to the influence of the Holy Spirit and live lifestyles that are very different to those of the world. If, however, the church were to lose this critical quality of being brothers and sisters in Christ, it would have lost its true essence and have little or no redeeming purpose for its existence.

There is no vertical structure of leadership power and authority that can safely exist among brothers and sisters in a flat organization. No one person or group of people have power over any other person or group of people. The only authority that leaders have in the church is the Word of God. Leaders and others with gifts in the church were endowed with them, not for positions of power but to function for the edification of the church. Gifts and talents are accorded church members as functional, not positional, tools.

The foundational principles by which the lives and relationships of Christians are guided are the same that undergird the church's operation. The primary one is that of love, love to God and one another. If this is applied in all areas of the church, numerous headaches would be avoided and many relationships would remain in tack instead of being shattered like Humpty Dumpty, never to be put back together again. In addition, the guiding fundamental principle of the church is that of *cooperation* and *collaboration* (partnership), not competition, in order to effectuate the mission of the church. And in the final analysis, the ultimate goal to be achieved is not black ink on the balance sheet, although this is always a plus in that of the church, but souls for eternity.

As one reflects on these significant differences between the church and secular organizations in reference to the sources of their philosophical assumptions and operational principles, it should become much clearer that although some leadership concepts have mutual applicability they must be redefined within the context of Christian theology and applied on the basis of Christian principles. The philosophical assumptions and structural principles that have no root in Christian theology and biblical principles are irrelevant and inapplicable to the church. And the practices that are based on those secular philosophical assumptions have no place in the church. Any practice, principle, or philosophy that even appears to have some relevance for the church must be analyzed and/or scrutinized on the basis of Christian theology and/or biblical principle before a decision is made to accept and use them in the church.

In summary, one needs to recognize the polarity that exists between secularity and Christianity in philosophy and principle. The predominantly broad principles that drive our secular culture are individualism, independence, and competition from which may be derived great productivity due to the incentive for individual gain. But the gain is not acquired at the exclusion of divisions and conflicts, bureaucratic infighting, and psychological warfare that can lead to unhealthy relationships and unproductive followers. Unfortunately, the church is not immunized against the invasion and/or importation of secular leadership practices in spite of its conversed nature and principles that are spelled out in the Word of God.

In the church, a type of collective philosophy/theology is stressed in that the individual is very important, but even his/her rights are to be sacrificed for the good or unity of the community of believers (1 Cor. 10:24, 31; Rom. 12:10; 15:2; Phil. 2:3, 4, 21) since there is a greater theological goal to be achieved in the final analysis, a greater witness that God so loved humanity He sent His Son to redeem the world through His death on the cross. This is what Christian unity can accomplish in our dying world. And instead of independence, the principle of dependence is stressed (John 15:5; Acts 17:28; Phil. 1:21) and that of cooperation and partnership are emphasized instead of competition (John 17:11, 21, 22; Gal. 3:28). And the ultimate result is not black ink, but souls for the Master.

Conclusion

In the beginning of this chapter, the scarcity of credible, effective, and exemplary leaders was mentioned, and many who have read this are probably questioning the reality of the scarcity. But now that you have read the information herein (broad-based, yet somewhat limited) as to what credible leaders do compared to what you have experienced from leaders in your life, would you conclude that there is a shortage of exemplary leaders?

There are relatively few leaders in the world who can be categorized as credible and/or exemplary in spite of their accomplishments in a dog-eat-dog world. It was probably a hazardous struggle to arrive at their current position because as they climbed the corporate ladder many of their colleagues were setting up road blocks to ascertain their stagnation and/or fall from grace. The experience of getting to the top of the corporate ladder is like that of a box of crabs trying to climb up and out. As one climbs up, there are two or more clawing at that one in their attempt to use it as a steppingstone to the top. It is also no means a lesser struggle to maintain one's position as leader. The "king of the hill game" is a vivid reminder of what happens to leaders at the top of their game. People are always trying to derail them in order to claim the position.

In secular leadership, leaders are still perceived, and in reality are, to be very competitive, assertive, egoistic, and controlling. Perhaps when the context of their leadership is objectively evaluated, based on followers' and stakeholders'

Chapter 4 Secular Leadership

expectations, leaders need to be all of these and more in order to survive in the survival-of-the-fittest game and to paint a certain color of ink that seems to matter most of all. In spite of the numerous responsibilities assigned to leaders, the high expectations of followers and the character of leaders, the bottom line of secular leadership has to do with the color (red or black) reflected on the organization's financial statements. Whatever operation is undertaken (building up people, creating a vision, etc.), it is pursued with an eye to the bottom line (ink color), which will determine whether the organization sinks or floats and the leader stays or goes. Black is the brightest and most acceptable color on the financial statements of all organizations, and credible leaders work with this in mind.

Chapter 5

Church Leadership

It was Pastor Ron Halvorsen who wrote in the Adventist Review that "no one would deny that the church needs reformation, revival, and spiritual revolution if we are going to revolutionize the world for Jesus Christ." And he concluded that "we leaders must recognize that the spiritual life of the church rises no higher than the spiritual life of its leaders" (*Adventist Review*, January 1999, p. 8).

When I first read this statement, I questioned the validity of such a high correlation of dependency of the church's spiritual life on that of its leaders. I began to wonder about the author's ego and why God would place such power in the hands of spiritual leaders to affect the eternal destiny of so many people. But then I realized that the leadership literature strongly supports the concept in reference to the power and authority leaders wield in organizations and that the Bible validates the idea in 2 Chronicles, 2 Kings, Micah 3:1–12 and many other scriptural passages, and that Ellen G. White confirms the said notion in the following statements:

> The church will rarely take a higher stand than is taken by her ministers. We need a converted ministry and a converted people. (*Testimonies for the Church*, vol. 5, p. 227)

> Satan is constantly endeavoring to attract attention to man in the place of God. He leads people to look to the bishops, to pastors, to professors of theology, as their guides, instead of searching the Scriptures to learn their duty for themselves. Then, by controlling the minds of these leaders, he can influence the multitudes according to his will....

It was the influence of such teachers [scribes, Pharisees, chief priests] that led the Jewish nation to reject their Redeemer. (*The Great Controversy,* pp. 595, 596)

When all of the above is considered, one cannot but conclude that it is scary to know the amount of power followers place in the hands of leaders and that leaders, particularly spiritual shepherd-servant leaders, have a grave responsibility to their followers. Just imagine that church leaders have, to a certain extent, the power to determine the eternal destiny of many church members. It is, therefore, incumbent upon the church (members and leaders) to ascertain that the revival, reformation, and spiritual revolution begin with the leaders of the local church and the administrative branches; that church leaders are selected/appointed on the basis of spiritual leadership criteria; that adequate education/training is given to all leaders prior to their occupation of those positions/offices/roles; and that leaders have accepted the godly responsibility to be ardent followers of our ultimate Leader, Jesus Christ. We need to ascertain that leaders have taken a solemn oath to lead the body of Christ to the Savior, and not to a savior, through their adherence to the principles, precepts, admonitions, and values of the Word of God. In other words, they must first learn to follow Jesus before they are able to lead others to Him. We must also informally and formally evaluate our leaders on an annual basis based on biblical or spiritual leadership criteria and hold them accountable, not only by the administrative branches (presidents of conferences, etc.) but by those people (church members) whom they lead instead of investing certain powers/influence in their "office" that provides the false perception that they are above the members.

Church Leadership Crisis

When one realizes the import of the above, it becomes much more difficult to accept the fact that there is also a crisis of leadership in the church. It is extremely unfortunate, but there is a leadership crisis in the church. In other words, there is a scarcity of effective, credible, exemplary, and authentic leaders in the Christian church. James E. Means refers to this as "the crisis of leadership deficiency may well be one of the most pervasive and pernicious problems facing contemporary Christianity" (*Leadership in Christian Ministry*, p. 18). It is not surprising, therefore, to discover that "Christian people everywhere," according to Dr. Lynn Anderson, "are crying out for spiritual leaders—men and women grounded in the Word of God, made wise by the experiences of life, and filled with the love and compassion of Christ" (*They Smell Like Sheep,* p. 1). The implication here is that for the most part leadership in the church is ineffective, inefficient, and unworkable with leadership styles and methods patterned after those of secular leadership. Although there are some functional commonalities between church/religious and secular leadership, there are very significant principle differences that separate the two, and these will be stressed later on in this chapter.

Another important aspect that contributes to this crisis is that too many church leaders perceive themselves as heads of the church. And they embrace the misconception of the church as a politically conventional organization that has a bureaucratically pyramidal structure with them occupying the pinnacle or lofty peak position. So they function like politicians and become very astute at playing the political game. They do whatever is situationally ethical and/or politically expedient to maintain their political friendships, save their positions, and give the impression that they are cooperative (they go along to get along), all at the expense of kingdom/body laws and principles.

I know of a situation in which a first elder in one of our churches was a member of both the church board and school board. He did a very effective job for both church and school. However, a new pastor was assigned to that church who wanted to get rid of the school principal for personal reasons. Unfortunately, the first elder was aware that the pastor was heading in the wrong direction, but he went along for the "ride" to safeguard his position. A few years later, the principal inquired of the first elder as to why the pastor and school board took such actions against him, and the elder confessed that the principal did nothing wrong, but that the pastor started the process and they all lacked the courage to stop him so they went along with him.

There are too many church leaders who believe that inherent in their positions are the illusive components of power and authority, which they allow to inflate their egos and make them comfortable dictating everything, having members "bow" down to them, controlling situations and members, and having things done their way. Ellen White has counseled that "No human being is to seek to bind their other human beings to himself as if he were to control them, telling them to do this and forbidding them to do that, commanding, dictating, acting like an officer over a company of soldiers" (*Testimonies for the Church,* vol. 9, p. 146). And for those who are acting like lords, she offers the following serious advice because of the detrimental effect such members have on the work of God. In this instance, she was shown or enlightened by God about the behavior or practice of lords in the church. "I have been shown that there is one practice which those in responsible places should avoid; for it is detrimental to the work of God. Men in position should not Lord it over God's heritage, and command everything around them" (*Testimonies to Ministers and Gospel Workers,* p. 301).

Leaders of this caliber are a significant distraction and stumbling block to the advancement of God's work. These are people who relish/bask in the sunlight of

Chapter 5 Church Leadership

their titles/positions with their twisted misperception of associating power with offices, and they will do almost anything necessary to remain in their positions. Take a moment and listen to those who are not reelected to their cherished positions and you will understand. Is this, however, an individual problem or is there something inherently wrong with the structure of the system that contributes to this manner of thinking and behaving? The answer is that, for the most part, the problem is systemic in nature. There is no doubt that the structure of any system influences relationships, thought processes, and behavior patterns of the people who are a part of and/or function in it. If a church, for example, has leaders and some members who believe that the church is an institution, quasi or not, with bureaucratic rankings, those people will act on that belief and relate to each other as they would in a secular institution with superordinates and subordinates. This type of relationship accords much power and authority to the leader(s) and others holding offices in the church, and this runs antithetical to the God-given nature of the church.

These bureaucratic-thinking leaders who are bent more on controlling church members instead of loving them dearly and sincerely are contributing to the leadership crisis in the church. Such leaders can surely be classified as modern-day scribes and Pharisees, and it is not surprising because human nature has not changed for the better over the last two thousand years. These are leaders who enjoy preeminence, the exercise of power and authority, and the prestigious seats at all functions. This reminds me of a business man who owned a business and directed every aspect of it. When he eventually decided to join a church, he looked for one that was operated like his business. He attached himself to one where "the pastor was the domineering autocrat just as I was in business." The man eventually attached himself to this autocrat and soon became second in command in the church as a result of his incredible loyalty to this pastor. His confession was that "between the two of us we very effectively and skillfully controlled the religious life of about five hundred people." In the final analysis, his proclamation was, "Our church is Christ's body and not an organization.... Helping people come together and be the body of Christ is a whole different 'ballgame.' My business skills don't help ... the Bible does" (Richards and Hoeldtke, *A Theology of Church Leadership*, pp. 79, 80). However, if you want to know who such leaders are, try the following and see if you hear from them directly or indirectly:

1. Don't invite them to certain functions to which leaders are expected to be invited.

2. Don't print their names or include them in programs of very special occasions.

3. Forget to inform them of certain critical information that you communicated to peers.

4. Assign them seats with the "regular" laity and not at the head table at special church luncheons, etc.

In addition to the above, there are some other critical things that contribute to poor and ineffective leadership that eventually helps to perpetuate the leadership crisis in the church. These are:

1. Maintenance of the status quo with no mission statement, no vision statement, no plans, and very superficial relationships.

2. Rejection of good and viable yet contrary ideas that are in disharmony with the current trends of thought and action, even though such notions may not be in contradiction to any biblical principle, and the negative actions of leaders and others to vilify members with such ideas, resulting in social isolation and classification of the said members as "trouble makers."

3. Use of politics and positional influence by leaders to circumvent members with the said ideas for fear of being perceived as less knowledgeable while building up their leadership image as opposed to the sound but apparently contrary notions.

4. Allowing members to sit and soak with no real involvement, while enhancing the importance of leadership through members dependence on it and creating a vacuum in the absence of leaders.

5. The building of a fortress mentality in which leaders think their ideas are ultimately the best and, therefore, there is no need for other leaders and/or ideas.

The result of such leadership can lead to conflict between leaders and followers that, if allowed to go on without correction or resolution, will lead to stagnation in the members growth and development, which can be very crippling to any church. This in turn will inevitably lead to membership reduction with the church's purpose/mission left unrealized and the eventual death of a congregation.

There are at least two other major factors that contribute to ineffective leadership and the said crisis in the church:

Lack of or Insufficient Leadership Education/Training/Mentoring

There are too many curricula in higher education institutions that do not provide for leadership education and training, and seminaries are no exception. So many ministers graduate from institutions and accept positions in local churches without any theoretical foundation in leadership, having no basis for how to lead the body of Christ. And it is often the case that many of them "dash into the fray with lots of heart and too few skills—and get demolished." Then there are "others with skills but no heart," and they "leave behind them a trail of trouble. Still others, with both heart and skills, are hamstrung by antiquated ministry methods and leadership styles" that according to Anderson are "patterned after business models rather than after Jesus." The serious consequences are that "too many good leaders burn out or give up. Some even become adversarial and wind up with broken spirits and broken churches," while "others plod on, but with little hope" (Anderson, *They Smell Like Sheep*, p. 2).

It is probably one of the most difficult problems for church leaders to come to terms with—the fact that they lack the necessary leadership expertise and wisdom to lead themselves and the churches they are in charge of in an effective manner. They probably assume that those who elected and/or appointed them recognized their leadership potential and/or expertise and consistently believe it to the point that when things are in disarray they blame their followers instead of themselves. Leaders must always take responsibility for anything that happens in their organization or church. However, these same leaders believe that once in a leadership position, their own need and expectations of others dictate/demand that they know the answer to everything and be in control of the situation (Schein, *Organizational Culture and Leadership*, p. 367). Leaders should come to grips as soon as possible with the fact that they do not have all the answers to all questions and neither are they equipped as they should for leadership positions, and the clergy is no exception.

John C. Harris has confirmed in no uncertain terms that the "basic problems in theological education arise from the fact that seminaries remain relatively uninformed by immediate, accurate, comprehensive knowledge of the leadership dilemmas of modern church life" resulting in the production of ministers/pastors who are ill-equipped and ill-prepared to contend with the turbulent demands of congregational leadership in a rapidly changing secularized society" (*Stress, Power, and Ministry*, p. 98). Unfortunately, one of the serious consequences of this dilemma is that the "clergy are thrown onto their resources to pioneer and accumulate tested knowledge of effective congregational leadership" (Ibid., p. 116). And based on my experiences with numerous pastors, it appears that no real significant improvement has been made in seminary leadership education in the last twenty plus years, which continues to contribute to the leadership crisis in the church.

The Recalcitrance of Leaders and Systems to Change

It appears to me that when individuals and collectives (groups or organizations) develop and become well established in terms of certain patterns of thinking and behaving that are based on well-founded standards over years of trial and error, changing such standards to alter the thinking, behavioral and performance patterns, or mode of operations is very difficult, even in the light of new knowledge that is relevant and applicable to and for the further development of those individuals, groups, and/or organizations. Changing the thinking and behavioral pattern of people requires the unlearning of those established and well proven standards embedded in the mindset, which is not an easy process. Even leaders who should be blazing the trail in envisioning a better future for their organizations are at times very reluctant to change their modus operandi, which eventually leads to organizational stagnation and even death.

Changing and the acceptance of change are difficult due to the uncertainty and anxiety caused by change. More importantly, however, leaders are reluctant to change because they are generally the most significant beneficiaries of the status quo and will struggle/fight to maintain the system as is. When leaders are reluctant to change, it becomes more difficult for organizations to change. There are times when leaders desire change and run smack into the face of organizational inertia.

Credible leaders, however, understand the significance of the flexibility attribute. They know that knowledge is fluid and change based on information is inevitable, so they accept the notion of stagnation as being unacceptable, and flexibility as a necessity of ineluctable change. These leaders are progressive in their thinking, look objectively at information and their systems structure and operations, and make changes that are beneficial for all. It is time to take a fresh look at the teachings of Jesus, Paul, and other New Testament writers to discern how we can cease our contribution to the leadership crisis in the church.

Armed with the information of the above leadership crisis in the church, it is time for the leadership of the church to take up the mantel and continue the revolutionary movement that Jesus started some two thousand years ago. However, political leadership will be reluctant to change due to the potentially significant loss of benefits for the beneficiaries in any attempt to reform the church. However, based on the significant influence of modernity on the church (some good and too much bad), there is a need to return to the biblical teachings (the New Testament in particular) on church leadership, including the qualifications, function, and return of the leadership responsibilities to the plurality of elders, instead of its substitute and embodiment in one leader who has displaced the genuine biblical local church leaders, if we believe that the Bible is the authentic word of God and our only rule of faith and practice. We have ignored for too long many of the teachings and have implemented in the body of Christ systems, methods, and styles that are not only secular, antiquated, and unbiblical but have contributed to our basic human craving for power and authority over others. Let us remember, as I wrote earlier, that human nature has not changed over the last two millenniums, and the same love of power and authority as was exemplified in the church leaders (scribes, Pharisees, and chief priests) continues to plague the church of God today through its leaders. Ellen White cautions that:

> Christ foresaw that the undue assumption of authority indulged by the scribes and Pharisees would not cease with the dispersion of the Jews. He had a prophetic view of the work of exalting human authority to rule the conscience, which has been so terrible a curse to the church in all ages. And His fearful denunciations of the scribes and Pharisees, and His warnings to the people not to follow these blind leaders, were placed on record as an admonition to future generations. (*The Great Controversy*, p. 596)

Anyone who has been following the unfortunate development of the misconduct of priests in the Catholic Church and listened to the victims' explanation of knowing that something was wrong with what the priests were doing to them, yet they continued to allow these men to perpetuate their twisted imposition on them because of their fear of going to hell if they exposed the priests' immoral behavior and of the priests' position of power in reference to their closeness to God, and their standing in society, which meant that no one would believe them as the victims. This problem was so pervasive and allowed to be practiced for hundreds of years that it became acceptable behavior and a part of the cultural milieu of that church. Think seriously for a moment and understand that these were (probably still are) well respected men and leaders in our society who taught the people that talking negatively about them would probably land people in hell, and this scare tactic worked. In addition, some parents would have believed them over their children. This is truly an act of brainwashing that allowed these trusted men to control and/or rule the consciences of so many.

As we follow leaders, and particularly religious leaders, keep things in perspective and remember that leaders are human beings, sinners saved by God's grace, and followers should not exalt leaders over themselves due to their position or role. Remember that "position does not give holiness of character. It is by honoring God and obeying his commands that a man is made truly great" (White, *Prophet and Kings*, pp. 30, 31).

It is very unfortunate, however, that when the leadership crisis monster raises its ugly head in local churches, so many of us are generally inclined to believe that these are isolated situations and that if the ministers are transferred the crisis will subside or come to an end and the incoming pastor will provide for a new beginning. Except for rare instances, the period between the outgoing and incoming minister is a time of great tranquility and/or some semblance of peace for some, but it is the calm before the next storm for others. The problem is that so many seem to think that what is needed is a change of environment for these leaders and all will be well. They fail to recognize that leaders, and particularly church leaders, must take responsibility for the state of affairs in the church; that the transfer facilitates moving the problem leader (so classified only because leaders are responsible and should be held accountable) from one church to another, which in actuality means, a transference of the problem to another environment; that the problem is partially systemic in that the current dependency model is inherently irrelevant to an educated/enlightened membership and most of all, to the nature of the body of Christ.

The critical question is, what type of leadership model is relevant and needed in the church based on our present understanding of its nature, structure, function, and mission as outlined in chapter 1 of this book? There are a number of theories of leadership (trait, situational, followership, eclectic, and McGregor's Theory X and Y) and leadership styles, which has to do with a leader's approach to their selective method of authority applied in the making of decisions, as well as what they do and say, and how they act in dealing with subordinates. They are:

1. **Authoritarian** – The leader's authority is derived from his/her office more than from his/her personality. This type of leadership provides for little or no participation from followers in the decision-making process due to the assumption that the leader knows what to do and may at times result in the sacrifice of followers' personal development.

2. **Bureaucratic** – This is based on a system of rules to be adhered to at all structural levels and under all circumstances. The authority of this leadership style is based on the level at which one is in the bureaucratic structure.

3. **Democratic** – Both leaders and followers participate in the decision-making process and no one dominates the process or group action. The selection of the best idea(s) is pursued, and it may not come from the leader.

4. **Laissez-faire** – In this model there is a great amount of permissiveness in the decision-making process. The group is allowed to proceed in any direction it desires based on its convictions. The leader supplies materials and contributes when asked to do so.

5. **Charismatic** – This is a personality-centered approach in which followers are attracted to or drawn to leaders with magnetic charm or appeal and/or special gifts and talents (Lall, *Dynamic Leadership*, pp. 22–25).

6. **Transformational** – This is a style in which the leader's approach is that of transforming organizations with or without the assistance of followers.

However, the only one that is embraced by the Word of God, as is reflected in the New Testament, is the unequivocal shepherd-servant model. Therefore, the following portion of this chapter will focus on this style or spiritual shepherd-servant leadership from a biblical perspective.

The Shepherd-Servant Model

Old Testament Shepherd Servant

In the Old Testament, God is portrayed as the Shepherd of His people. Israel, in his blessing of Joseph, referred to God as "the God who has been my shepherd all my life to this day" (Gen. 48:15, NIV), and in Genesis 49:24 as the "Shepherd, the Rock of Israel." David, in Psalms 23, provides a more detailed description of God's role as a Shepherd. He wrote:

> The Lord is my shepherd, I lack nothing.
>
> He makes me lie down in green pastures,
>
> he leads me beside quiet waters,
>
> he refreshes my soul.
>
> He guides me along the right paths
>
> for his name's sake. (verses 1–3, NIV)

Isaiah mentions Him as the One who "tends his flock like a shepherd: He gathers the lambs in his arms and carries them close to his heart; he gently leads those that have young" (Isa. 40:11, NIV). And in Psalms 100:3 and Ezekiel 34:31, God is mentioned as the true Shepherd and His people as the sheep of His pasture.

The Old Testament also mentions or portrays prophets, priests, and kings as human shepherds in 1 Samuel 13:14 and Psalm 78:70–72. However, God is the One who sets the standards for shepherding, and human shepherds are required to follow in His footsteps as far as is humanly possible, the results of which is the implementation of a dependency model. In other words, men—inclusive of women—appointed by God or any local or administrative body of Christ become dependent on Him to implement His will in their shepherd-servant leadership role. In other words, these men and women function in both followership and leadership roles. They have a sacred responsibility to learn how to follow Jesus to the fullest extent as is humanly possible before they should attempt to lead His people to Him. Their primary duty is to first learn how to walk in the footsteps of Jesus, (they need to have that personal experience with Jesus in order to learn the direction in which they will lead others) and become dependent on Him for all they need to help others step in and then walk in the same footsteps. A shepherd-servant leader cannot lead others on a path that he/she does not know unless he/she is planning to end up anywhere. Shepherd-servant leaders are not perfect human beings, but they need to be exemplary in all spheres of life if they are going to genuinely represent the character of Jesus for others to see and become convinced to invest their time and energy in following Jesus through them.

New Testament Shepherd Servants

Jesus declared Himself, in John 10:11, to be the "the good shepherd. The good shepherd lays down his life for the sheep," and as a good shepherd, He said, "I know my sheep and my sheep know me" (verse 14, NIV). Jesus could not have remained in heaven and become our Shepherd, so He left the grandeur of heaven and came down to our global pasture to become one with and one of us. As a shepherd, He led His disciples to places they had never been before. He fed them spiritual food they had never eaten before; He gave them water and drink they had never drank before; He lived with, mingled with, cared for, touched, and was touched by many; He laughed, smiled, cried, sweated, suffered, and eventually died in order to conquer sin and death for His sheep. He did not come and live a secluded, isolated, and monastic life in which He separated Himself from the people. He identified with His human sheep and served them. He did not wait to be served by them but was present and always available to meet their needs. He left us an example of servant-hood (slave hood) and service. His shepherd-servant model of leadership is one that should be used as the model in our training/education of all perspective church leaders. "I am the way and the truth and the life" (John 14:6, NIV), and "if you love me, keep my commands" (verse 15, NIV).

Human Shepherd-Servant Leaders

God the Father and Jesus were never shepherds in the sense that they did not shepherd literal sheep, but the dominant leadership model in the Bible is that of the shepherd-servant. The shepherd concept is used about 500 times, but for it to be clearly understood, the shepherd-sheep relationship needs to be explored.

As was mentioned earlier in this book, sheep were a prized possession of shepherds in biblical times, and they could not stay at home and shepherd their sheep. They traveled great distances to find green pastures and watering holes for their flock. They spent days and nights, weeks and months at times with their sheep. During those times, they lived with their sheep, and their major role was to care for them. When accidents occurred, they bandaged broken bones and wounds. They nurtured the young and assisted mothers experiencing birthing difficulties. They slept in the pasture with them or at the sheep pen door to protect them; they placed their lives on the line in their defense against wild beasts, and the sheep did little or nothing for the shepherd. The shepherd was there at their beck and call; he was the true servant of his sheep, and at the end of the day, the shepherd smelled just like his sheep (Anderson, *They Smell Like Sheep*, p. 19).

This is exactly what the Chief Shepherd, Jesus, did. He, through His incarnation, left the pristine splendors of heaven and came down to this sinful world to be one with us in order to shepherd us into His kingdom. Shepherding from this perspective is a role He could not have performed from heaven. It cannot be effectively performed from a long distance.

The shepherd had a special relationship with his sheep, and it was not based on a ruler over servant, nor strong over weak, nor lord over servant perspective. It had nothing to do with title or position. It was based on the following:

1. **Knowledge** – The shepherd knew his sheep and they knew him. Even when several shepherds brought their sheep together in one pen for their safety during the night, at the dawn of day when each shepherd departed and called their sheep, each shepherd's sheep followed after the voice of their shepherd. Jesus said unequivocally that His sheep knew Him and He knew His sheep (human sheep). This concept of mutual knowing by both sheep and shepherd is critical to their relationship and the trust factor which is next on the list.

2. **Trust** – This is one of the fundamental pillars of all relationships. It may even be the major factor underpinning human endeavors. Many people work together who do not necessary like each other, but if the trust factor is completely absent, relationships will deteriorate and that will in turn affect the accomplishment of any meaningful progress or achievement. The following may be an extreme example, but it will clarify the point. A con artist who cultivates a friendship with another con artist must trust that he/she is believed by the other for both to be successful at their illicit endeavors (trust must be mutual). In these types of relationships, trust may be a more critically important factor than love.

   For the Christian, or from a theological perspective, love is the primary factor in all meaningful and/or redemptive relationships. The important point here is that trust develops with knowledge. The more one knows another, the more likely it is that he/she will trust or distrust based on the nature of the knowledge. People who know their leaders and like what they know about them are more likely to trust them, and when one trusts, one is more likely to follow the said leaders. Such leaders appear to be credible in the perception of such followers and the more credible they seem, the greater trust will be accorded them.

3. **Commitment** – Shepherding is not something that shepherds seldom do. It is a full-time responsibility that requires real dedicated commitment. A parent who intends to shepherd a child to become a productive member of any society cannot be an off-and-on parent. Parenting requires complete dedication if the expected outcome will be realized. Shepherding requires the same commitment to the task of leading. Shepherds must consistently give of their time and effort for the achievement of the outcome desired by both sheep and shepherd.

4. **Presence** – In biblical times as well as today, shepherds could not and cannot shepherd their sheep in absentia without risking the sheep's endangerment. For human shepherd leaders, absence does not make the heart grow fonder. Being present, not necessary all the time, but the greater portion of the time, is critical to shepherding. Providing effective shepherd leadership also means generous presence, making oneself available to those being led for many reasons.

The shepherd-servant leader concept revolves around the shepherd-sheep relationship and its implications, with greater emphasis on that of Jesus' shepherding His disciples. His relationship with them was not based on power and/or authority but on love and other kingdom principles. He had the authority because of who He was, but He chose the principles of love, kindness, mercy, and compassion on which to base His leadership, and I am convinced that His disciples were extremely comfortable around and with Him.

When we look at Christian leaders, we need the assurance that by the way they live their lives they are caring, loving, trustworthy, and unselfish, and that their leadership styles are patterned after Jesus. Paul, the great shepherd-evangelist leader, directed the focus of the Ephesians to "be ... followers [imitators] of God" (Eph. 5:1), and to the Corinthians, he wrote, "Follow my example, as I follow the example of Christ" (1 Cor. 11:1, NIV).

This is an exceptionally critical idea for followers to understand. There are too many who follow Christian leaders for the simple reason that they are called Christians, and they generally do so blindly with the end results being disastrous at times. Remember Jim Jones!?! How can this pitfall be avoided? Christian followers should know when to follow human shepherd leaders and when to look to Jesus only. They should know what is required of their leaders and be able to distinguish between when leaders are following Christ and when they are not. They should be cognizant of Christ's example through His Word, and when their leaders depart from His path, it is time to turn their mind's eyes to Jesus only for leadership. Christian leaders are humans and, therefore, sinners saved by God's grace, and if they are not guided by the Holy Spirit, they will lead themselves and others astray. There are too many Christian leaders who begin their leadership journey with good and wholesome intentions, but the position/office and power (as some see it/them), if not kept in proper perspective, will intoxicate them to the point in which they begin to perceive themselves as saviors, leading followers to themselves and into a dependent relationship with them, instead of leading them to Christ.

There are also too many Christian professional leaders who are just hired hands (hirelings). They are primarily in their office/position for the fame, glory, and prestige inherent in those offices and, in many cases, for the money. They care little for God's people; they are wolves in sheep clothing, selfish and full of pride. When things go wrong (when there is danger and they are most needed), they bury their heads like ostriches in the sand, or they leave town, or they are very willing to leave the "sheep" for the wolves to devour. As Jesus said: "The hired hand is not the shepherd and does not owns the sheep. So when he sees the wolf coming, he abandons the sheep and runs away" (John 10:12, NIV).

A story is told about a tour bus driver who was driving some tourists in the countryside of Israel while explaining to them the great relationship shepherds have with their sheep. Suddenly, he looked across a field and saw a "shepherd" chasing and whipping some sheep, actions that ran counter to his description of a shepherd's care for his sheep. The driver became so enraged that he stopped the bus and ran across the field to confront the shepherd, only to discover that the man driving the sheep was a butcher who had acquired some sheep and was taking them to the slaughterhouse.

The reality is that some politicians compromise their principles; cowboys drive; dictators rule with an iron hand; hirelings run away in times of danger; and butchers "kill" the spirit and soul; therefore, members must be made aware or educated not to place their eternal destiny in the hand of human leaders. They should be critical thinkers who make their decisions based on God's Word—kingdom principles—and they should be prepared to be courageous enough to depart from the path of any leader who does not lead them to Jesus.

There is no doubt that the church is in need of authentic, credible, spiritual shepherd-servant leaders who are walking in the footsteps of Jesus and are "able to draw people to Christ and to help them to grow in their relationship with Christ" (Clark, *Building Christian Communities*, p. 135). It seems very important at this juncture to take a careful look at the local house-church leaders in the New Testament in order to discover who those leaders were, how they were selected, and what criteria were used as the basis of their selection/appointment.

Elders in the New Testament House Churches

Leadership is one of the gifts given to the church by the Holy Spirit according to Paul in Romans 12:8 (NIV), and those to whom it was/is given are expected to utilize it in shepherding God's people. But who were these people who were given the said gift and responsibility in the New Testament body of Christ?

The disciples/apostles, including Paul, were given a significant leadership responsibility in terms of the gospel dissemination to all the world. As they, and particularly Paul and others, traveled to numerous cities and towns, and preached/taught the gospel to the Gentiles, many accepted Jesus as their Lord, which necessitated their coming together in house churches for approximately two centuries (some claim 120 years) subsequent to the departure of Christ for His heavenly abode. The establishment of such churches inevitably resulted in the appointment of leaders to shepherd those bodies as is stated in Acts 14:23, "Paul and Barnabas appointed elders for them in each church and, with prayer and fasting, committed them to the Lord, in whom

Chapter 5 Church Leadership

they had put their trust" (NIV). Paul also reminded Titus of the reason why he was left back in Crete: "The reason I left you in Crete was that you might put in order what was left unfinished and appoint elders in every town, as I directed you" (Titus 1:5, NIV).

There were also elders in the Jerusalem church to whom the famine gift from the Antioch church was presented by Paul and others. In the Philippi church, these appointed elders were addressed as "overseers" as well as those in the Ephesus church. The elders in the latter church were called to Miletus and given a final farewell speech by Paul that was emotionally moving and spiritually uplifting, and they were counseled to: "Keep watch over yourselves and all the flock of which the Holy Spirit has made you overseers. Be shepherds of the church of God, which he bought with his own blood" (Acts 20:28, NIV).

But who were these elders and why were they referred to as "shepherds," "overseers," and "bishops"? The transliteration of the Greek word for elders is *presbuteroi*, which simply means "older ones" who lead on the bases of their age and spiritual experience. These, however, were not the only criteria used in their appointment as is evidenced in Titus 1:5-9; 1 Timothy 3:1-7, and 1 Peter 5:1-4, which will be addressed later in this chapter. The word for shepherds is *poimaenoi*, which has been mistakenly translated "pastors" and "preachers," since it literally means "shepherds." The word for overseers is *episkopoi*, which is generally translated "bishops." A more precise translation is that of "guides," "caretakers," "leaders," or those who watch on behalf of, as referring to the function of spiritual shepherd leaders. The word, however, is generally given the meaning of an "office" instead of a function. For example, 1 Timothy 3:1 reads, "If a man desire the office of a bishop, he desireth a good work." Fortunately, the New Testament does not refer to spiritual leadership as an office or position but as a function and/or task. Dr. Andersen continues to explain that the text could be more accurately translated to read, "If anyone desires to bishop," or to do the work of overseeing/guiding, and not to function in the office of a bishop. He also mentions that when the Greek Old Testament uses the word *episkopeo* or *episkopos* it does so as a description of what shepherds do when caring for their sheep in Jeremiah 23:2 and Ezekiel 31:11, 12 (*They Smell Like Sheep*, p. 189).

Unfortunately, the institutionalization and commercialization of the gospel, professionalization of the ministry and the seventeenth century mistranslation of the word "shepherd" to mean bishop or pastor (office and not as a function), have created a type of invisible emanation of authority around the office of bishop/pastor. Inherent in this is the potential for intoxication, abuse, and a very rigid two-tier class structure in the body of Christ. The power-intoxication issue was dealt with in the previous chapter and will be again later in this chapter. The potential for office/

positional abuse has a long list of historical evidences for its own substantiation and should serve as a caution sign to granting ecclesiastical power/authority to any individual without proper accountability to those being led and a structure for a balance of "power" in the church. The absence of such a structural arrangement gives the impression that leaders are superior to followers due to their education, office, or ordination.

When this type of thinking becomes a part of the structure of members' mindset, the belief of their inferiority will manifest itself in their interaction with leaders, which runs contrary to the church of God being a brotherhood and sisterhood, and operates on organismic principles. The current structure of things creates certain leadership expectations, some of which are followership submission, while ignoring the mutuality of submission mentioned by Paul, and deference which has found its way into our organizational policy. Unfortunately, when some courageous members act in ways that contradict the deference policy, statements such as "I am the pastor" suggest that he has power, authority, and the right to act that way and be accepted by the inferiors even when those actions are in blatant contradiction to the whole body. I have been in situations in which the pastors were unequivocally in the wrong, yet the majority of members supported them by turning a blind eye to that which was so obvious. This is a critical issue that needs to be addressed in a way that will create some balance of "power" in the church.

The three words *presbuteroi* (elders), *poimaenoi* (shepherds), and *episkopoi* (caretakers) have had and continue to have, since New Testament time to present day, very significant meanings for church leadership. In reference to the first word, elders were the only ones trained, appointed, and given broad responsibility to lead, guide, and take care of the church or house congregations. They were the only ones instructed to shepherd God's flock (Acts 20:28, 29; 1 Peter 5:1–4), and they were and are still to be summoned to offer intercessory prayers and anointing for the sick as is found in James 5:14: "Is anyone among you sick? Let them call the elders of the church to pray over them and anoint them with oil in the name of the Lord." And they were the ones instructed to "bishop," "oversee," guide, or take care of God's church. The words shepherd and bishop are directly linked to and cannot be divorced from the function of elders. The elders were instructed to shepherd, guide, and watch the flock they shepherded. Elders and bishops were one and the same; leaders of the local congregations (*Seventh-day Adventist Bible Commentary*, vol. 7, p. 297). So whether they were called shepherds, elders, or bishops, the role was the same and there was always a plurality of elders appointed to each house congregation.

Multiple Elder Leaders

I do believe that Paul was cognizant of the inherent danger and potential for abuse in the appointment of a single leader with "power" and authority over the entire house congregation and, therefore, instituted the appointment of a plurality of leaders without rank. Particularly if the leader perceives his/her position from a conventional perspective as having power and authority, it would not take very long for the intoxication to take place.

As was mentioned previously, Paul and Barnabas appointed elders in each house congregation they established (Acts 14:23) and Paul called/summoned the Ephesian elders (plural) from the single church in Ephesus to meet with him in Miletus (Acts 20:13–30). There is no doubt that "multiple leadership, a plurality of elders, was the norm of the New Testament churches, if not the imperative of Scripture" (Means, *Leadership in Christian Ministry*, p. 25). However, Carlos G. Martin intimated a singularity of leadership (a single leader as is equivalent to our current pastoral system) in each local church in Ephesus when he wrote that "probably each of them [elders] summoned from Ephesus by Paul would have been in charge of a congregation meeting in someone's house" (*Adult Sabbath School Study Guide*, p. 156).

Was Carlos Martin unaware of the plurality model of elder leadership in the New Testament church or was he extrapolating from our current one-leader many-elders system to that of the New Testament churches? Or was he providing a justification for the present pastor-elder system? Some people attempt to perceive pastors as elders and see no real distinction between them. The reality is that church members in general see their pastors/ministers/priests as the qualified, ecclesiastically appointed spiritual leaders of local congregations, and they, including the elders, look to these men and a few women for leadership in the local congregations in spite of its antithetical nature to the New Testament model. In most of our churches, elders are placed on the back burner. They have become almost irrelevant, particularly in North America, and have been relegated to sitting on boards, committees, and on platforms for the announcement of various components of the divine service. They are generally asked to preach primarily in the absence of the pastor.

Another reality is that by referring to the professional pastor as an elder is generally unacceptable and does not change the social barrier nor the mindset and neither the behavior of those considered to be superior in ecclesiastical ranks. When the church sanctions such ideas as "he has charge of his pulpit" and "directs his church by influence rather than by any authority vested in him" (*Seventh-day Adventist Bible Commentary*, vol. 10, p. 1083), it has to bear in mind the serious psychological, social, and/organizational consequences. The intent of the use of the possessive adjective "his" may have been free from any structural ranking and ownership, but these notions are directly linked to and contribute to the solidification of a ranking structure that places the pastor/minister/priest in a superior position and negates the principle of equality within the priesthood of all believers. As an educated/trained Adventist minister/elder, I have often wondered why pastors would claim ownership of the pulpit (they did not build it, nor did they pay to have it built, the people did), inherent in which is the authority to grant approbation and disapprobation of its use. It is understandable that some speakers, due to the negative trend of their lives, should not be issued an invitation to any pulpit, but should one person in the church be given that decisional responsibility to make unilateral determination as to whom should be invited, knowing how subjective/political we can be in spite of our offices? Let us remember that there is wisdom in the advice of a multitude.

There is a need for some structural changes, for the elimination of all ranking, particularly in the local churches. Members need to come to the realization that they are entrusted with certain gifts, not positions, to serve God directly and indirectly by serving the body of Christ and others. The key words are "service," "servants" and "self-denial," not domination and bureaucrats, and there is no place for the latter in God's church. We ought to learn from a particular denomination with churches located in the Arizona/New Mexico area. They were having so many clergy-elder difficulties that were ripping their churches apart that they decided to merge the clergy with the elders and create an elder leadership system that has turned out to be the best thing for those churches. If we are reluctant, as a denomination, to institute such a change, why not accord CEO status to the pastors in the local churches. Many function in a similar manner, so why deny them the privilege of such a title? However, Ellen G. White advised in *Selected Messages*, volume 1, that "the secret of unity is found in the *equality* of believers in Christ" (p. 259, italics added).

The significant question to be asked and answered is, how did we, as a denomination, arrive at our current quasi bureaucratic structure and for the most part, clergy-dependent congregations in our local churches? Does our present church body structure reflect the New Testament elder-shepherd leadership model? Adventism in its infancy appears to have been theologically closer to that model. In a series of articles written by G. I. Butler on church government as is quoted in volume 10 of the *Seventh-day Adventist Bible Commentary*, he expressed that "while the office of elder was recognized as the principal one in the church, his powers were regarded as merely advisory, since the body of the church was the deciding authority" (p. 299). In another article, he affirmed that "the work of correcting, admonishing and overseeing in the church belonged to him far more than to anyone else" (Ibid.). And in the

Chapter 5 Church Leadership

September issue, he also wrote that the "minister and the members were to support him [the elder] against gossip and against idle complaints" (Ibid.).

In another article written by H. A. St. John relative to the duties of church elders, he stated that, "They [the elders] should visit the members and seek the wandering, baptize, and conduct the ordinances in the absence of the evangelist, and call business meetings before the conference session, at the close of the year, and other times when necessary" (Ibid.).

The above information seems to place the full leadership responsibility on the elders in the local churches, something that was in keeping with the New Testament leadership model in the local house churches.

There is sufficient historical evidence in our denominational literature to conclude that in the initial stages of its evolutionary development, there were first deacons who provided leadership in the church and elders were appointed later and accorded full responsibility for oversight of the said churches. However, with the introduction of professional clergy (pastors) came the power struggle for leadership supremacy in the local church. This power struggle did not emerge from the church's attempt to better organize itself for a broader or global dissemination of the gospel. It was a function of parochial politics designed to capture control of leadership in the local churches. Armed with a higher level of education and the people clamoring for pastoral leadership as were the other denominations, the clergy gained the victory and assumed, to this day, the primary functional responsibilities of the elders. This changed the New Testament model and dynamics of the local church leadership through the transfer of the elders' task, influence, and "authority" into the hands of a single leader, the pastor. If pastors, therefore, have the ecclesiastical imprimatur to function as they do, then the difficulties inherent in the current leadership structure can be considered both as individualistic and systemic. So when we hear pastors referring to the elders, deacons, and members as "my elders," "my deacons," "my members," or "my church," they are only expressing that which is part of our denominational unwritten policy. Let us not forget, however, that if one thinks that he/she owns something, that individual's behavior toward that thing will be reflective of the thought process.

Some people may think that the current system has served the church exceptionally well and is responsible for the relatively phenomenal growth over the years. It (the system) is based on the dependency model and keeps churches dependent on their pastors with most members sitting, soaking and leaving, and coming back on a weekly basis for more spiritual food with no substantial progress being made in terms of discipleship making for the effectuation of the gospel—members going into the world and making disciples of others.

Russell Burrill points out that "once Adventists adopted the dependency model and settled pastors over local churches, church growth ebbed." He further explains that "one of the most amazing developments in Adventism has been that the only parts of the world not showing significant church growth are those areas, such as North America, that have adopted the dependency model" (*Radical Disciples For Revolutionary Churches*, p. 61). In reference to this model, Ellen G. White wrote that "the ministers who are hovering over the churches, preaching to those who know the truth, would better go into places still in darkness. Unless they do this, they themselves and their congregation will become dwarfed" (*The Review and Herald*, February 9, 1905).

Getting back to the New Testament multiple elder-shepherd church leadership model will probably make our members more dependent on the Holy Spirit and lead to more in-depth study of the Word for a greater understanding of the gospel in preparation for its dissemination that will usher in a greater membership involvement in the effectuation of the church's mission. We need a genuine revolution for Jesus, and all church members must play a leading role to make it happen.

Elder Qualifications

As was mentioned earlier, wherever Paul went and evangelized, he organized house churches and appointed local elder leaders to shepherd the flock. The appointment process appears to have been taken very seriously and involved a great amount of solemnity when one considers the criteria utilized for the selection of those elders. These criteria are as follows:

Titus 1:5–9

1.	Above reproach	2.	Husband of one wife
3.	Children obey them (him)	4.	Not self-willed
5.	Not quick tempered	6.	Not a drunkard
7.	Not pugnacious (not ready to fight)	8.	Not a money lover
9.	Hospitable	10	Loves that which is good
11.	Sensible	12.	Just
13.	Devout	14.	Self-controlled
15.	Holds the word dearly	16.	Able to refute objections

Chapter 5 Church Leadership

1 Timothy 3:1–7

1.	Temperate	2.	Gentle
3.	Manages family well	4.	Not a new convert
5.	Good reputation with outsiders	6.	Do things willingly
7.	Not a money lover		

1 Peter 5:1–4

1.	Not lording it over God's people	2.	Serve as overseer
3.	Serve as examples to members	4.	Willing to serve
5.	Not motivated by monetary gain		

These men/elders were expected to be humble, vigilant, loving, and caring, not perfect, but being led by the Holy Spirit in their spiritually maturing journey with Jesus. A modern elder was once heard saying that if these criteria were to be applied to the election of elders today, no one would be elected. This is a very sad commentary on the state of affairs of eldership in the modern church, but if the church is going to be guided by elder leaders, it cannot ignore or push aside the above-mentioned criteria for their election/appointment today. It is probably best not to have elders instead of lowering the standards.

The New Testament elders were responsible to lead the local flock or church to Jesus in their spiritual journey by developing healthy members and relationships through equipping, modeling, teaching, and unity preservation in order to create effective functioning members for internal and external purposes (evangelism). It can be assumed that those elders clearly understood that a healthy church is not measured by the size of the house/building, number of members, or number of programs but by its unity and equipped members in ministry participation.

Major Biblical Functions and Attributes of Elder Shepherd-Servant Leaders

Credible shepherd-servant leaders (elders) "do not dominate, they serve … do not demand, they guide … do not manipulate, they teach … do not subjugate, they inspire … not lords, but models and ministers." And Means continues to write that "when these truths are forgotten or ignored, church leaders become dictators, overbearing and ugly" (*Leadership in Christian Ministry*, p. 99). But from a biblical (New

Testament) perspective, what are the major functional roles elder-shepherd-servant leaders are expected to perform in the body of Christ? The following is not an exhaustive list, but it represents the important functions of elders in the church:

They Lead Themselves by Following the Mandates of Jesus

These are leaders who allow themselves to be led by the Holy Spirit and the Word of God. In other words, those members who desire to be shepherd-servant leaders (including elders) must first learn to lead themselves by using the principles of the Word as the basis for all their thoughts, words, and actions. Self-mastery (being guided by the Word and Spirit) is a prerequisite for leading others, because if one cannot lead oneself, it becomes extremely difficult for others (especially God's people) to allow themselves to be led by such a leader. From a Christian perspective, self-mastery is based on knowing Jesus and His kingdom laws and principles, wholeheartedly embracing them as the foundation for their lives and totally surrendering to the leading of the Spirit. Self-mastery or self-control is partially achieved through one's efforts but more so by the power of the indwelling Spirit working through each individual for consistency over time.

Self-control is one of the criteria used by Paul and others in the selection and appointment of elders to lead church members. He further emphasized this attribute in his final visit to Miletus from where he summoned the Ephesian elders for a farewell counsel session/meeting and told them in Acts 20:28 (NIV), "Keep watch over yourselves and all the flock." Paul unequivocally understood that self-control was not a once-in-a-lifetime achievement, but an ongoing struggle in which the born-of-God shepherd has to remain vigilant or on high alert against the attacks of the enemy or suffer the serious consequences of what the lapse in good human judgment can create. Ellen G. White writes about the consequences of hurrying men or elders who lack self-control into positions:

> In many places we meet men who have been hurried into responsible positions as elders of the church when they are not qualified for such a position. They have not proper government over themselves. Their influence is not good. The church is in trouble continually in consequence of the defective character of the leader. Hands have been laid too suddenly upon these men. (*Testimonies for the Church*, vol. 4, pp. 406, 407)

When members of the bodies of Christ (churches) recognize the criticality of church unity as was mentioned in chapter 1, they will probably begin to apply sound judgment through the implementation of kingdom principles to the selection process of its elders and other leaders. A necessary change of this "magnitude" mandates the elimination of all politics in the process, and this will not be easy, particularly for those who have formed convenient friendship alliances for the perpetuation of their control over the church or certain positions. Based on the structure of the election process also, body members who are aware of ongoing irregularities in the process and uncorrected character qualities in many current and potential leaders should be lovingly and caringly courageous enough to become righteously indignant and speak up in the name of Jesus for that which is right and wholesome in and for the body of Christ, irrespective of the social isolation and other consequences. Leaders should have the moral courage to take the lead in this direction.

They Understand the Biblical Origin, Nature, Structure, Function, Mission, and Culture of the Church They Lead

The right understanding of the nature, structure, function, mission (purpose), and culture of any organization is critically significant for the leader to know if he/she is going to lead it successfully. In reference to addressing some characteristics of admired leaders (honesty, forward-looking, inspiring, and competent), Kouzes and Posner stated unequivocally that even more than being competent, the leader needs to take "the time to learn the business, to know the current operation before making changes and decisions that affect everyone in the organization" (*Credibility*, p. 17). The church is no exception. Its leaders need to have the right and comprehensive understanding, from a biblical perspective, of the church if they are going to be at least partially successful in leading it to its destination. In addition, because of the unconventionality of both the church and its leadership role, it is even more important to understand those valued components and their underpinning principles in order to avoid the wholesale application of secular conventional principles of organization and leadership in the church and to lead effectively the body of Christ for the realization of the original purpose for which God brought it into existence.

There are many churches that have become nothing more than stagnated social clubs, repeating the same hum drum processes year in and year out, seeking primarily to maintain the established organizational structure at the exclusion of all others. They spend more time and money attending meetings (including services) and paying bills respectively than fulfilling the mission of the church. The lack of the right understanding of the above-mentioned church components and the substitution of the leaders' personal ideas as to what it should be contribute to a great extent to the ongoing and many of the unresolved conflicts and other issues that have become part of the cultural fabric of the body. The consequences are very serious and may lead to member attrition and negative church growth.

It is, therefore, vital for church leaders to study very carefully chapter 1 and this chapter, and be prepared to implement those principles and leadership attributes that should be applied in the church. Shepherd-servant leaders must understand, from a biblical perspective, the nature, function, mission, culture, and destination of the body in order to lead/guide/shepherd the church to its destination.

They Shepherd God's Flock by Serving Them

There is an AT&T commercial in which a shepherd is shown leading a flock of sheep by walking in front of them with a shepherd's rod. This is symbolically a powerful image depicting AT&T as the leader in its area of business while the others are following its lead. This image coincides with what Jesus said about the shepherd who enters the gate and "when he has brought out all his own, he goes ahead of them, and his sheep follow him" (John 10:4, NIV). Shepherds take the lead and make positive things happen for their flocks. They lead by taking the initiative in providing, through others and themselves, all the services needed for the growth and development of the flock. They lead God's people by taking care of their needs and preparing them to take care of the needs of others in their service to God. As a caretaker, Peter counseled the elders to "be shepherds of God's flock that is under your care, watching over them" (1 Peter 5:2, NIV).

Unlike secular CEOs and other leaders who are paid significant sums of money to lead their companies successfully (many of them have at their disposal people to serve them in various capacities), shepherd-servant leaders (elders and ministers) are called to a life of "servanthood" and/or "slave hood." To the secular mind, these descriptive terms appear to demean and/or denigrate, and may even serve to undermine the personal worth and value of those serving as servant or "slave" leaders. But what Jesus did was to take man's elevated position of leader and give it the lowest status and then attach tremendous value, worth, and meaning to it in His kingdom under construction on earth. Jesus knew about the self-centeredness of people and how much they enjoy power, authority, high positions, and being served, and He stated in no uncertain terms that these antithetical attributes were of greater value (humble servants and slaves) in His kingdom.

Humble shepherd-servant leaders serve God's people through counseling, advising, mentoring, modeling, and teaching with an eye to building up the body of Christ by leading it into a deeper spiritual relationship with Jesus and making disciples/leaders to lead out and advance the work on earth by His grace. To accomplish these important things in His body, leaders must be humble and willing to be led by the Spirit in order to do things from Jesus' perspective. He took a basin and towel, got down on His knees and washed the dirty feet of His disciples. Does washing the feet of others create that sense of humility in us today? What does it really take to make us humble in this modern era? Look to Jesus and do what it takes to make you humble!

They Feed and Equip God's People

There is a warning given in Jude 12 in which we are admonished to look out for the selfish and ungodly "shepherds who feed only themselves" (NIV). Unselfish, loving, and caring shepherd servants (elders) are advised in John 21:15–17, Acts 20:28, and 1 Peter 5:2 to feed God's people. But how do they accomplish this significant role?

1. They develop a leadership style and a body infrastructure that lends itself to or supports teaching and learning and eventually sharing. It is important for leaders to understand and demonstrate in the things they do and say that such things are designed to teach some idea, value, and/or lesson for the edification of those being led. If these things are neglected, it becomes much more difficult for teaching and learning and effective sharing for mission realization.

2. They study and learn from their own and others' experiences in order to teach and preach effectively. Shepherd-servant leaders cannot share what they do not know and have. Being a good student (continuing education) is a serious obligation for all leaders, including teachers and preachers. Learning increases one's knowledge and understanding and sharing reinforces it.

Great leaders are generally great teachers because they are great learners. They have a vision, ideas, and values that must be communicated with clarity to followers for greater understanding, acceptance, and implementation for the advancement of their organizations. Elders were required to be "able to teach" (1 Tim. 3:2, NIV) even though they were not seminary trained (and based on my experience in a seminary, teaching was not a priority) nor educated teachers. The idea, however, of being able to teach "indicates a capacity to guide others into godly living by an application of the Word of God to the practical issues of life" (Richards and Hoeldtke, *A Theology of Church Leadership*, p. 132).

Jesus did not attend a seminary (this is not an indication that a seminary education is of no value), but He was probably the greatest teacher of all times. He spoke with authority and His teaching amazed those who listened to Him (Matt. 7:28, 29;

13:54; 22:23; Mark 6:2; 11:18; Luke 4:32), and He led numerous people to God. Paul did not attend a seminary, although he was an educated man, instead he depended upon the guidance of the Holy Spirit and became the best known Christian theologian who was very successful at leading people to Jesus. His experience with Jesus through the Spirit was of greater value and influence than any seminary education. Jesus is our ultimate Leader and all church shepherd-servant leaders must learn to lean on Him.

Remember, who we are as teachers and leaders speaks far louder than what we say and/or teach. Irrespective of how loudly we teach or preach, people will not hear because of who we are. Living what we teach and preach is of far greater influence than lessons taught and sermons preached. People hear very clearly what you do and see dimly what you say.

3. They (elders/leaders) impart to members the knowledge and skills necessary for ministry and provide opportunities for feedback. It is a false assumption of too many leaders that becoming a Christian and reading the Word of God (something many seldom do) are sufficient preparation for ministry involvement, so some leaders neglect this critical component of their role—equipping body members. The effectuation of our God-given commission to go and make disciples of all nations is dependent upon body leaders making disciples of body members. This is not a one-time act but a continuous process and a theological mandate. Keeping God's people in a state of ignorance due to your negligence is antithetical to God's desire for His people and the great work to be completed prior to His second coming.

4. They feed/equip not only through formal and informal learning sessions, but also through the cultivation of healthy relationships with body and community members. Through their communication and actions in the socialization process, they share their values, beliefs, principles, ideas, and experiences; they share their experiences and expertise in mentoring as many as possible by taking them under their "wings" and showing them the "ropes" or how to deal with critical situations based on their lifelong experiences and how they successfully dealt with them. This is an instructive way of demonstrating how much they (elders/leaders) truly care.

5. In the final analysis and for reinforcement purposes, they provide opportunities for potential disciples to learn by teaching and leading.

This is a way for disciples to demonstrate their grasp of knowledge and skills and the chance to apply them in the process of discipleship making.

They Protect Body Members

Another of the major functions of the elders/leaders is to operate as spiritual sentries or watchmen, keeping guard or watch over God's flock, the church. Paul instructed the elders from Miletus to "keep watch over yourselves and all the flock" because he was sure that after he left "savage wolves will come in among you and will not spare the flock" (Acts 20:28, 29, NIV). He further cautioned them that "even from your own number men will arise and distort the truth in order to draw away disciples after them. So be on your guard" (verses 30, 31, NIV). Peter, who chose to be an elder, corroborates Paul's counsel when he advised the elders to be on the alert because their high powered "enemy the devil prowls around like a roaring lion looking for someone to devour." Then he admonished them to "resist him, standing firm in the faith" (1 Peter 5:8, 9, NIV).

Shepherding God's flock is a daunting and risky responsibility. Not only do elders have to protect the body from those whom they can see and hear proclaiming their antithetical teaching to the Word, but also from the unseen enemy who works through body members to disseminate false information and create discord in his attempt to destroy the church. The fortunate thing is that the identification of the external enemy can be done relatively easily. Unfortunately, the internal enemy is far more difficult to identify and is generally not discovered before the damage is done. And the possible divisions/schisms created by these disputes may take years to repair while the church continues to suffer and its mission realization is negatively affected. Another group or body members the church must be guarded against are those who genuinely believe in many customs and practices that have been imported into the church from the world and made a part of the fabric of the church's culture. The bride of Christ must remain pure of secular customs and practices in preparation for the wedding.

Whatever the negative circumstances, God's people need protection, and sometimes it comes at the cost of the shepherd's life. On May 20, 2001, the television show *60 Minutes* documented a story about a Catholic priest who ran into some difficulty with the political establishment of Kenya and resorted to locking "his" members in the church to safeguard them while he slept at the door on the outside. Unfortunately, his body was later discovered at the side of a road with bullet wounds. Here was a "shepherd" who apparently gave his life for God's flock in that area. Was it a wise thing to do? Difficult to provide an objective answer due to a lack of all the facts involved in the case, we can at least conclude that he probably thought he was acting in a protective role.

One of the most effective ways of protecting God's church is to educate/equip it in the Word of God. When church members are properly grounded in the Word of God; when members unequivocally comprehend the Word—God's plan of salvation, His laws, principles, and values and their application to their lives—such people are not easily shaken, mislead, or drawn from the faith. They become like the farmer's seeds that fell on good ground with their roots penetrating far into the soil for an exceptionally stable foundation. They, in turn, will bring forth much fruit. It is, therefore, incumbent upon the elders/leaders and others to educate and/or equip God's people with His Word and the skills necessary to continue His ministry on earth.

They Live Exemplary Lives

There is no doubt that leaders, especially those with excellent credibility capital, exert a significant amount of influence in the organizations they lead. Their influence can be such a potent force that many followers attempt to imitate them in numerous ways. Leaders, therefore, must be extremely careful not only about the words they use in communicating with their followers but more so with the lives they live. Leaders live their lives in "fish bowls," and followers are constantly evaluating everything they see them do and hear them say, and even what they hear about them. And the conclusions at which they arrive affect their perception for good or bad about the leaders. Therefore, leaders, and particularly Christian leaders who are held at a higher standard, "must be careful how [they] walk, where [they] go, for there are those following who will set their feet where [theirs] are set" (Robert Lee, quoted in Water, *The Encyclopedia of Christian Quotations*, pp. 599, 600).

A story is told about a man and his son who were walking on a white-sandy beach one evening. The man became so engrossed in his reminiscent thoughts that he lost track of his son for some minutes as he continued to walk. Suddenly, he came to himself, and as he turned around to check on his son, there he was walking in his father's footsteps. Parents are also leaders, particularly to their children, and they need to live exemplary lives in the event that their children decide to walk in their footsteps.

Another important reason why Christian leaders need to live exemplary lives is that they are in the ministry of life transformation, leading people to Jesus and helping them see the necessary changes required to live in His presence. Those people are first attracted to leaders and other Christians before they are to Jesus. Changing lives requires changing mindsets (this is a very difficult and time-consuming process) and "people's minds are changed through observation and not through argument" (Will Roger, quoted in Tan, *Encyclopedia of 15,000 Illustrations*, p. 6851). What people see and hear in reference to how leaders live, *principled lives*, have a longer and more forceful impact upon them than what they hear. This is so vividly reflected in the following prose by Edgar Guest:

> I'd rather see a sermon
>
> Than hear one any day;
>
> I'd rather one should walk with me
>
> Than merely tell the way.
>
> The eye's a better pupil
>
> And more willing than the ear,
>
> Fine counsel is confusing,
>
> But example's always clear.

Christian leaders must be the ones pulling the string in General Eisenhower's string demonstration of leadership example. He placed a string on a table and pulled it, and it followed his wishes—went where he wanted it. Then he pushed it and it went nowhere. Shepherd leaders do not push, coerce, or force anything on anyone. They encourage, counsel, advise, love, and let the lives they lead do the pulling.

Shepherd leaders understand very clearly that at various times they function as leaders, peers (colleagues), and followers. The latter can present some difficulties for many leaders due to the mindset of numerous leaders that they should always function in a leading capacity because they are smarter than or more informed than other people, or that they have the best ideas and are entitled to the position. Nothing could be further from the truth, and no further explanation is necessary. In order for shepherd-servant leaders to take the lead and live exemplary lives, they must first follow the lead of or become imitators of the Chief Shepherd because they are followers or sheep also. They must learn to walk in the Master's footsteps and become good followers because they function first as followers (sheep) of Jesus before that of being a leader.

Credible shepherd-servant leaders are not perfect nor stagnant, but are daily maturing spiritually in Christ. They lead by going first and setting the example. They are in compliance with the word of the Good Shepherd who said in John 13:15 that "I have set you an example that you should do as I have done for you" (NIV). Peter and Paul confirm that Christ left an example that all leaders and others should imitate. Remember, elder shepherd-servant leaders imitate Christ—

they have integrity; they live exemplary lives; they model the way; and they set the example for others to follow.

They Envision a Better Future State for God's Church

The Bible is very explicit in reference to the consequences to be experienced by the church or God's people who lack a vision. "Where there is no vision, the people perish" (Prov. 29:18). Although this verse may be referring more specifically to a prophetic vision or a message given to a prophet by God for His people, one cannot deny the significance of a healthy vision for God's church generated by shepherd-servant leaders. And the vision of which I speak is not physical eyesight. It is the ability to see or envision through the mind's eyes that which does not currently exist in the church but that which is embedded in the Word of God (due to the fact that whatever we formulate must be a reflection of what God wants for His church). Furthermore, it is the ability to develop programs and activities for the effectuation of the said vision. If your church does not have an existing mission and vision statement, it is time to formulate them and develop programs and activities for their realization.

Unfortunately, there are too many shepherd-servant leaders (elders and pastors) who are journeying through life and "leading" God's people without a biblically-based vision. They have no idea of where they are going or where they are taking God's people, and they generally end up anywhere with "their" churches experiencing negative growth and the possibility of closing their doors. If it can be said that they are genuinely leading, it is virtually impossible to provide credible leadership without a vision. Authentic shepherd-servant leaders know where they are going (heaven at last), where to take God's people, and how to get there by God's grace.

Fortunately for the church, its ultimate destination vision has been formulated and provision has been made for its realization through the redemptive act of Jesus on the cross. It will become a reality with His second coming. In the meantime, however, we are to occupy until He comes and develop goals and objectives for the work that has to be accomplished prior to His coming. These are related to (1) the spiritual preparation of the body (the church members) to meet Him and (2) transmitting the gospel message (making disciples for Christ) to all "four corners" of the earth—to all nations and people.

The cliché, "salvation is an individual matter," is probably a half truth. It places the responsibility upon the individual to develop faith in a vital relationship with Christ for his/her salvation. If this is the way to salvation, then why does the Bible teach us not to forsake the assembling of ourselves together? I assume that there is a collective and individual spiritual benefit for the coming together. It would also allow for the abdication of a leader's obligation to the individual and the body at large to feed, protect, watch over, and care for, and the eventual nullification of church leadership. We are our brothers' keepers; we contribute to the redemptive preparation of each other through encouragement, love, and kindness; and shepherd-servant leaders (elders) need to collaborate with members for the development of a shared vision and goals that will contribute in significant ways to the maturing of the church in Christ as it prepares itself and others to meet Jesus. Much more will be written about vision and its importance in the following chapter.

They Develop Disciples for Leadership Multiplication

There are church leaders who wallow in their self-importance and feel that nothing seems to go right in their churches in their absence. This situation seems to magnify the importance of their status and presence and make their churches more dependent on them as "true followers" should be. But for those who are cognizant of the critical role of leadership in the multiplication of leaders in organizations, including the church, will understand the necessity for credible leaders who will plan, structure, and program their institution and/or church for the development of leaders in order to ascertain the effective functioning of the church in their absence.

Thomas Monaghan, founder, president, and CEO of Domino Pizza from 1970 to 1985, was once asked about the reasons for the phenomenal growth of his company, and his response was, "I programmed everything for growth ... Every day we develop people [because] ... the key to growth is developing people" (Tan, *Encyclopedia of 15,000 Illustrations*, #6826). Ralf Nader was also quoted as saying that "the function of leadership is to produce more leaders, not more followers" (Water, *The New Encyclopedia of Christian Quotations*, p. 600). A confirmation of this notion was written by Kenneth Gangel who claimed that "good leadership always breeds leadership" (*Competent to Lead*, p. 47). This multiplication/reproduction of leadership is critical, not only for the successful operation of organizations, but for the smooth succession of leadership. For Noel Vose, "Success without a successor is failure" (Water, *The New Encyclopedia of Christian Quotations*, p. 600).

Unfortunately for the church, according to Lowell Streiker, it is "today ... raising a whole generation of mules. They know how to sweat and to work hard, but they don't know how to reproduce themselves" (*Big Book of Laughter*, p. 69). Fortunately, for the church, its Founder, President, and CEO (Jesus Christ) left us an excellent example of leadership multiplication and gave direct instruction in this regard. He chose/selected twelve men of varied backgrounds and developed them into leaders through education, training, empowerment (Holy Spirit power), and the opportunity to lead. Then

He commanded them (and us) to "go and make disciples of all nations ... teaching them to obey everything I have commanded you" (Matt. 28:19, 20, NIV). Discipleship making is a major function of the church, and disciples do not sit idly by and wait for instruction from church leaders, they act like leaders because they are leaders and they set about making disciples of others for Jesus.

Ellen G. White is quite unequivocal in stating that the church is to be organized for service with its watchword being ministry. Then she proceeds to write that "Christian ministers, physicians, teachers, have a broader work than many have recognized. They are not only to minister to the people, but to teach them to minister. They should not only give instruction in right principles, but educate hearers to impart these principles. Truth that is not lived, that is not imparted, loses its life-giving power, its healing virtue." She concludes that every member should be involve in some line of work for Jesus and that "many would be willing to work if they were taught how to begin. They need to be instructed and encouraged" (*Ministry of Healing*, pp. 148, 149).

The implication of leadership multiplication is very clear in her statement to teach people to minister and to educate them to impart principles. The significant notion here is that the making of disciples is critical for at least three reasons:

1. It is easier for one leader to educate one hundred people to do the work of one hundred people than for one leader to do the work of one hundred people.

2. The rapidity with which the church can disseminate the gospel is greatly enhanced through the multiplication of leaders.

3. Because credible leaders make incredible followers, it becomes easier for such shepherd leaders to maintain the focus on Jesus Christ as their ultimate leader whose will is to be realized.

They Endeavor to Maintain Church Unity

I recall a very painful situation that occurred in a church with which I was closely connected many years ago. This situation cast a dark shadow over the church for many years. Without going into all the details, the pastor was in disagreement with many board members, including some elders and the treasurer, about a significant issue. The inevitable occurred in that the matter was taken to the whole body, and the people supported the pastor without a right understanding of the issue and an objective consideration of all the facts. Unfortunately, there was a significant disturbance that developed immediately following a divine service that eventually led to the excommunication of a few elders and the treasurer. This created a division in the church that lasted for years and negatively affected that redemptive relationship, that cohesively critical factor needed for the church's smooth operation and also for the realization of its mission. Fortunately, the excommunicants were restored to church membership years later without having to be re-baptized.

Attaching blame to any of the involved parties may be counterproductive to what needs to be achieved in this section. Let it be known in plain language, however, that leaders are responsible and should be held accountable by the administration and the local people whom they lead for the cultural atmosphere and performance of their organization, including the church. Christian leaders have a sacred obligation to maintain the unity of the church and this cannot be overemphasized. Jesus prayed for the "complete unity" of believers because it is a potent testimony to the world that God sent Jesus here and that He loves the people of the world (John 17:23). He knew that when believers are united and functioning in a redemptive manner that there is something exceptionally magnetic about such a situation that it almost compels others to want to be a part of it. He knew the consequences of being a divided kingdom or house—it "will not stand" (Matt. 12:25, NIV). He also knew that there is something very ungodly about disunity because it sends a negative message to the world; destroys "body" relationships; and creates distrust and fear that are anathemas to the Christian faith.

Anything, therefore, that will create division in the church, except for public or known sin that will potentially cast an aspersion on the church, is to avoided and/or dealt with in a manner that will lead church members to a *consensus*, or create an atmosphere in which members can lovingly disagree without being disagreeable and unrelenting in their pursuit to have their ideas heard and accepted at any cost. Even the parliamentary procedures (Robert's Rules of Order) that we employ in conducting our meetings can be very divisive. It is fundamentally a political tool that is used by governments and other organizations to arrive at political decisions. It is also used to circumvent opposition or people with contrary ideas. There is no doubt that it has its pluses and minuses, but it should be applied with great understanding and wisdom and transcendent common sense.

If a potentially divisive decision is mandatory all attempts should be made to arrive at a consensus or reduce the divisiveness to its least common denominator—a point where it has the least impact on members' relationship. Even when this situation arises, the stress and focus should be on the significance of remaining united after the vote is taken. The ideal would be the removal of Robert's Rules of Order and the building up of a church in which loving members can come together in various group circumstances to make decisions for the operation and advancement of the church. Before this can occur, it is important for all leaders and members to come together and agree and set the stage for a cultural change in the way church members conduct "business." This is something that should pervade the entire atmosphere of the church and all should work together for the realization of such an outcome. It will not be easy, but when one realizes the negative consequences and the impact of such on the health and mission accomplishment of the church, it is worth straining every sinew to make it happen.

Consensus may be considered ideal and too time consuming, but if it preserves the unity of the church, it is worth pursuing. It is also the goal to be reached, and leaders should endeavor, in their decision-making approaches, to make unity preservation become an important aspect of the cultural fabric of the church. Christ prayed for it, and it should be a priority for all members, and all should work for its realization in the church.

They "Empower" Members

Two things that people generally associate with leaders are power and authority. Power is usually defined as the ability or might of a person or thing; the strength or force exerted or capable of being exerted; or the ability or official capacity to exercise control over others. Authority, on the other hand, is normally defined as the right and power bestowed upon someone to command, enforce laws, and exert obedience. The sources of origin of these two concepts according to William Oncken Jr. are competence, position, personality, and character (*Colorado Institute of Technology Journal*, p. 273, quoted in Richards and Hoeldtke, *A Theology of Church Leadership*, p. 137), and I would also add, the possession of money.

When we consider carefully the nature of the church as is revealed in chapter 1, would it be appropriate for shepherd-servant leaders to be endowed with this type of power and authority? The answer is an unequivocally "NO!" Why? Because God's church is an organism (the body of Christ) and should be operated like a family with brothers and sisters who function on organismic principles that are unlike those on which secular institutions operate. Some of these organismic principles, which may have been mentioned previously, are, but not limited to, love, mercy, kindness, cooperation, compassion, service, humility, mutual submission, and mutual suffering. It logically follows that any conventionally organizational structure, genuine or quasi bureaucratic, in which there are members holding positions or offices that even seem to accord any semblance of power or authority over body members will not contribute in any positive way to the realization of an organic operation based on the aforementioned principles.

It appears that the only structure that will accommodate the application of those principles is a flat church structure with all members being on the same level, yet performing different functions or roles/ministries—all sinners saved by the grace of God. This is unlike the hierarchical structure employed in worldly organizations that accord its employees relative power and authority based on the level of the positions within the structure. In other words, the lower one is positioned in the organization, the less authority one is accorded, and the higher up in the structure one is positioned, the higher is the rank and the more power and/or authority one is accorded. Not so with the church.

Many members in the church are quick to deny the existence of any hierarchical structure, but when church policy gives credence to the ranking of members in positions or offices in the disguise for organizational order and good governance, it is stating by implication that some members holding certain positions/offices have more power and/or authority than others and that they are functioning within a hierarchical system in the church. A clear indication is the policy that states that in the absence of a pastor, "the office of elder ranks as the highest and most important" (*Seventh-day Adventist Church Manual*, 16th ed., p. 47). However, the assignment of an ordained minister undermines or lowers the ranking status of the elder when the extension of the policy states that "an ordained minister ... should be considered the ranking officer, and the local elder as his assistant " (Ibid., p. 120). Not only is the "status" of the elders—the Holy Spirit appointed New Testament leaders in the local church—reduced, they have become the ordained minister's assistants and are referred to as "undershepherds" when they have been given the biblical mandate to shepherd and protect and feed God's people (Acts 20:28). In addition, they are expected to show "proper deference" to conference representatives, ordained or not, when they visit the local field (Ibid., p. 121).

This ranking and according of deference seem to be a very formal and business-like arrangement devoid of any brotherly love, which introduces, by implication, the unintended superior-inferior relationship between ordained ministers and elders and members. This makes it difficult for the "inferior" to relate to the "superior" in a loving and redemptive manner as a brother or sister in God's family should do. It also gives the false impression that ministers/pastors are closer to God because they are His representatives and their word is to be adhered to. No wonder that many in such positions are so inclined to believe their own press and act upon that belief that can be very detrimental to the operation of the local church. This situation is probably the fault of the system rather than that of the individual. One should be cognizant of the serious consequences inherent in ranking:

1. It gives the appearance of a bureaucratic structure with the pastor/minister/shepherd leader at the pyramid apex or head of the church.

2. It provides body members of higher ranking offices with delusionary power and authority over others.

3. It lends itself to formality and destroys the intimate brotherly and sisterly love relationship and collegiality that need to exist among members in church.

4. It places leaders in a more controlling role than one of shepherding.

5. It also determines expectations of both high and low ranking parties/individuals. For example, the king expects his subjects to bow to him and the pope expects his church members to kiss his ring.

A story is told about a boy who drove his grandfather's cows from pasture to their barn. They were usually herded in a very orderly manner as they went to their assigned stalls. One day a few cows went to the stalls that belonged to other cows that noticed their stalls were occupied by others. What a confusion and commotion that created. The cows had learned what was expected of each other. A change in the established routine or expectation was very upsetting.

Now think about church. If you sit in the seat where Brother Big normally sits, you will probably hear from him. Mention something that an "inferior" is not expected to say to a "superior," and you will hear from that person. Call a pastor an elder and you will hear the unequivocal distinction between the two. But it is time to get back to how shepherd leaders can "empower" church members.

Shepherd-servant leaders do not have positional power or authority because their functional role in the body of Christ is to serve, not to control and dominate. Therefore, they cannot empower anyone in the conventional sense because it (power) "is lodged in the whole church; members have control over their piece of power and must finally give consent, time, ideas, energy, and money" (Weems, *Church Leadership*, p. 81). And when members are dissatisfied with the operational dynamics of the church, they vote with their feet or withdraw their funds or time and/or become uninvolved as an expression of their veto power.

The types of power/authority that shepherd-servant leaders have are the Word of God, character, and the Holy Spirit's power working through them, not the spirit of commanding and controlling. Shepherd-servant leaders (elders) need to know the

Chapter 5 Church Leadership

Word of God, which is sharper than any two-edged sword. This knowledge should not be utilized to beat members and anyone else over the head, nor is it to be used for self-glorification. It is for the building up of the body of Christ as it journeys to maturity in Him, and this is the authority for which Paul gave God thanks (2 Cor. 10:8), not for the power of command and control. A Christlike character is a powerful influence for good. Character is a leader's credit card rating as to his/her integrity, reliability, honesty, loyalty, sincerity, and personal morals. Respect for their character will reap greater rewards for leaders and the church.

It is character that counts with God, not money, position, power, or authority because God is no respecter of persons. When people see and hear the harmony between what leaders say and do (integrity), they are more likely to be influenced by such word/action congruence than even by the Word of God. And the Holy Spirit is the true source of power to which leaders should direct people. Micah claimed that when he rebuked the corrupted leaders and prophets of Israel, he was "filled with power, with the Spirit of the LORD, and with justice and might" (Micah 3:8, NIV) because "power belongeth unto God" according to David in Psalms 62:11. Prior to His ascension, Jesus instructed His disciples that "all authority in heaven and on earth has been given to me" (Matt. 28:18, NIV), and He delegates to whom He deems necessary through the power of the Holy Spirit on earth. It is He who empowers us, the church, to accomplish its mission, and that power is available for all who by faith in Him will lay claim to it.

Anyone—elder, pastor, treasurer, president, etc.—who thinks that he/she is in charge and has the power/authority to control God's people should be reminded that the power issue was settled by Jesus many years ago. Jesus (and I repeat this idea again for emphasis and reinforcement because of its criticality) saw the intoxicating effects of power and authority on the religio-political leaders of His day (Pharisees, scribes, Sadducees, elders, and chief priests). He experienced the military strangle hold of the Roman government to which the Jews were subjected and the enormous amount of power exercised by the said political power.

Thus, Jesus decided that His blood-bought church, the community of believers, would be devoid of any such controlling powers because it is antithetical to the organismic principles of His kingdom, and counterproductive to the relatively smooth operation of His body on earth. He, therefore, instituted a very significant paradigmatic change in leadership theory and practice. This idea was written in a previous chapter, but it cannot be overemphasized due to the fact that this matter is a very significant source of conflict and confusion in the church that is yearning for resolution. Jesus turned conventional leadership upside down on its head because those who want to lead in His church must come to the stark realization that there is no corporate ladder to climb because there is no potentially vacant place or positional spot to be filled at the top of the ladder or peak of the pyramid structure. The only CEO in that position is there for eternity. Therefore, earthly spiritual shepherd leaders must lead as servants and slaves with their towel and basin on their knees. In our secular society, leaders get their "feet" washed, but in the community of believers, leaders wash the feet of the followers of Christ.

As Jesus said, "'You know that the rulers of the Gentiles lord it over them, and their high officials exercise authority over them. Not so with you. Instead, whoever wants to become great among you must be your servant, and whoever wants to be first must be your slave—just as the Son of Man did not come to be served, but to serve, and to give his life as a ransom for many" (Matt. 20:25–28, NIV).

At the Last Supper, without much fanfare, Jesus got down on His knees with His towel and basin and washed His disciples feet as an example for all to follow (John 13:4–17). Unfortunately, too many church leaders are cognizant of Jesus' position on this issue but their love for authority, power, preeminence, greatness, control, and the spotlight leads them to completely ignore, overlook, and/or pay pure lip service to His instruction in this regard. It was Anthony Campolo who wrote that "few people know the rhetoric of servanthood better than the clergy. And yet so many of them, even unconsciously, are on power trips." He claims that "may be ... some of them were attracted to the ministry because they saw in the role of the minister the opportunity to exercise power. Clergymen of this type have learned to play their power games with a cleverness that keeps most people from ever suspecting what they are really about" (*The Power Delusion*, p. 42).

Church leaders who pay lip service only to Christ's teaching on this issue need to clearly understand the One whom they serve. They also need to be aware that they may be able to fool some of the people some of the time, but they cannot fool all the people all the time, and most important of all, they cannot fool God. In addition, if such leaders are attempting to achieve greatness through their control of God's people, they should remember that "true greatness, true leadership, is achieved not by reducing men to one's service but in giving oneself in selfless service to them" (J. Oswald Sanders, quoted in Water, *The New Encyclopedia of Christian Quotations*, p. 600).

Ellen G. White also warns against the high handed power developed through positions that tends to make men gods and creates fear. She claims that it is a curse that leads to insubordination and distrust, and a "loss of confidence even in the management of faithful men" and that the consequences of "Satan's methods [which] tend to one end—to make men the slaves of men. And when this is done, confusion and distrust, jealousies and evil surmising, are the result" (*Testimonies to Ministers and Gospel Workers*, p. 361). And these results are anathemas to the nature of the church and its leadership.

There is a significant difference to what may appear to be no contradiction between what Jesus mentioned about leaders becoming servants and slaves of the people and Satan's methods to make men slaves of other men as is written by Ellen White. The difference lies in the fact that it is fundamentally a matter of choice in that potential leaders who are asked to serve do so with the right understanding of the "position" from which they lead. On the other hand, even though a choice is involved, men become slaves of other men due to their vulnerability—lack of knowledge, the courage to act on knowledge, the current structure of the church—and the power and authority of those who ignore the teachings of Jesus in their attempt to seek that which should be given to God alone.

The exercise of power and authority creates dependency of church members on leaders and distracts their attention or ultimate focus from their Savior. It tends to stifle creativity and initiative and causes members to sit and wait for instructions and orders instead of functioning as leaders. This inevitably leads to organizational stagnation, undeveloped minds, and the death of the spirit, which becomes a real liability to the church. Many of these same leaders who in their attempts to control and dominate meetings and individuals without much success will resort to the evocation of their much esteemed "position," and you will hear such things as, "I am the pastor" or "I am the leader" or "I am in charge," etc. These expressions are an indication of the failure of these leaders to create healthy working relationships with those whom they lead because doing so is a critical component to getting things done, and it also indicates that they, the leaders, have little left. Keep a keen eye out for those who are obsessed with being in charge and play the political power game to keep themselves in positions and/or offices. They are not ready for shepherd-servant leadership in God's church.

Shepherd-servant leaders are expected to take loving care of God's people and maintain a yielding and open disposition in light of sound counsel. They are to be more concerned about service than the power and authority to control. The authority they have is the Word of God, which is used to "empower" or build up the saints and to lead them, not to themselves, but to the Chief Shepherd who is the genuine source of power. These shepherd servants build warm and loving relationships, which provide them with the type of influence needed to lead the church.

They Love God Supremely and People Dearly

God is the Leader of all and He is a loving God. Shepherd leaders should love God supremely because they are cognizant of who He is and how much He loves the human family; that the foundation of His government is love; and that love is also the fundamental principle of His kingdom on earth. They are to be the personification of His love on earth because they bring their lives into conformity with His Word, which reads, "If you love me, keep my commands" (John 14:15, NIV). And in order for them to live in such a way, they must earnestly and prayerfully seek the guidance of God through His Holy Spirit as they immerse themselves in His Word. These leaders (servant type) must exemplify their love for God not only in public worship and on God's holy day, but in every encounter with God's people and others. It is their responsibility to go first, to be the example, and reflect the character of God through their consecrated lives. According to Paul, "Love must be sincere" (Rom. 12:9, NIV), and if it is, what a powerful witness the lives of leaders will be in and out of the community of believers.

The above is not an indication of perfection on the part of shepherd leaders, nor is it a suggestion that they will not make mistakes, but we should bear in mind that Jesus said, "by their fruit you will recognize them" (Matt. 7:20, NIV), which also includes their love for God. They are frail human beings made strong only by the grace of God. They will make mistakes, but if the trend of their lives reflects an unconsecrated spirit, the church has a spiritual obligation and a right to ask them lovingly to step aside until they get their lives in order so that they can more rightfully represent Jesus to the body and others.

Loving God supremely is a sacred and unequivocally personal obligation of shepherd- servant leaders and a prerequisite for loving dearly the community of believers and others. Shepherd-servant leaders know about the "new commandment" that Jesus issued to "love one another. As I have loved you, so you must love one another" (John 13:34, NIV) and also about the second greatest commandment which is to "love your neighbor as yourself" (Matt. 22:39, NIV). This love knows no national, racial, ethnic, or socio-economic boundaries. It is unconditional and transcends all manmade distinctions. When body members and leaders accept Jesus Christ as their Lord, they come together as one under a new set of divine principles that should obscure all distinctive differences and create a principled mono-cultural church in which love is expressed and experienced by all with Christ at the center of our focus. In order to maintain that principled position, they avoid the corruption of gift-taking or bribes for future favors from members (Exod. 23:7–9). That is the way it ought to be. Leaders and members cannot proclaim their love for God while harboring a dislike for members who may not be of the same racial, ethnic, religious, economic, or national origin—they cannot love God whom they cannot see and hate their brothers/sisters whom they can see. We are a world church.

Shepherd-servant leaders must take the lead in demonstrating their love for all people and must do all within their sphere of influence to eradicate or lessen divisively manmade distinctions that create a tremendous amount of conflict in His church. They ought to create a climate of acceptance, tell the truth in love, and inform body members what God expects of His people. They have a grave responsibility.

They Are Compassionate and Passionate About What They Do

Unless they are hirelings or very good actors, it is virtually impossible for shepherd-servant leaders to perform their function/role devoid of compassion. Body members are human beings who have not escaped the unsavory effects of sin. They have problems, issues, and needs that they cannot resolve or deal with on their own. Just as the Chief Shepherd knew His sheep and their individual needs and demonstrated His compassion through His presence and action on their behalf and others, current shepherd-servant leaders have a serious responsibility to members of the church body. They must develop relationships with members and create opportunities for members to get to know them. Even though leaders may not be qualified in every need area, they should be compassionate enough to refer or seek the necessary professional assistance rather than attempting to administer ineffective help.

As was mentioned previously, shepherd-servant leaders must be an example for others to follow. A story is told about a church luncheon in which members were all dressed up and moving in a line to be served their lunch. As they waited in line, a small boy became ill and emptied his stomach on the floor in the presence of everyone. Due to the repulsive nature of his action, the members stepped aside without thinking. The assistant minister, realizing the boy's dilemma, stepped forward and placed his hands around the boy and comforted him. Then the senior pastor stepped forward and cleaned the area, and things returned to normal. There is no doubt that the assistant pastor, in taking the lead and showing compassion, set the example for others to see and follow, and I can just imagine how high his "credit rating" soared.

In addition, shepherd-servant leaders need to be passionate about what they do. I remember some years ago my home church was without a pastor for many months, probably over a year, and lethargy had almost set in. Then a certain literature evangelist was assigned to the island and given some leadership responsibility in the church. In his first sermon, he asked a critical question which in essence was, "If your house was on fire, would you walk down the road and say in a soft tone, 'My house is on fire,' or would you run and scream at the top of you voice, 'MY HOUSE

IS ON FIRE!'?" The point is, being inspirational or passionate about what you do is critical to leaders because they are expected to supply the energy needed to fuel the organization.

Good leaders understand the power of the word and use it in appropriate contexts to light "fires" for Jesus and to motivate members for greater involvement in ministries and other things. They also know that members enjoy and are motivated by inspiring, not dull, sermons or speeches. In other words, they cannot light a fire with a wet match. Imagine for a moment Jesus walking into the temple and seeing its desecration but reacting in a nonchalant manner to those aggressive money changers and merchants. Would they have left the temple? Christ reacted with great passion (He was passionately indignant), and without even using the whip, He successfully chased them out. So why is it that shepherd-servant leaders do not show greater passion for what they do?

Ellen White wrote about an occasion in which the celebrated actor, Betterton, was dining with the Archbishop of Canterbury, Dr. Sheldon, who asked the actor, "Pray, Mr. Betterton, tell me why it is that you actors affect your audiences so powerfully by speaking of things imaginary?" Mr. Betterton's response was, "… it all lies in the power of enthusiasm. We on the stage speak of things imaginary as if they were real; and you in the pulpit speak of things real as if they were imaginary" (*Evangelism,* p. 179). Credible shepherd-servant leaders do not have to pull strings, play political games, or use unethical tactics such as gimmickry, cajolery, and false appeal to revelation. They need to be lovingly and enthusiastically honest and lead with a Christlike passion that will light the "engines" of all members, encouraging them to take off and soar to unprecedented heights of involvement with and for Jesus.

Shepherd-Servant Leaders are Principle-Centered

They are Christian people who lead God's children from a principled perspective. This means that it is critically important and, I daresay, compulsory for them to know the Word of God, the scriptures, not on a superficial level but on an in-depth level that provides them with the knowledge of God's commandments, precepts, values, admonitions, warnings, and all the principles that undergird the aforementioned and guide their thoughts, words, and actions. It also requires great courage to implement these in one's life and leadership service due to the fact that there are those who are ready and willing to fight for political decisions or that which is politically expedient. Under such circumstances the leader must focus on that which is right and endeavor to humbly communicate this position in such a manner as to lead the congregation or

Chapter 5 Church Leadership

members to a principled understanding of the situation(s) for them to comprehend the need to perceive the biblical perspective and do that which is right.

The shepherd-servant leader should never succumb to any decision that is contrary to God's will and/or principles. Even if a perceived decision serves the leader's political purpose temporarily, something that is deemed or seems correct, but is not rooted in any biblical principle, it should be rejected by the leader on the basis that it is not the right thing to do. This would be an opportune time to demonstrate to followers that even the leader's perceived decision(s) can be faulty and needs to be rejected. This will serve as an excellent precedence for future decisions.

The leader's public rejection of his/her own perceived but biblically baseless decision sets the right standard for all to follow. The leader is to stand firmly on principle even in the face of universal scorn or death. Ellen White stated in no uncertain terms that the world needs "men who will not be bought or sold ... men who do not fear to call sin by its right name ... men who will stand for the right though the heavens fall" (*Education*, p. 57). Bill Robinson supports this idea of standing for what is right except he uses the term "truth" and states that "truth means standing firm no matter whether it yields returns or not, whether it meets with universal recognition or universal condemnation, whether a fight for truth leads to success or to absolute scorn and to obscurity" (*Incarnate Leadership*, p. 97). This idea of standing for the truth or what is right is further extended by Dr. Peter Koestenbaum when he wrote that "the bottom line, when it comes to principle, is the willingness to die.... for what is right" (*Leadership*, p. 176).

There are so many who have given up or made the ultimate sacrifice for truth or that which is right over the many centuries since Christ returned to heaven. Many of us will find ourselves in similar positions if we live long enough to experience the end of time. Furthermore, there are numerous Christians who are currently suffering and even dying for the truth because they have that Godlike courage to stand when all the odds are against them.

Other Shepherd-Servant Leaders' Responsibilities

There are some other leadership and administrative responsibilities that fall within the scope of shepherd-servant leadership and these are:

- **Planning** – This will be discussed in great detail in the last chapter, but it is important to understand the eighty/twenty (80/20) rule of planning. It is to spend 80 percent of your time planning and 20 percent in execution of the plans. The idea is that if sufficient time and effort are placed or spent in the development of a detailed plan, it becomes relatively simple and less costly to implement.

- **Organizing** – This is a part of the planning and implementation processes. Organizing system structures of large or small groups for the effective implementation of the plan(s).

- **Managing/Supervising/Leading** – This is the area and time that leaders spend in an aerial perspective to ascertain the effective and coordinated operation of all departments/ministries for effectuation of the church's plans/goals/mission.

- **Decision-making** – All decisions made in the planning and implementation processes should be principle oriented. It is critically important to exclude politics and do what is right at all times.

- **Communicating** – This is critical to all processes and should be conducted, not with a forked tongue, but with honesty and integrity.

- **Evaluating** – This is another vital function that is needed to assess the performance of all involved in both the planning and implementation processes, but it must be performed in an honest, fair, and objective manner.

- **Budgeting** – This is critically important and should never be underestimated, since it, to a large extent, determines the scope of the plan and its implementation.

For those individuals who may be seeking a quick biblical summary of shepherd-servant functions only, the following may be very helpful:

- Acts 20:28, 29 – They keep watch or guard, oversee and shepherd
- 1 Timothy 3:15 – They take care of God's church
- 1 Timothy 5:17 – They direct the affairs of the church by preaching and teaching
- Titus 1:5–14 – They encourage and yet refute falsehood
- James 5:14 – They pray over and anoint the sick
- 1 Peter 5:1–4 – They shepherd, serve, and are examples to the flock
- Ephesians 4:11, 12 – They prepare God's people for works of service

Shepherd-Servant Leaders Plan Work for and With Body Members

One of the significant functions of shepherd-servant leaders is planning work for the body of Christ, His church, and the development of structures (within scriptural guidelines), programs, and activities for the effective implementation of those plans. This function requires certain knowledge and skills that have to be outlined in more detail for the reader to clearly understand and be in a better position to apply in the church. Therefore, due to the length or volume of information required for this section, it was decided to place or make it into a separate chapter.

Conclusion

It was J. Oswald Sanders who wrote that "great leaders who have turned the tide in days of national and spiritual declension have been men who could get angry at the injustices and abuses which dishonor God" and do something that we fear so much, "enslave men" (*Spiritual Leadership*, p. 61). Shepherd-servant leaders have a solemn responsibility to God first and then His people. They unequivocally need to comprehend the fact that they are first followers of God and must learn through theory and practice all that He desires of them in their walk with Him before they able to lead others to Him. As a result of their dependency on Jesus and willingly allowing Him to lead them, it becomes amazingly easier for them to step aside, under the right circumstances, and allow others to lead in both their presence and absence.

Human shepherd-servant leaders are servants, mentors, equippers, caretakers, protectors, and overseers of the body of Christ, and when there are digressions from the path established by Jesus in His Word, shepherd-servant leaders have an obligation to redirect the foci of members to Jesus Christ and what He requires of them. This process may require some critical and innovative thinking on the part of leaders that may lead to approaches or methods of dealing with critical situations that may seem revolutionary, but as long as there are no principle digressions, they should be courageous to stand firm and be counted for Jesus irrespective of the political cost.

Shepherd-servant leaders are to be fully committed to God and His church; reliable, dependable, and available when needed; and consistent in their teachings and lifestyles due to the exemplary nature of their role in the church. They keep the destination (heaven at last) and path before the people in all they do, and they provide the fuel to keep the members "engines" running on track through the destitute wilderness of life to the Promise Land.

In the final analysis, because of the healthy relationships they have cultivated with body members that lead to extraordinary collaboration between them, they will be able to say by the grace of God that "we have done it together," and as Lord Byron wrote, "when we think we lead we are most led" (Stevenson, *The Home Book of Quotations*, p. 1094) because shepherd-servant leaders who allow themselves to be led by Christ through the Holy Spirit and influenced by their brothers and sisters will be in the best position to provide credible, authentic, and Christlike leadership to the church of God. This type of leadership is not motivated by financial gain because such leaders are "not given to filthy lucre" or "must not be grasping and greedy for filthy lucre (financial gain)" (Titus 1:7, KJV, AMP). Peter supports unequivocally the concept of the elder performing his responsibilities with a willing mind and "not for filthy lucre" or "not dishonorably motivated by the advantages and profits … but eagerly and cheerfully" (1 Peter 5:2, KJV, AMP). What are the implications for others who serve in the church?

Chapter 6

Planning for God's Church

I flew out of Puerto Rico one summer night en route to Trinidad. When the plane leveled off at about 30,000 feet, I looked out the window closest to me straight into an impenetrable darkness, and I began to wonder what the pilots were seeing and whether we would ever get to Trinidad alive. For a few brief moments, I completely forgot that the pilots flying the plane had a flight plan and properly functioning navigational instruments; that they were well trained and experienced in the system operations of the plane, and that I would, by the grace of God, get to Trinidad safely, which I did. Conversely, if the pilots lacked the relevant knowledge, skills, and training and had no flight plan, the probability of ending up anywhere would have been 100 percent. Similarly, a ship that leaves port without a well-trained captain and crew, a navigational plan, and properly functioning navigational instruments is likely to end up anywhere, even on the rocks. A church without a plan and well-trained leaders is like a rudderless ship adrift in an ocean without a destination.

Abraham Lincoln once said, "If I had ten hours to cut down a tree, I'd spend the first eight sharpening my ax" (Beausay, *The Leadership Genius of Jesus*, p. 35). The sharpening of the ax is symbolic of the amount of time he would put into planning/preparing to cut down the tree. Planning is an exceptionally significant function of leadership, and if leaders are operating without a plan in their organizations/institutions, they will drift into the port of nowhere. I remember my elementary school principal, the late Pastor Allyne from Trinidad, saying to the school then, "What you will be you are now becoming." The essence of this idea lies in the fact that, consciously or unconsciously, we are creating our future by the things we do on a daily basis because "today" is both yesterday and tomorrow, the past and the future.

Therein lies the link that connects our past, present, and future destination. This idea was captured by John Sculley, CEO of Apple, when he stated that "more than anything, we believe the best way to predict the future is to invent it" (Nolan, Goodstein, and Pffeiffer, *Plan or Die*, p. 76). With all things being equal, organizations and individuals can shape their destiny by the plans they develop today and how effectively they implement them. As the cliché' reads, "If you fail to plan, plan to fail," and if you fail to plan, remember that you will end up anywhere because you are leaving yours and the church's destiny to chance.

Questions: If your church continues on its current path, with or without a plan, where will it end up or what will it accomplish in the next five to ten years spiritually, socially, numerically (growth), or relationally? If your church has no plan, "road map," or GPS (Global Positioning System), do you know precisely where it is going, why it is going, how it will get there (anywhere), and when it will get there? If your church has no plan, you can rest assured that it is heading in no specific direction. A plan is a significant tool needed by individuals, organizations, and/or institutions that will provide a guide as to where they are going in reference to some destination. And the type of plan I am referring to is not one of an abstract and/or very complicated nature, but one that is realistic, strategic, and simple enough for all involved to understand. It involves a process that requires a plan and a planning process.

Plan: Definition and Purpose

A plan is the end product produced by those involved in the planning process. It is a "road map" document intended to be used as a guide by organizations and/or individuals in their decision-making. It is not just an end product, however, resulting from a planning process because it may not be beneficial to you or your church if it is the product of an extrapolative process in which church board members take their current church calendar and transfer all the programs and activities to the next calendar year. A more beneficial approach is the strategic planning process, which by definition is "the process by which the guiding members of an organization envision its future and develop the necessary procedures and operations to achieve that future" (Goodstein, Nolan, and Pfeiffer, *Applied Strategic Planning*, p. 3). In other words, strategic planning involves envisioning an ideal future state for your church, determining its current state, and deciding the path necessary to take for the realization of the difference between the two states. It is developing a better road map for your church (Ibid., p.325). This is one of the major responsibilities of leaders and other guiding members of your church. This may best be achieved by the election and/or appointment of a planning committee.

Planning Committee

The guiding members or leaders of a church are generally on the board, and it is the guiding policy of the Seventh-day Adventist Church in reference to the boards' function that the "chief concern is the spiritual nurture of the church and the work of planning and fostering evangelism in all its phases" (*Seventh-day Adventist Church Manual*, 15th ed., p. 79). Unfortunately, I have never experienced or heard of any church board that has implemented this policy in any significant way, and particularly the planning aspect, never mind strategic planning. This is not to suggest that there are no boards engaged in this process, but based on my experience in the church, I have never seen it done. The reality is that church boards are generally too occupied or bogged down with the nitty-gritty administrative issues (financial, departmental, and other problems) that consume too much of their time and disallow for any serious consideration to real planning.

However, this specific function of leadership and the church board is far too important to be neglected. Ellen G. White gave credence to its significance when she wrote:

> Those who have spiritual oversight of the church should devise ways and means by which an opportunity may be given to every member of the church to act some part in God's work.... Plans have not been clearly laid and fully carried out whereby the talents of all might be employed in active service. There are but few who realize how much has been lost because of this.
>
> The leaders in God's cause, as wise generals, are to lay plans for advance moves all along the line. (*Testimonies for the Church*, vol. 9, p. 116)
>
> The best medicine you can give the church is not preaching or sermonizing, but planning work for them. If set to work, the despondent would soon forget their despondency, the weak would become strong, the ignorant intelligent, and all would be prepared to present the truth as it is in Jesus. They would find an unfailing helper in Him who has promised to save all who come unto Him. (*Evangelism*, p. 356)

God's church is saturated with so many talented and gifted members, the utilization of whose services can turn the world upside down. But all the parochial politics and relational problems prevent too many from serving in the work. There are leaders whom I know who are reluctant to use some of those gifts for fear of members stealing the spotlight or being perceived as more informed and skillful, and probably better leaders, and the "lost" that Ellen White speaks about continue to plague numerous churches. All are to be given the opportunity to serve or use their gifts in the service of God, and if the board is too overwhelmed, my recommendation is to elect and/or appoint a planning committee with the mandate to develop and monitor the implementation of an established plan. This committee should become a permanent part of the local church structure and should include the leaders of all departments, including members with training and experience in this area (the process of planning will be dealt with later in this chapter).

If your church is not prepared to make such a bold move and the leaders are not ready in terms of their interest and commitment to pursue such a programmatic activity and embrace all the cultural changes that are inevitable and concomitant with this process, it will continue to experience, according to an unknown author, one, two or all of the following:

1. Mediocrity or mediocre performance that does not measure up to its full potential. Much more will be written about the contents of a strategic plan and its impact on the church. The church's performance under such a plan can be measured/compared with that of a written plan.

2. Complacency sets in when there is a lack of challenge, stimulation, and motivation to move the church forward in terms of its growth and development to fulfill its major purpose, its mission. It should be remembered that comfort and leisure are things we enjoy as a people, but they are never sufficient, in our estimation, for a completely fulfilling life (Leider, *The Power of Purpose*, p. 72). As humans we are inclined to sense feelings of empty and shallow existence when our lives are devoid of challenging and difficult experiences. When these situations are confronted and conquered, growth and development are realized.

3. Science and technology are changing our world at such an exponential rate that if individuals and/or organizations are not staying abreast of those advances, they are not only stagnating but retrogressing. Churches that are not growing toward spiritual maturity and their numerical capacity (even beyond) are being fundamentally stagnant, and this condition can lead to negative growth, slow decline, and eventual death. Before the latter occurs, dissatisfaction normally sets in, and this generally acts as a catalyst or spring board for drastic/revolutionary changes with cultural implications.

It is important to note here that if your church is ready to divert from its current path of mediocrity, complacency, and/or stagnation, it will not be easy. This to a large extent will depend on the size, age, and socio-economic background of the members. There will also be church (organizational) inertia and outright resistance from some members because the uncertain results of change can be intimidating, and the beneficiaries of the current system will be exceptionally reluctant to accept any change due to its perceived negative impact on their positions and/or benefits they receive from the present organizational arrangement. If the inertia and outright resistance are permitted to prevail in the leaders' attempt to create a better future state for the church, failure is inevitable. In reference to the church, failure is an unacceptable condition. Leaders must, therefore, identify, evaluate, and deal with them (inertia and resistance) in ways that will enlighten, persuade, and reduce the uncertainty in order to bring the entire church along, and not just a majority, if it is going to fulfill its mission in an effective way.

Remember, any church that is engaged in strategic planning and implementation will experience changes that are, at times, very problematic to deal with, particularly if the whole church is not, in principle, behind the proposed changes. Effective leaders, under such circumstances, should step backward, take a seat, and wait for followers to catch up. If you as a leader move forward without them, you are not leading. Moving forward in a united front is critical to the unity, witness, change, and growth of the church.

Reasons for Strategic Planning

I am cognizant of certain problems that are plaguing many churches, and these are generally left unattended. Too many church members are uninvolved in any kind of ministry. They attend church services, sit, listen, and more or less soak up presented information and depart until they return again to repeat the process while hoping for the presence of an evangelist to grow their church for them. In addition, the spiritual condition of many churches appears to be on the decline; members' relationships are fractured and/or shattered and are left unresolved due to the absence of or ineffectiveness of leadership; and too many members walk out the backdoor unnoticed and never return. In other words, many churches are moving fast to the destination of anywhere, and unless members understand the situation and become dissatisfied with the current state of affairs and move to change course, a slow death is inevitable. They should also have a felt need for a better future state for their church. When these two conditions exist, extrapolative planning (calendar programs transferring from year to year) will no longer be an effective planning tool. The only option that will be most effective is strategic planning.

Benefits of Strategic Planning

The many significant benefits that may be derived from strategic planning are as follows but not limited to:

1. It provides a unifying theme for all church programs and activities (Adair, *Not Bosses But Leaders*, p. 99). Instead of each department, board, or committee going in its own direction, a strategic plan provides for all these to go in the same direction toward the realization of the church's purpose for its existence.

2. It provides a framework for decision-making and action (Goodstein, Nolan, and Pfeiffer, *Applied Strategic Planning*, p. 6). The plan becomes the focus of the church (not at the exclusion of Christ), and whatsoever decisions are made or actions taken, they are done within the parameters of the framework.

3. It unleashes the church's energy behind a shared vision with the understanding that the plan can be accomplished by the grace of God (Ibid., p. 6). Strategic plans by nature have a way of drawing people and energy to them because of their shared vision. Because the plan is based on the shared vision of the people, there is that willingness to ascertain its success.

4. It gives substantive visibility to psychological ownership (Ibid., pp. 140, 327). In strategic planning, all members are given the opportunity to contribute ideas every step of the way. It is not the leader's plan. In the final analysis, it is the plan of the entire church. We should always remember that "plans fail for lack of counsel, but with many advisers they succeed" (Prov. 15:22, NIV). When the advice of all members is sought, given significant consideration, and integrated into the plan, it belongs to the members, not the leader only. When this is the case, people are more inclined to be involved in the implementation process where it is critically needed.

In addition, the more members involved in sharing ideas, the more ideas there are from which to select for plan inclusion and the more opportunities there are to question ideas for greater clarification. Ellen White indirectly endorses this idea when she wrote that "may God pity the cause when one man's mind and one man's plan is followed without question" (*Testimonies to Ministers and Gospel Workers*, p. 302). This high level of involvement will provide members with a clearer understanding of the potential changes necessary for the plan to work; how their lives will be affected; and what their contributions need to be for the realization of a better state.

William C. Bean presented some additional benefits (some of the following may overlap some of the above) of strategic planning in his book *Strategic Planning That Makes Things Happen*:

1. It is visionary, yet realistic
2. Is thorough, not piece meal
3. Develops direction, not confusion
4. It is cross environment
5. Proactive, not reactive
6. Aggressive, not passive
7. Is expansionist, not protectionist
8. Priority driven, not add-on driven
9. Realistic, not political
10. Implementation is the key, can produce great results
11. Results-bound, not shelf-bound
12. Is measurable, not ethereal
13. Is ongoing, not episodic
14. Purpose/mission driven (pp. 18–21)

The said author warns about some strategic traps into which many may fall. These are bigger is better, elegance and flashy, spread too thin, do not raise the bar, complacency, mere extrapolation, cheaper is better, if it ain't broke don't fix it, analysis paralysis, makes the number, and ignore corporate culture. The final three are ego, politics, and bureaucracy, which are the most difficult, if not impossible, to deal with or erase due to the fact that they are so fundamental to what goes on in an organization. They are referred to by Bean, the said author, as "the greatest and most frightening enemies in the history of business" (Ibid., pp. 29, 30), and the church is no exception in regards to these. It is one of the exceptionally important reasons why strategic planning is needed in the church. Members will be compelled to deal with their egos, parochial politics, and the quasi bureaucratic structure of the church.

A reflection on chapter 1 of this book reveals an earthly unattainable idealism if our dependence is on generic man (self), but with God nothing is impossible. The said perceived idealism can become a realism only within the context of a complete surrender to the working of the Holy Spirit. When this is realized, egos will be replaced by mutual submission, politics by principle, and bureaucracy by a flattened church structure with love and easy accessibility to all members. Changes and results of this nature are a true reflection of what a reformation and revolution for Jesus will accomplish in His church when submission to Him is genuine.

The Planning Process

Where Do You Begin?

The beginning of the planning process, which is planning to plan, is critical to the success of the entire process due to the need for the establishment of a sound foundation for the plan. In the commencement of the process, therefore, leaders must take the lead in the discovery of the answers for the following questions according to Leonard Goodstein, Timothy Nolan, and William Pfeiffer in *Applied Strategic Planning* (p. 9):

1. **How much commitment to the strategic planning process is present in the church?** Leaders must sense the frustration and dissatisfaction of members with the current state of affairs in the church and the need for a new direction to head off the present deterioration and the potential for closing the church permanently. When these conditions exist in the church, acceptance of the said process is made easier, and members are generally more likely to contribute their resources and become involved in the process that they perceive will bring the necessary directional changes to their church.

2. **Who should be involved in the planning process?** It is advisable to select members who are willing to commit the necessary time to complete the plan, which may take between six to twelve months, probably less, depending on how often and for what duration they meet and the availability of needed information. The planning committee or team should be comprised of a cross section of all departments,

Chapter 6 Planning for God's Church

ministries, leaders, and non-leaders. This type of representation will produce a wide variety of ideas and questions critical to the production of a substantive strategic plan.

3. **How long will the team or committee meet each session, how often will it meet, and for what time frame or how many months?** This is important since members of the team need to be cognizant of the time to which they are committing in the event that they may have other significant obligations during this time period. Once they are on board, members should be expected to stay for the duration and complete the plan. Remember, this calls for true commitment.

4. **How does the fiscal year fit in the process?** Timing is very important. If the plan is comprehensive in nature and will be implemented at the beginning of the fiscal year, it should be completed in a timely manner for its budget to be integrated into the overall or general budget of the church. It will become the focus of the church's operations and, therefore, cannot be excluded from the budgetary process.

5. **How will all stakeholders be involved in the process?** In the context of the local church, this question does not hold much relevance except for its relationship with the conference administration, and whether the church is a part of a district, and how the plan will impact upon that relationship. Whatever the circumstances, it is important to keep informed all those whom the plan will affect or who have to contribute in significant ways to its implementation and success. All those involved in the process should be given a copy at the end of the process.

Remember, this will be a challenging process, and if church members are not ready because they perceive strategic planning as unimportant, failure is inevitable.

The Planning Team or Committee

After the questions have been successfully or reasonably well answered, the next logical step in the planning to plan stage is to select, elect, or identify the members of the team. The number may include five to twelve members depending on the size of your church and the number of quality people necessary to be involved in the process for its success. Although it was mentioned earlier to select a cross section of departments and ministries, members of the team should possess the relevant knowledge, skills, and behaviors that are critical to the success of the planning process. The lack of these will retard the progress of the team. It is also important for team members to know that principled decisions should take priority over political ones and should be in the best interest of the church and its mission.

The Initial Meeting

At the initial meeting of the planning team, great consideration should be given to the wise counsel of Solomon who wrote to "commit to the LORD whatever you do, and he will establish your plans" (Prov. 16:3, NIV), and then earnestly come to the realization that "many are the plans in a person's heart, but it is the LORD's purpose that prevails" (Prov. 19:21, NIV). At the completion of this aspect of the initial session, the team should do some assessment of the strengths, weaknesses, opportunities, and threats (internal and external) and make inquiries into the following from both leaders and members:

1. What are the critical activities of the church?
2. What are the challenges facing the church?
3. What is occurring in the church that should not be happening?
4. How well equipped are the church members to meet the challenges?
5. What information and skills are absent and needed presently and in the future?
6. On a scale of one to ten, where does your church stand in reference to the fulfillment of its purpose/mission? (Modification of information taken from Giber, Carter, and Goldsmith, *Linkages Inc's Best Practices in Leadership Development Handbook*, p. 109).

Why Is This Information So Important?

The planning team/committee needs to understand very clearly the current state of the church and how that state is impacting or contributing to or not to the realization of its mission. It should also provide the team with a sense of the current knowledge and skills present in the church versus what are needed to move the church into a better future state. In other words, the planning committee needs to know where the church is, where it needs to go, how it is going to get there, when it will get there, and the reason(s) why it needs to do so.

Mission/Purpose

It was Ron Halvorsen Sr. who wrote that "when people forget their purpose, they forget who God is and what life means." Thus, "we are left with a religion and a church seemingly without meaning" (*Adventist Review*, January 1999, p. 10). I have been a member of several Adventist churches that seemed to be going nowhere. They seemed to be marking time, stagnated and to a large extent, regressing. The members appeared to understand that they were not fulfilling their mission but just never moved, while I was there, in the direction of the generally understood church mission. These are churches that either had full-time or part-time pastoral leadership, but they were on their way to nowhere. They needed credible/effective leaders who clearly understood the significance of the mission of the worldwide church to take the gospel to all the world, as well as the need to develop or formulate a mission statement for the local church. Each church plays an important role in the realization of the gospel to all the world, but each church will not take it to all the world. Therefore, each needs to clearly define its local mission within the context of the overall worldwide church mission. It is, therefore, the responsibility of the planning team/committee to engineer/develop a clear and concise mission statement of less than 100 words for the local church.

Some members may now be asking, what is a mission statement? It is a clear and concise statement of the purpose or reason for the existence of your church. It is what Leider referred to as "the heart and soul of why we exist as an organization" (*The Power of Purpose*, p. 96). So without this common statement, church members, including departments and ministries, are left to go in diverse directions and are "incapable of moving in a cohesive, integrated fashion" (Goodstein, Nolan, and Pfeiffer, *Applied Strategic Planning*, p. 328). It also provides a specific direction(s) and focus and compels the church to concentrate its resources and energies on its real priorities because it is apolitical; it provides the scope of the church's programmatic activities; it is the rallying point for the entire church; and it provides a clear understanding of what is to be done in the church (Ibid., p. 184).

Without a clear, distinct, and transparent purpose/mission statement and a concentration on a path for its realization, your church is fundamentally on a road to nowhere or is like a ship without a rudder adrift in the middle of the ocean on its way to the rocks. You may, however, be asking, what does a mission statement look like? I was once asked to lead a committee to develop a mission statement for a small church. On my way home one evening as I thought about what a sound statement should be, a thought came to me, and I immediately asked my wife for a pen and paper so she could write it down while I drove for fear of forgetting when I arrived home. I took it to the committee some days later, and it was accepted without any change. It is now the official mission statement of the Gethsemane Church of Seventh-day Adventists in Brockton, Massachusetts. It reads:

> To live in loving fellowship; walk in the Master's footsteps; reflect the character of God; lead others to Jesus and membership in His family; and equip them for ministry.

Once the planning team has completed the formulation of the mission statement, it should be taken to the church board and the church at large for their input—questions, discussion, and contributions. Any added information of value gained through this process should be taken back to the committee and integrated into the original statement, and then taken back to the church for its approval. This is very important because psychological ownership is critical to both the planning and implementation processes. Upon the completion and approbation of the mission statement, the team or committee turns its attention to an examination or evaluation of the core values of the church.

Values Examination

As a church (Adventists), our core beliefs and values are at the heart and soul of who we are, what we do, and how we operate. They should drive our thought processes, decisions, and actions (behaviors), but unfortunately, we do not always utilize those guiding principles as reference points for what we think, say, and do. I have experienced and have been told of numerous situations in which church members (some have been misled by their leaders), including individuals, groups, boards, etc., have used politics, hate, envy, and revenge as their guiding principles in decisions made against certain members.

Part of the problem is that many church members coming out of the secular workplace are not properly informed and/or educated about our foundational values and beliefs and are inclined to transfer those from the secular world to the church. It is also a problem of leaders not applying the core values in the decision-making processes and keeping them before the people at all times. As a church, we have become too negligent and complacent in our compromise of those beliefs and values for political reasons on a conscious level. Leaders need to stand firm on principles regardless of the consequences when others are conveniently or otherwise going astray. But what are values? A value is a concept or something that is of invaluable worth to us. It is "an enduring belief that a specific mode of conduct or end-state of existence is personally or socially preferable to an opposite or converse mode of conduct or end-state of existence" (Ibid., p. 13; as quoted in M. Rokeach, *The Nature of Human Values*, p. 5).

The planning team/committee needs to examine the current prevailing values and beliefs that guide the thinking and actions of the church versus those of a theological nature by which it should order its life; any philosophy and/or assumptions of its operations; and the culture of the church in order to sense where the church is in reference to these things versus where it ought to be currently and in the future. It is worth noting that our values, beliefs, and assumptions form our mindset and are at the heart of our church culture. If, therefore, our theological values, beliefs, and assumptions are flawed, so will be the church and its operations. These are some of the reasons why these must be brought to the surface and discussed for all to become cognizant of them and how to apply them in all phases of the church's operations.

It is also important for the planning team to examine it own values and beliefs on an individual and collective bases for clarification purposes, otherwise there will be little or no agreement about vision or goals and how to achieve them or whether they will meet the current and future needs of the church. Unless these are brought to the fore and conflicting differences are resolved, there will be continuous conflict on the team and very little will be achieved. We all understand the significance of unity among church members and how we are instructed to resolve our disagreements. As a Christian church, conflict should be kept to a minimum if it cannot be completely eliminated. The next step is to conduct an evaluation of the church's environment.

Assessment of Your Church's Internal and External Environments

One significant aspect of this assessment is the internal environment of the church in reference to (1) its cultural climate, which should provide the committee or team with a sense of the quality of members' relationships and how these are impacting negatively or positively on the operations and productivity of the church, particularly in regards to its mission; (2) its resources, particularly the human and financial, in order to determine the availability of sufficient human power for the effective implementation of the planned program as well as to decide the scope of the plan (the available resources will affect the scope of the plan in significant ways since it would be unwise to develop a plan that requires greater resources than are present in the church); (3) the infrastructure or how the operational capabilities of the church are structured and whether these are impacting the operational processes and end products in a negative or positive manner (if a negative impact is discovered, it is time to restructure for a more effective operation); (4) policies, how the current policies are contributing to the present state of affairs in the church; and (5) goals and objectives, what are the present goals and objectives of the church and how are these being achieved.

It is also of great significance to get some sense of the external environment of your church. Be cognizant of the political, economic, social, industrial, and technological developments and the demographic changes in both the immediate and broader community. Make an attempt to know about the demographic characteristics of those living in the area as well as those moving in. Monitor the churches in your area and try to understand what they are doing and how all the above-mentioned components are impacting your church and what your church can do to make a positive difference with those in your immediate area and the general community.

Develop a Substantive and Realistic Vision

Too many of our churches go through the motion of programs and activities, going around in circles week after week and accomplishing little or nothing. We attend our regular weekly services and may conduct an evangelistic crusade in the summer, if at all, and at the end of the year, we have no idea as to what we have accomplished. This is because we go through the same hum drum programmatic routine without realizing how deeply we are settling into a complacent mode of operation due to a lack of a challenging vision, a "destination," and how to get there.

Churches need leaders who can assist or lead them in the formulation of a vision that will light a fire in the hearts and minds of all members and redirect the churches to a different path for the realization of God's will/purpose/mission for His church. If there is no vision and "leaders are unclear about their direction and destination, their constituents will suffer from discomfort and stress" (Conger, *Learning to Lead*, p. 96) and will soon languish. Remember, if leaders do not know where they are taking their congregations, they and their constituencies will end up some place. Churches with no vision are generally very stagnated and on the decline, and we know, according to the Italian proverb, that those "who will not be ruled by the rudder must be ruled by the rock." But what is a vision?

By definition, a vision is "an ideal and unique image of the future" (Kouzes and Posner, *The Leadership Challenge*, p. 97). Burt Nanus defines it as a mental model of a future state that exists in the imagination and is "a realistic, credible, attractive future for your organization. It is your articulation of a destination toward which your organization should aim, a future that" by design "is better, more successful, or more desirable for your organization than is the present" (*Visionary Leadership*, p. 8). In other words, a vision is a future projection of what you and your members would like the church to become within the guideline of the mission statement. This is a very creative and proactive process and is a method of taking charge and creating

Chapter 6 Planning for God's Church

your church's future, something that should not be left to chance, all things being equal.

The following are some samples of vision statements that may help you in your attempts to develop your own. Allied Signal Corporation's vision statement is to be "one of the world's premier companies, distinctive and successful" (Stewart, *FORTUNE Magazine*, November 30, 1992). The United States constitution is a visionary statement of the founding fathers of this country.

Based on what has been written so far about vision, leaders and members may understand the concept of a vision, but what are the reasons for a vision? Why do churches need a vision statement? According to Goodstein, Nolan, and Pfeiffer, it is needed because:

1. Members of the church perceive a need for a shared or common vision to place their church on a more successful path.

2. Members desire greater control to shape the destiny of their church.

3. Members sense that the current state and operations of their church are inadequate and failing.

4. They know that their church is in trouble and need a way out.

5. They sense a need for more resources for the operations of their church.

6. They sense that the current state of affairs in the church is unworthy to be passed on to the next generation. It is broken and needs to be fixed. (*Applied Strategic Planning*, pp. 39–41).

The understanding of the reasons for the development of a vision statement is critical for members to willingly give their support to the planning committee. If the members of a church do not sense their inadequacy or failure to fulfill their mission or the reason for their existence as a church, their support for such a statement will be lukewarm or nonexistent. It should be borne in mind that new visions for churches are generally "most important when people are ready to pay attention, and they are only ready to pay attention when they are consciously or unconsciously hurting" and "because of the accumulation of disconfirming information" (Schein, *Organizational Culture and Leadership*, p. 301). Members must perceive the need for something better for their church than the current state of affairs and must hunger for it with such intensity that they are willing to utilize their resources for the realization of that vision. In addition, the planning team should be aware of the characteristics that make up a good vision. One should not be developed just for the sake of having a vision statement. It should meet the needs of your church and should be one that:

1. grows out of but is different from the mission statement, and is clearly stated for all to understand.

2. is unique and more specific than the mission statement.

3. focuses on the preferred future state of the church.

4. meets the future needs of the members.

5. is realistic in the sense of having a reasonable chance of succeeding.

6. is lofty, unlike the present, with high standards and noble values.

7. is inviting in that it attracts the hearts and minds of church members and stakeholders.

8. contains bad and good news in that it changes the status quo; breaks with the past; it is a judgment on the past, and it creates uncertainty and much anxiety particularly for those whose cherished positions may be negatively affected.

9. provides hope in that members believe it will change things and make a difference in their lives.

10. is a shared vision; psychological ownership is critical to the successful implementation and realization of that vision. (Weems, *Church Leadership*, pp. 41–45).

Functions of a Good Vision Statement

There is something mystical about a well written shared vision statement. It has several distinguishing functions, unlike any other component of the planning and implementation process, and these are as follows:

1. It transcends the status quo and provides a paradigm shift from the old to a new way of thinking and doing things in your church.

2. It becomes the organizing and guiding principle for day-to-day decision-making.

Chapter 6 Planning for God's Church

3. It provides a unifying theme that draws church members together in collaborative effort for its realization.

4. It sets the agenda and provides direction and purpose to church members.

5. It focuses attention on what is important and what is not.

6. It provides the attention on which members energies should be focused.

7. It is a forward-looking and idealized image that causes members to focus on the future.

8. It provides a challenge and a sense of being engaged in something important.

9. It sets the standard of excellence and becomes the invisible leader (Conger and Benjamin, *Building Leaders*, pp. 40–43; Kouzes and Posner, *The Leadership Challenge*, p. 111; and Nanus, *Visionary Leadership*, p. 17).

It is also important for the planning team to bear in mind that there are some significant factors to be considered in the process of developing the vision statement in order to avoid vision failure. Jay Conger has identified the following four reasons for vision failure:

1. Leaders project and incorporate their own personal needs in the vision over those of the church.

2. Team members develop a blind and over ambitious vision and miscalculate the resources needed to achieve the vision.

3. Unrealistic assessment of the current and future needs of the church.

4. Failure to identify the major internal and external environmental changes and redirect the vision (*The Charismatic Leader*, p. 139).

The role of leadership after the implementation of the vision is also critical in order to avoid failure. New visions generally call for a change of actions and behaviors that are relevant to the success of the new vision. If, however, the leaders and followers fail to change course and adapt the needed actions and behaviors, the vision is bound to fail. Leaders are also responsible for keeping the visionary fire burning in the hearts and minds of the members. If they fail to keep it alive or before the people on a consistent basis, sooner than later, the flame will be extinguished. It is very similar to driving to a certain destination without keeping one's eyes on the gas gage. If the fuel that keeps that engine burning is not replenished or added from time to time, the engine flames will go out and the destination will not be reached. Remember that leaders supply the psychological fuel to keep that visionary flame burning in the minds of the people. And a change of leadership can adversely affect the vision. If for example, the pastor is transferred and the other visionary local elders and leaders are not reelected to their current "positions," those coming in may not have the same vision, see the necessity for one, or be enthusiastic about the current one. The end results are very obvious due to the influence of leaders in organizations.

Now that the planning committee/team is armed with the above information, it is time for the group to write the vision statement, which is different from the mission statement. Bear in mind what you know about your church—members strengths and weaknesses and what they are thinking in reference to the future of their church. This is an aspect of the process that will not be easy. It will require both left- and right-brain thinking. Members of the team will have to put on their creative, intuitive, insightful, imaginary, analytical, and holistic caps to arrive at a winning vision.

The completed vision statement (five to twenty years down the road) should be shared with the church board, or in order to save time, taken to the church in a business session. Sufficient time should be allowed for thorough digestion, discussion, and feedback by all members. They should be encouraged to get involved and not hold back, to share what is on their minds because nothing is too dumb to contribute. Now is the time to speak (or hold one's peace after) in order to avoid the "trip to Abilene" or what is known as the Abilene paradox, which has to do with a family who drove many miles to Abilene, Texas, for dinner one hot summer night in a non-air-conditioned car. It was a very uncomfortable experience, and it turned out that no one in the family had really wanted to go. What happened is that when someone suggested the idea, although no one really agreed with it, each thought that the others wanted to go and was unwilling to express any opposition. Thus, the whole family took a trip that no one wanted to take. Needless to say, it was a miserable experience.

Although it is understandable for church leaders to desire smooth, lovey-dovey meetings, this is the time to legitimize disagreement, to agree to disagree, if possible, in a Christ-like manner and let all the sacred cows be brought to the surface and dealt with in an objective manner. Take the time to do this now before moving on, or the road ahead will be filled with huge potholes that may require greater effort to maneuver. Don't be afraid. You will get through it, and the church will be a more united entity if it really wants to change course.

Information of value gathered from the general meeting with all members should be taken back to the planning team and integrated into the current vision statement. This may also mean the rewriting of the vision, which may result in it being very different to the original one. Remember, however, that the new vision will reflect the input of and be owned by the people who will work to make it a reality. Psychological ownership is critical to its successful implementation. A shared vision statement of this nature will jump start the church's future because it will attract people, talents, skills, and other resources needed for the effectuation of the vision. The final written version should be shared with the whole church for its final approval.

Develop a Future State Model for Your Church

The development of the future state model for your church is important and requires the planning committee/team to write in some detail what it desires the church to be like in the next ten to twenty years based on both the mission and vision statements, and most of all what God wants for His church as is reflected and/or embedded in His Word. This model or prototype is to surpass, in quality, value, and worth, the current state of affairs of the church. If it does not, the time spent and the end product will only be an exercise in futility. As this model is drafted, remember that it should be very well thought out and written in language that is understood by all church members. It should not be a lengthy boring document but one that is written in short sentences.

As the committee thinks and writes, bear in mind that God's ideals for His church are embedded in His Word. It is, therefore, important that the following questions be kept in mind as the prototype is developed and/or articulated:

- Who envisioned and commissioned the building and/or establishment of His church?

- What are the ideal nature, structure, function, and mission of His church that need to be included in any church plan?

- What should be the ideal quality of our relationship with God through Jesus Christ our Lord that currently is not very obvious in the church?

- What is the ideal quality of our relationship with one another in the body of Christ that does not currently exist in the church?

- What is the ideal quality of our relationship with those on the outside of the church or the secular society that is currently absent in the church?

- What are the ideal methods and approaches necessary for the effective proclamation and/or dissemination of the gospel in our limited world that are not currently utilized?

It should not be understated nor overemphasized that any plan for God's church is not about the individual nor collective desires of the members. *It is all about God's revelatory instructions in His Word.* This means that we must delve into or study sagaciously the scriptures in order to discover those ideals that may be synthesized for all to see, read, and understand if leaders are going to even attempt to change mindsets and light fires in the heart of people for their maturation in Christ and the transformation of the world for Him.

The following scriptural passages will provide some of the answers to the above-mentioned questions that should be integrated into the prototype and final plan product:

- God's children are called out of darkness (Eph. 5:8–14)

- Sons of God (Gal. 3:26–28; Rom. 8:14; 2 Cor. 6:18; Heb. 12:7)

- Nation of priests (Exod. 19:5, 6; 1 Peter 1:16; Deut. 4:20; 7:6; 28:9; Isa. 43:21; 61:6)

- Love for one another (1 Cor. 13:1–13; Matt. 22:37, 39; Luke 10:27; Mark 12:30; Rom. 14:15; Eph. 2:2; 4:2, 15; 1 Peter 1:22; 2:17; 4:8; 1 John 3:18; 4:7, 8, 16, 20)

- Honoring others, even above ourselves (Rom. 12:9, 10, 15, 16; Gal. 5:15; Eph. 4:2; 1 Cor. 10:24; Phil. 2:1–5; 1 Peter 5:5)

- Do not show favoritism, God does not show it (Deut. 1:17; Isa. 3:8, 9; James 2:1–9; Rom. 2:10)

- Restoration of relationships (Exod. 22:3; Lev. 6:1–5; Num. 5:8; Rom. 13:6–8)

- Nothing done out of selfish ambition (Eph. 4:2–6)

- Gifts given to all (Rom. 12:4–8; 1 Cor. 12:12–31; Eph. 4:8–16)

- Leadership selection/election (1 Tim. 3:1–13; Titus 1:5–8)

- The church should not be hasty in placing anyone in the role of leadership (1 Tim. 5:22)

It will be a serious challenge to develop programs that are designed to change minds and behaviors and are acceptable to the entire church body. Therefore, be

Chapter 6 Planning for God's Church

resolute in your determination to get the "job" done. There will always be those members whose positions are threatened and will fight to maintain the status quo. But if there is a will and need to change course for the development of a new and better state for God's church, do not become discouraged, the battle is not yours but the Lord's, and He will fight for you. The team should remain focused and steadfast until the work is accomplished.

Upon due consideration and integration of the above into the completion of this model, the team should turn its attention to an objective and comprehensive assessment of the church. This should include but not be limited to the following ten items.

1. **Leadership** – The team should determine the quality and effectiveness or credibility of the leadership, and determine if the type discovered is sufficient to lead the church to the realization of the desired future state, or whether a change is in order.

2. **Growth** – The team should determine, as far as possible, whether there has been any spiritual, relational, educational, financial, and numerical growth in the church. If there has been growth in these areas, try to understand the factors that contributed to it and how to improve on them for greater growth in the future. If growth has been lacking, determine the level of growth needed to reach the desired future state and the factors, concepts, and methods needed to produce the desired growth.

3. **Departments and Ministries** – There are no sacred cows. All departments and ministries need to be assessed for their viability and effectiveness in fulfilling their purpose and to determine if they are needed and how they should be restructured, if necessary, for the realization of the new future state.

4. **Stewardship** – This is to include both the human and financial resources of the church. The team is to determine if the human resources in terms of the available talents/gifts and time and finances are sufficient to achieve the desired future state. If they are insufficient, determine the additional resources needed, and if they are not available in your church, tailor your future in terms of reducing some aspect of your plan. The reality is that if the resources needed to make your future plans come true are not available in your church and the team cannot definitively determine the acquisition sources for that which is needed, the grand future state you so desire must be tailored

to the available current resources. Remember, the knowledge, skills, time, and finances of church members are critically important to the realization of the planned future state, so these must be carefully evaluated to determine their presence in the church.

5. **Budget** – this is one of the significant aspects of the financial resources that needs meticulous assessment. It will take money to build a new and better future state for your church. Additional funds will be needed and spending priority will be required. Therefore, if conflicts arise when the new plans are assessed against the current budget, they should be resolved immediately or before moving on with further planning. The ideal thing would be to develop a budget based on the new future state. If this is initially impossible and additional funding is needed, make plans for the acquisition of the additional financing by raising new money and/or making some hard choices in the reduction of some programs that have little or no bearing on the achievement of future state. It is critical to secure the additional funds or the plan may fall flat on its face. This is not to exclude the exercise of the church's faith in God that He will provide for their needs. (I have experienced some miraculous things happen over my years as a member of the church in particular reference to church buildings and/or acquisitions, so this approach should not be discredited.) Let us also remember that this must be balanced by hard work to raise the necessary funds because faith without works is dead and so will the new plans. Bear in mind also that the scope of your plans for a better future will be based on the availability of both your human and financial resources.

6. **Individual Involvement** – It is very unfortunate that in most churches there are relatively few members who bear the operational burden of their churches. Whatever the reasons (political, economic, educational, social) are for this current situation, it falls extremely short of God's ideal for His church and what He can accomplish through His children. He gave gifts to His people, and all should be given the opportunity to serve through the use of their gifts in the body of Christ. The team is to determine the gifts in the church and how they may be utilized to effectuate the new future state of the church. If necessary, assign certain functions/responsibilities to individuals to ascertain the involvement of as many people as is possible, particularly in the implementation process.

Chapter 6 Planning for God's Church

7. **Technology** – We live in a technologically driven society and age, and we cannot afford to bury our heads in the sand and pretend as though it has no use in our church. There are tremendous benefits to be derived from the use of available technology in the church. Some examples are computers, satellite dishes, digital projectors, large-screen televisions, etc. that can be used for the building up of the body of Christ if the church can afford to make such purchases. The planning team should assess the current use of any technology and what is needed for the realization of the better future state of the church.

8. **All Programs and Activities** – All current church programs and activities are to be assessed to determine their value, worth, and relevance to the mission of the church and their potential use in the fulfillment of the new mission and vision. Those that are deemed to exist for the mere existence of a program should be eliminated and those that have some contributive value to the new future state should be integrated into the programmatic aspect of the plan. This will not be an easy process for many who are heavily invested into these programs. The assessment may unearth some sensitive issues and sacred cows that will make many emotionally uncomfortable and inclined to defend the status quo. However, honesty and integrity are very critical to this process, not politics, if team members are to be objective in their assessment in order to move the church toward a better and brighter future state.

9. **The Building and Parking Lot** – The entire church building and parking lot are to be examined to determine possible deterioration, structural damage, or other needed repairs. In addition, its future needs in reference to building additions to accommodate the new future state is to be determined. Every aspect of the building is to be examined, including room utilization. Do a thorough job and make some recommendations for its improvement and accommodation of the new plans.

10. **Goals, Objectives, Methods, Strategies, and Paths** – All these are to be assessed to determine their relevance to the new future state of the church. The team may discover the absence of one or all of the above. If this is the situation, begin to think very seriously about the formulation of some goals and objectives and strategies, methods, and paths by which these may be achieved. The goals and objectives

must be based on the new mission and vision of the church. This aspect of formulating goals is normally done after the assessment of the entire church.

Bridging the Gap

Now that you have determined what you want the future state of your church to be and you have completed the assessment of the current state of affairs in your church, compare both to discover the inevitable gap between them. Then turn your attention to how you will bridge the gap. In other words, begin to write in some detail how the church will get from where it is to where it wants to be. This is to be a systematic step-by-step approach that should include some long-term goals from which to derive one, two, or three short-term goals. The long-term goals represent the things the church wants to achieve in the long run. The short-term goals are the ones it wants to achieve in the next month to a year.

This section should also include the relevant programs and activities needed for the realization of the goals. In other words, the team or committee is to select those programs and activities and develop the strategies and methods or the path that the church needs to take to fulfill its chosen goals. Assignments should be made to departments, ministries, and individuals in order to make sure that the plan becomes a reality. It is a way of taking the program off the pages and bringing it to life. Members are to take responsibility for its implementation.

In addition, all infrastructural changes (doctrines are excluded) necessary to achieve the new future should be proposed. That is, any change in reference to eliminating department(s) or ministry and replacing it or them with those that are deemed important to the fulfillment of a better future for the church. As the team writes this aspect of the plan, it should be done in such a way that all departments and ministries, the whole church, are working toward the realization of the same goals. This approach is to ascertain that departments and ministries are not going in their own direction but are working together for the general good of the church. Remember, the entire scope of the gap will not be covered in one year, but working on a systematic basis, year by year, it will be accomplished by God's grace.

Tracking the Progress and Results of the Planned Program

This is clearly one of the failures (shortcomings) in the body of Christ. We plan programs and activities, and if lots of people show up and have an emotionally good time or experience, we automatically judge the event as a success, which is a very

Chapter 6 Planning for God's Church

subjective way of evaluating any program. Too often we plan programs without establishing in advance, or during the planning process, the objectives or critical success indicators (determinants) by which to measure the success or failure of the program.

A system of tracking the success or failure of all programs and activities should be developed by the team. The committee should write in some detail how it or the church will track the progress and results of the plans, as well as to determine mistakes, missed opportunities, and misguided suggestions, and how they will be corrected. In other words, develop some danger signs that will clearly indicate that things are not going as planned so that correction may be made before disaster sets in.

Submission of the Proposed Future Prototype

Upon completion of this aspect of the plan (the prototype) it is mandatory for the team to share it with the church board and/or members of the church. The board should study it carefully (it should have no veto vote), and a presentation should be made to the entire church in a meeting for this purpose only.

Prior to the meeting, each department, ministry, and individual should give due consideration to the plan to determine its role in the new future plan. Sufficient time should be allotted for the careful study before a final decision is made. All members should be given the opportunity to question, discuss, challenge, object to, and eventually vote on the prototype. Members should endeavor to remain as objective as possible by laying aside all political inclinations (parochial politics) and all personal sacred cows for the advancement of the whole body in its achievement of a better future state. Remember, this is a plan of great value and should not be rushed. If it takes several meetings to reach a consensus or at least 95 percent agreement, take the time to do so.

In the final analysis, when the vote is taken by the body, the planning team goes back into session to integrate the suggested corrections or recommendations and to extract the rejected ideas from the proposed plan. When the work is completed, the document is to be shared with the entire body and particularly with those who are assigned certain responsibilities in the implementation of the plan for them to develop their action plans or the more fine details of how they will accomplish their assignments if not worked out by the planning committee and approved by the church. This, to a large extent, depends upon the approach of the planning team or committee.

Operational/Action Plans

If the planning team chooses not to include action plans in the plan, all current departments, ministries, and individuals should be given the finished document and allowed to work out how they will implement their assigned portion of the plan. This is the operational "nuts and bolts" aspect of the plan that will transform the future plans from its paper existence to action. According to William C. Bean, this aspect of the plan decides how the comprehensive plan works; weak and troubled spots will be discovered; and the plan will be carried from concept to reality, which means that each unit of the plan must list (1) specific programs and activities (not general and fuzzy); (2) measurable, tangible with clear results; (3) deadlines, has a starting and ending time (unless continuous by nature); (4) the individual person responsible for performing duties or assignments (no "we"); and (5) assignments to be followed through to completion and beyond (*Strategic Planning That Makes Things Happen*, p. 57).

When the action or operational plans are developed by the persons or departments to whom they have been assigned, these should be reviewed by the planning team and taken back to the body for its confirmation. However, prior to doing so, the team should develop an alternative or contingency plan in the event that things do not turn out the way they are planned.

Alternative Plan

It is inevitable that something will go wrong along the way because all aspects of a plan never turn out the way they are planned. This may be a reflection of the imperfect human beings behind the development of a "perfect" plan. Take an objective look at the whole plan and try to discover some things in the plan that you think are likely to go wrong and decide the impact they will have on the plan and the church, and then develop some countering alternatives as an insurance policy against encountering a flat tire. It is almost like going on a road trip and preparing for the most obvious things that are likely to go wrong, such as a punctured tire for which there is a spare tire, which can only be used if it is in good condition.

At the completion of this unit, a comprehensive plan for your church is now ready for your church's confirmation and for the implementation process to begin.

Comprehensive Plan Implementation

Now that you have planned the work (a better future state for your church), it is time to work the plan or take it off the paper on which it is written and turn it into reality. Here is where the rubber will meet the bumpy and pothole-filled road, and

Chapter 6 Planning for God's Church

as you may suspect, it will not be an easy ride. Many strange things will happen, but if you view the plan as a road map, rest assured that if you follow it you will reach your destination. There are those who will try their best to follow the guide and take some wrong turns. Know the plan and what your assigned responsibilities are, and determine by the grace of God to get to that better future state.

As I mentioned previously, this stage of the game will not be easy. Challenges will arise, problems will surface, but the body of Christ must face the challenges and problems head on, deal with them, and make sure the church stays on course. It is at this point that some people's courage and will to endure will be sorely tested, but the church must remain focused and determined to achieve its goals. Strangely enough, this is the stage when many companies pour millions of dollars down the drain for failure to activate their plans and recognize what Timothy Galpin calls the seven deadly sins of implementation, which are:

1. Lack of leadership (if leaders do not want it , it will not happen. Change leaders when necessary)

2. A focus on one or two influence systems instead of all (no sacred cows)

3. Unclear or inadequate project management

4. Poor communication throughout the process

5. Insufficient resource application to effort or plan

6. Easing into and through changes to the influence systems (remember, no exception to any aspect of the church. All must conform to that which is necessary to make the plan into reality)

7. Waiting until the strategy is completely developed before commencing implementation activities (*Making Strategy Work*, p. 141)

Now that we are cognizant of those "sins" that can cause the death of plans, let us turn to some good things that will breathe some life into the implementation process and produce the intended results. These are as follows:

1. Credible Leadership – Without this type of leadership, purposeful change of any significance is virtually impossible. Credible leaders are needed to keep the vision and the path before the people as well as to keep the fire burning in their hearts and minds; provide the necessary training, knowledge and skills for plan implementation; and maintain the momentum.

2. Psychological Ownership – There must be that conscious awareness or feeling that the plan is not the leader's but that of the church because all members were given the opportunity for input, which was taken into serious consideration and integrated into the plan. This is referred to as a shared plan and shared ownership. Without this, implementation difficulties will multiply many folds.

3. Goals and Objectives are Measurable – Goals and measurement tools must be clear. This is critical to the success of the process. There must be no doubt in the minds of all participants as to what they are attempting to accomplish and the standards that will be used to measure their performance. It is the responsibility of leaders to work closely with all participants and provide performance feedback. This will give leaders the needed information as to what is being accomplished; how participants are performing; whether they need assistance; and whether the program is on track. This is an opportunity for leaders to discover problems and take corrective measures if things are not going as planned. It is a way of providing psychological support to those who need it.

4. Resources: Human and Financial – In order to keep the program on track, those aspects that require financial support should be funded in a timely manner to keep the momentum going. A lack of funding could create a reduction in impetus and program continuity. It is also important to have people who are trained and possess the required knowledge and skills, are creative, energized, persistent, committed, and thorough in the right places doing the right things.

5. Training and Development – This is an ongoing process that leaders use to educate and train members with the relevant knowledge and skills to transform the planning concepts into reality. My recommendation is to equip as many people as possible. In the event that a few have to leave, there will be sufficient qualified people to fill the created gaps and ascertain a smooth transition, and/or if some decide to neglect their responsibilities. This is a way of securing the continuity of the program without significant lapses in its forward movement.

6. Open Communication – Open and honest communication is a critically important factor in the implementation process. And healthy relationships are a key component of good communications. Leaders should, therefore, strive to build and maintain such relationships and

Chapter 6 Planning for God's Church

establish communications systems that will facilitate the easy transfer of knowledge between all participating members. Remember, effective communication will reinforce the vision, direction, and methods of how to achieve the proposed new future state.

7. Structural and Operational Changes – Change is very difficult for many due to, but not limited to, the uncertainty and anxiety it produces. However, church members must be courageous (God has not given us the spirit of fear) enough to make the necessary structural and operational changes in their churches to accomplish the Master's plan—His mission or purpose for His church through His people. There may be resistance by those who have a vested interest in the current status quo. Do your utmost to work with such people by helping them to see the benefits for all and how the church will fulfill the purpose for its existence. Stay focused.

8. Rules and Policies – There is something very incompatible about making and maintaining structural and operational changes while adhering to the old policies and rules. The new future state requires new rules and policies that are compatible with that new environment. It will require changes in members' behaviors and mindsets, so be patient, but perform the needed revision in this area.

9. The Physical Church Environment – The implementation process will take time before significant results begin to surface. In the mean time, it is important for members to sense the beginning of the new future state by making some simple changes in their church's physical environment where needed. Change the wall hangings, including posters and other things such as letterhead and logo of the church; make a large print of the new mission and vision statements and hang them in very conspicuous places (the mission statement with some real artistic creativity should be mounted to the back of the pulpit area). Whatever you create, let it be professionally done. It is for the church of God, and it should get the best. Small prints can be made and framed and hung in other places where they can be easily seen. People will begin to sense the dawn of a new and better future.

10. Celebrate and Give Thanks – It is important to take some time out of the busy schedule of creating this new future and celebrate the accomplishment of certain landmark achievements by giving God thanks in very meaningful ways. Do not forget, as leaders, to thank

people and recognize individuals for their submission to the call of duty by the Holy Spirit to utilize their gifts and work hard for the realization of certain major goals and objectives or landmarks of the plan. Take the time to celebrate (Ibid., pp. 26–35).

Remember, it is of great importance for leaders and the planning team members to monitor the implementation process in a meticulous manner for the spotting of errors and those who are not on track in order for them to take corrective actions in a timely way as the program moves forward.

Positive Results

There are probably only a few things that are as exhilarating as experiencing positive results from a challenging situation. I recall the emotional agony that probably all Americans experienced many years ago with the unfortunate explosion of the space shuttle Challenger and the loss of some brilliant astronauts. After a mourning period, it was back to work to correct the problem and put the space program back on track. Then with the successful launch of the next space shuttle came a revived exuberance and an unspeakable exhilaration. NASA confronted what appeared to have been insurmountable problems, and the results were as sweet as honey. Success is always sweet but it is never cheap. The emotional pain and agony you may experience going through the process may seem unbearable, and the human inclination is to feel threatened and run or fight. However, be persistent, the battle is not yours but God's, and He will fight the fight for you. Face the challenges, obstacles, and conflicts head on, and do your best to resolve them in a manner that will not negatively impact the implementation process.

It cannot be overemphasized that it will take time for substantive results to be evident, so do not seek for a quick fix or you may be disappointed. Once you begin the process, do not look back, press forward in the name of Jesus and success will emerge. It may even take one, two, or three years to experience very good results, but the real test is how the process is impacting in a positive way the behavior of church members as they move to a new and much better future state.

In addition, the planning process may appear to be very lengthy and complex for many. If it does, start on a smaller scale. Choose a goal and go through the process, and after positive results are evident, you will gain sufficient confidence to pursue something greater. Remember, the unseen hands of God are ever-present and ready to help, so claim it by faith and attempt the impossible because nothing is impossible with Him.

Conclusion

Planning is exceptionally significant to the success of any venture or organization. If you fail to plan, plan to fail. Organizations, including the church, without a plan are like a ship adrift in the middle of an ocean, being tossed around in every direction, that is likely to end up anywhere, even on the rocks or to a watery grave, as was stated earlier.

Conventional organizations are generally formed to accomplish a specific purpose or mission and if the work and people are not effectively planned and structured respectively, those organizations will never function to their optimal level nor achieve the high expectations of their leaders. In addition, if leaders lack a sound vision and fail to develop a shared vision and plan with the people of their organizations, failure is inevitable.

The church is not a conventional organization, but it is also subject to the said failures and disintegration (on an individual congregational level) as well. God has given to His church more gifts and talents than it needs to accomplish His work. Too many of us have selected to bury those talents, but you can rest assured that if you do not use them, you will lose them. Even our leaders have failed to recognize the distinct difference in the nature of the church being the body of Christ and not that of a conventional organization. Instead of acting on organismic principles as they should, they have become caught up in the power and authority issue, and who is in charge in the church—parochial politics. They have failed to hone their leadership skills in this direction and have generally failed to lead the church to a "destination" it has never gone to before in terms of exceptionally high numerical growth and spiritual maturity in Christ. And one of the significant reasons for this is their failure to develop an integrative plan for their churches.

Unfortunately, our leaders (pastors) continue to lead our churches down the extrapolative path, transferring programs from one year's calendar to the next that has brought little or no success in many churches in North America. All churches need an integrative plan as is outlined in this chapter, a road map that informs us of where we are going, how we are going to get there, a timetable for getting there, what the future will look like, and how the name of God will be glorified when we get there. It behooves leaders, therefore, to provide the direction by looking to the Word of God for His road map or GPS, and then energize the membership to successfully travel to the planned "destination." Plan the work with the people and work the plan with the people. Amen!

Chapter 7

Conclusion

The central issues about which I was very concerned initially that led to the writing of this book were the type and functional qualities of both leaders and followers that should be exemplified in the church of Christ. My conclusion, based on my reading/research and personal observations of numerous church leaders and followers over the years was that too many of them (leaders and followers) were thinking and operating/functioning far more extensively on secular rather than on Christian leadership/followership principles. Then I thought that something was radically wrong with this approach due to the nature of the church. It is not a social/political club nor a conventional organization but the body of Christ, an unconventional organization that functions like an organism, according to Paul, that requires leaders and followers to operate on biblically organismic principles that are distinctively different to those of the secular leadership/followership principles and dynamics.

One of the most critical things that all Christians should keep in mind is that the church belongs to God and He made Jesus its Head and the people its body. This means that the body is in subjection to the Head and looks to it for its "marching orders" through His word and the Spirit of God. In other words, all we need to know in reference to the church's origin, ownership, nature, structure, function, culture and mission are all outlined in His Word. The Bible provides all the directions, principles, precepts, and values that we need to guide us in the development of healthy relationships and the dynamics of our interactions as we work cooperatively for the realization of God's will for His church. Whatever we do in His church should be based on biblically-oriented principles and not manmade values. Christ is the Head, not man; He is in charge, not man; and each individual, leader,

Chapter 7 Conclusion

or follower has a personal responsibility to read/study/research His Word in order to be well informed as to what Christ's will is for him/her and the collective body, the church.

In reference to the church's nature, let us remember that we (Christian leaders and followers) have been called out of spiritual darkness (the secular society) into God's marvelous light—His kingdom under construction on earth, a community of loving and redemptive relationships with Jesus and each other. Christians are referred to as "saints" by Paul; they are "holy," set aside for holy purposes, and, therefore, should think and conduct themselves based on a distinctively different set of kingdom principles from which they have been called. The implication here is that the wholesale transfer and/or application of secular leadership/followership styles and principles/rules of conduct or operation in the church is inappropriate due to the fundamentally significant differences in the nature of the body of Christ, the church, to that of secular organizations or institutions. What is needed, therefore, is an unambiguous theological understanding of the origin, nature, mission, structure, and function of the church as is outlined (although in limited form) by Jesus, Paul, and other New Testament writers. This should provide or help us discover the organismic principles that form the foundation upon which all leaders and followers are to base, not only their relationships within the church, but the totality of their lives in and out of the church.

The said biblical/kingdom/organismic principles of love, mercy, compassion, justice, unity, patience, humility, cooperation, partnership, preferring one another, and submitting to one another that govern our relationships in the body-of-Christ community are applicable to the roles of both leaders and followers. However, followers should be independent and objective thinkers like Jesus, yet dependent on Him for directions and guidance, not just the reflectors or rubber stamps of human leaders' thoughts. They should also be God-fearing, exemplary, courageous, and principle-centered people whose self-worth is wrapped up in their relationship with Jesus and not in human leaders because they should only be followed when they are following Christ. Christian followers allow themselves to be led by the Holy Spirit and do not follow on the basis of political alliances, connections, need for vicarious power, personal gain, nor self-glorification, but with the understanding that they are in the church to serve God through service to His people, all people. Thus, they follow to fulfill the will and purpose of God for His church's existence, the realization of the great gospel commission.

Jesus was a distinguished follower and a very unconventional, yet eminently exemplary leader. He was totally dependent on the Father and independent of human leaders. His connection with the Father was unbroken, and He demonstrated no personal interest in the secular and religio-political leadership components of power and authority, but in the towel-and-basin principle of humility and the redemption of those said leaders and followers. He was a praying shepherd leader, educator, disciple developer and a compassionate, principle-centered, mission-oriented visionary—a revolutionary for God. He lit a flame in the hearts of His disciples that continues to burn in the hearts of His followers today. His exemplary leadership is more than worthy of imitation. All Christian leaders should endeavor to walk in the leadership footsteps of Jesus.

In reference to leadership in general, there are some common elements in both secular and Christian leadership that are primarily due to the fact that leaders in the two camps lead people. The distinctive differences are based on the socially acceptable manmade principles for the secular, inherent in which are power and authority, with profit as its bottom line. On the other hand, Christian leadership is based on a God-given set of principles outlined in His Word and is devoid of power and authority. They, Christian leaders, do not get their marching orders from a governing board or board of directors but from God through His Word; they do not articulate their own personal philosophical or theological perspective on church leadership but look to God through His Word; and they do not ultimately strive to change the color of the church's financial statement from red to black, although this is also important, their bottom line is the saving of souls for the Master. This is the reason why Christian leaders are to be different in how they think, behave, and function in the body of Christ. Personal gain and self-aggrandizement are not their motives; power and authority are not inherent in their role; and the color of their ink on paper is not the sum total of what they do. They serve God by providing shepherd-servant leadership to His people, resulting in the replication of leaders or disciples for Jesus and the redemption of souls for the kingdom of God.

A very significant aspect of Christian or shepherd-servant leadership is planning work for God's people. Ellen G. White rightfully stated that it is the best medicine for the church. Although she did not specify a method of planning, God's church should employ the most effective and efficient method for the best results. The extrapolative method, although systematically applied in many churches, is somewhat regressive in nature in that it does not provide for a sound integrative planning foundation on which to move the church forward. Strategic planning, on the other hand, is attractive, inherently comprehensive, and very integrative since it ties together all programs and activities for the realization of the church's mission and vision. The end product of this type of planning is a better road map for guiding church members to a better future state that is based on the embedded ideals in the Word of God.

Remember, those who fail to plan can plan to fail, and a church without a plan, inclusive of the Holy Spirit, is like a ship without a rudder that is ruled by the waves as it drifts into the port of somewhere.

Appendix

Plan Development in Local Churches

More and more church leaders are coming to the realization as to the significance of developing a plan for their churches, and they are not talking about a calendar plan in which the board inserts programs and activities in the dates of the months for a calendar year. They are referring to a systematic and/or strategic plan that can be very involved depending upon its complexity or relatively easy based on its simplicity.

There are many who are somewhat paranoid about this daunting approach due to the fact that such a plan development is not a part of the operational norm of numerous churches, so many have no knowledge of and are inexperienced in this matter, and do not know where to begin nor how to proceed. There are those who have limited knowledge and experience but are full of zeal and end up wasting much time, energy, and other resources. I have seen some leaders attempting to extract from departmental leaders their vision for their departments without first having a vision for the church, as well as informing them as to what a sound vision is about. So what they end up receiving are goals and/or objectives they want to achieve for that year.

Another significant problem or impediment in the application of this method or approach is the lack of knowing where to begin, the right process to follow, and where to end. The planning process begins with knowing the mission statement of the church or organization. For example, one church organization has adopted "this gospel into all the world in this generation" as its mission statement. All other branches and local churches of this organization must take into consideration this statement when developing their local mission statements as is clearly demonstrated in the following said statement of the Gethsemane Community of Seventh-day Adventist Church. Inclusive in this statement is the desire of the church to play its role in helping the larger church organization achieve its mission even though both mission statements are not identical.

Let us look at a real planning guide that may be helpful to many who are beginning the process. The following is an incomplete plan or a work in progress but one that may serve as a guide to many who are thinking about such a process or those already involved in the process but need some guidance along the way. I think the process is clearly outlined in the document and in the last chapter of this book.

Gethsemane Community Church

of

Seventh-day Adventists

OUR PLAN

Theme: Rebuilding Gethsemane for Mission Realization

Motto: Edify, Beautify, and Evangelize

    Gethsemane's Planning Committee

    Dr. Earlington Guiste, Chairperson

    Beatrice Guereiro

    Patience Mwosu-Dike

    Esther Chandler

    Charles Milburn

    Andrew Joseph

    Elodia Perry

    Maria Williams

Background Information

It is important to understand that since the inception of our church (Gethsemane Community Church of Seventh-day Adventists) with approximately seventy-five members, no well-planned and meaningful personal nor large-scale successful public evangelistic effort has been undertaken in the city of Brockton in an attempt to reach and lead its citizens to Jesus and a place in His earthly family. As a result of our failure to adequately plan for and implement those necessary/pertinent processes for the effectuation of our mission, our church continues to experience an annual attrition rate that will eventually lead to its extinction if corrective measures are not taken.

For approximately eight to ten years or more, our church leadership pursued an extrapolative process of planning through the transfer of annual programs and activity information (dates included) from one year to another in an attempt to achieve something that continues to elude our church. In addition to the relatively high attrition and low addition rates, our church is currently in a stagnation mode or going around in annual circles with no destination nor direction in mind due to the lack of a simple or strategic plan that is critical for the success of the journey.

INTRODUCTION

Any ship leaving a port needs a navigational plan or direction/destination, properly functioning instruments, and a qualified captain and staff to guide it to its destination or it may end up anywhere. Any organization or institution without a plan (simple or strategic) is like a ship adrift in the middle of an ocean, being at the mercy of waves and currents, which could carry it anywhere, including the rocks and/or a watery grave.

Our church is in need of a plan of direction to guide it to its selective destination. All vital church signs are indicating the need for a change of direction in order to avoid the "rocks." The future state of our church will not be shaped by osmosis but will be determined to a great extent by the things we plan to do on a consistent basis today and tomorrow because "what we will be, we are now becoming." It was John Sculley, former CEO of Apple, who once said that "more than anything, we believe the best way to predict the future is to invent it." This is what the power of the Holy Spirit can do with a sound plan and its proficient implementation—the invention of a better future state for our church. By His grace, it can and will be done.

Appendix Plan Development in Local Churches

Why We Need A Plan

It was President Abraham Lincoln who once said, "If I had ten hours to cut down a tree, I would spend the first eight sharpening my ax." The latter or time spent in sharpening the ax represents planning and preparation done prior to starting the job.

1. Our church is adrift or stagnated and, if allowed to continue in its current path, will end up anywhere.

2. We need a destination, direction, and energy to guide/lead us to a predetermined destination.

3. There is widespread dissatisfaction with the current state of affairs and a felt need for a change to something better.

Importance of a Plan

1. A plan is like a road map that shows the destination and gives direction as to how to get there.

2. It shows a picture of what the future state of the church could be like by the grace of God.

3. It provides a unifying theme and central focus for the whole church.

4. It is a shared vision that draws members together and unleashes the energy for its realization.

5. Members are more likely to identify with and become more involved because of the feeling of psychological ownership.

6. It is result oriented (getting things done).

7. It avoids failure and future extinction.

Delimitation of the Plan

This plan provides a relatively broad framework for the operation and realization of the church's mission beginning in the year 2005 with the sustained intervention of the Holy Spirit's power. It is not a detailed documentation of every aspect/thing that needs to be addressed in the pursuit of its mission, but it provides the guidelines for those pertinent aspects of the operation that are critical to its success. The detailed contents of the programs, seminars, and activities are delegated to the discretion of the presenters and those assigned the responsibility for their development and implementation.

The plan is limited to an introduction, mission statement, summary of an on-site/perceptive evaluation of almost every aspect of the church, a vision statement, and long-term and short-term goals, including the programs, seminars, and activities that are the means/tools used for the implementation of the goals in order to bridge the existing gap that lies between the current state of our church (based on the evaluation summary) and the vision statement, which reflects the visionary future state of our church.

The short-term goals are deduced from the long-term goals and will have to be formulated on an annual basis and prior to the year in which they will be implemented.

Mission Statement

Our mission: To live in loving fellowship; walk in the Master's footsteps; reflect the character of God; lead others to Jesus and membership in His family; and equip them for ministry.

Theme: Rebuilding Gethsemane for mission realization

Motto: Edify, Beautify, and Evangelize

Church Evaluation

Purpose: To discover a more realistic view of the current spiritual, physical, and social/relational condition of the church.

The evaluation included the following:

1. All aspects of the church building, internal and external, including parking lot and fence.

2. All departments and programs such as the Pastor and Board of Elders, Church Board, Sabbath School Council, Divine Hour Service, AY Council and its meetings, Women's Ministry, Personal Ministry, Treasury and Finance Committee, Boards of Deacons and Deaconesses, Risk Management, and the Building Committee. We tried to leave no stone unturned and gave our honest evaluation based on

our knowledge and information gathered from leaders and members of the departments and church in general.

Appearances can be very deceiving. What we discovered was very unsettling to many, so I have decided to exclude the evaluation results from this published document. However, it provided a realistic insight into the current culture of our church that left much to be desired. The following aspects of this plan may be very helpful to many, which is the reason for its inclusion in the appendix of this book.

VALUES AND BELIEFS

On the surface, it appears that Gethsemane's members committed to the principles, values, and beliefs (e.g. trust, patience, understanding, compassion, family, doctrines, Sabbath, family worship, open and honest communication, etc.) as are outlined in the Bible and the Seventh-day Adventists Church manual. A more in-depth examination seemed to reveal that some of the things we do and say as Christians are in contradiction to some of the things we value and believe. As Christians, integrity is a critical component/attribute of our character, and it is used as the basis by which we are judged whether we like it or not. It behooves us to be conscious at all times of whom we profess to be and whom we serve and represent here on earth. We should do our best by His grace to bring credit and glory to His name by reflecting His character in our daily interaction with others.

ASSUMPTION

It is at this particular level of the church's culture (the assumptive level) where certain assumptions lay the foundation for the good or ill of both individual members and the church. Assumptions about members determine to a very large extent how others interact with them or how they are treated. If false assumptions about people whom we do not know are made and acted upon, the church may be deprived of the use of certain gifts that can help it to make significant progress. It is, therefore, significant that assumptions are avoided and information sought before decisions are made. The only exception is to assume that all members have something positive to contribute to the church.

VISION STATEMENT

We, the members of Gethsemane Community Church of Seventh-day Adventists, are cognizant of the truth inherent in the proverbial expression that "where there is no vision, the people perish" (Prov. 29:18). The following is, therefore, what we envision the future state of our church to be. Our vision, as is presented in six major areas, is to:

1. **Church Structure (Building)** – make both the internal and external appearance of our church reflect to the Brockton community and surrounding areas the beauty, grandeur, and majesty of the God whom we serve (see Old Testament sanctuary description). This will be accomplished through the repair/restoration and further beautification of all defective, unclean, dilapidated rooms, hallways, sanctuary (place signs and announce from pulpit), ceilings, balcony area, including the addition and/or replacement of many or all existing pews, chairs, tables, and windows for the transformation of the entire church edifice.

   This transformation is to include the replacement of the hot water/steam system to avoid future leaks and further damage to the building structure and costly repair bills. The current system will be replaced by hot blow air that will easily accommodate the addition of an air conditioning system, which is needed particularly during the summer months.

2. **Church Leadership/Operations/Administration** – have our church led by well informed/trained, multiple, exemplary, Christian servant leaders (at least one being full time) who are converted and truly committed to the success and realization of our church's mission. This type of leadership would transform the operation of the body membership through the application of Christlike methods, biblical models, and organic principles for a more effective and efficient operation. The outcome/change should be reflected in starting and ending all services, programs, meetings, and activities on time; allocation of church funds for priority needs and mission realization; and educating members in effective human/Christian relational techniques for more harmonious working relationships as well as to lead others to Christ and His earthly family.

3. **Membership** – numerically increase our membership to the full physical seating capacity and overflowing; edify and educate all members for (1) a more profound understanding of God and His Word, (2) a more in-depth and personally consecrated experience with Jesus, (3) improved interpersonal relations, and (4) a spiritually cultural

transformation in which the total lives of members are brought into conformity with the teachings/principles of Jesus and those of other biblical writers (behavior patterns are changed—members are walking the talk and talking the Christian walk) and healthy Christlike relationships are developed/realized, which should lead, by the grace of God, to a more loving, caring, and unified body in Jesus.

4. **Finances** – have all our church members fully educated about the principles of stewardship and its implementation and cognizant of their significant role as stewards of God's creation/property. This will include their contribution of their God-given time, talents/gifts, and finances for the edification/development of the body and mission fulfillment. This education combined with their personal consecration should/will lead to increased giving. Inherent in this idea is more than sufficient funds for the solvency of the church's normal operation as well as to finance the cost of all other programmatic, evangelistic, social, renovations, beautification, mission needs, and other unforeseen needs of our church.

5. **Evangelism** – have all our members consistently involved in some form of evangelism (all net programs, personal, telephone, public, written, etc.) which is central to the purpose for the existence of our church. This will require an ongoing education and training program for all members in the Word of God, the doctrines of the Adventist Church, how to give Bible studies (techniques, methods, approaches etc.), how to influence people, and how to make friends—all theories and practices are to be included.

    Public evangelism (tent meetings, church meetings.) will be entered into only after all necessary preparations are made in advance and members are engaged in different forms of evangelism that will culminate in a public effort. Baptism, the end result of the above processes, will be conducted only after potential candidates are thoroughly indoctrinated/educated and demonstrate the necessary commitment to follow Jesus. It is also our vision to involve all members in post-baptismal programs and activities that are designed to integrate all new members into the body of Christ. This process will create a sense of belonging and oneness with the body, thus reducing the potential for back-door withdrawal.

6. **Community (Brockton and adjacent communities)** – The city of Brockton will be the major focal emphasis in reference to our outreach programs. Our church will serve as a clearinghouse for the collection of food, clothing (in good condition), and information (religious, medical, social, linguistic) for distribution to community members; as well as having a significant membership presence/involvement in the various community service agencies (AA, etc.) with a dual purpose of providing services to the needy and sharing the love of God and the soon return of Jesus.

BRIDGING THE GAP

Now that we are cognizant of the current state of affairs in our church and our vision for its future, it is incumbent upon us to chart out a course to get us from where we are to where we want to be. The following section is a representation of that path with its goals, objectives, programs, and activities designed to "sail" us into our future destination port. Very careful attention is to be given to this section for the meticulous implementation of the following as well as making any needed adjustment for the realization of our vision.

GOALS

Long-Term:

1. To provide the necessary educational/training services for the mental, physical, and emotional development of our members and lead them to spiritual maturity in Jesus.

2. To fulfill our mission through community/public evangelistic meetings (including personal evangelism), Revelation Seminars, Bible studies, and baptisms in our endeavor to reach community members for Jesus and membership in His earthly family.

3. To educate our members to the fullest extent possible on the principles of stewardship for their awareness of their God-given responsibility to the solvency of His church and the gospel dissemination.

Appendix Plan Development in Local Churches

4. To complete the total renovation and beautification of our church building, including the installation of hot-blow air and air conditioning systems within ten years.

5. To phase out the annual election of church officers over a seven-year period and phase in a voluntary spiritual gifts/talents identification and placement into appropriate/relevant ministries

6. To transform our church into a community clearinghouse/haven for the administration of social programs to meet the needs of the community.

Short-Term (2005):

1. To educate all members for greater functional efficiency and lead them into a deeper spiritual/consecrated relationship with Jesus and a closer redemptive relationship with each other.

2. To increase our church membership by a minimum of 10 percent.

3. To clean the entire church building/property and raise $12,000.00 for some repairs and restoration.

4. To increase our membership financial giving by a minimum of 10 percent.

GOALS' IMPLEMENTATION

Short-Term Goals (2007):

Goal #1: To educate/train all members for greater functional efficiency and lead them into a deeper spiritual/consecrated relationship with Jesus and a redemptive relationship with each other.

PROGRAMS/SEMINARS/ACTIVITIES

A. **Bible/Doctrinal Study Class**

1. Organize an annual Bible Study Class.

2. Announce its organization at Sabbath School, Divine Hour and place in church bulletin.

3. To be conducted on Sabbath afternoon following the Divine Hour and prior to AY.

4. To include all 27 doctrine doctrines of the S.D.A. Church.

OBJECTIVE: To teach in detail all twenty-eight doctrines of the Seventh-day Adventist Church (one doctrine per class or pace as needed). Additional subjects may be added according to class interest.

ORGANIZER: Board of Elders

TEACHER: Elder or Pastor

CENTRAL SUCCESS INDICATORS (CSIs):

- Attendance: number to be determined
- Consistency: regular meetings or class sessions
- Coverage of all twenty-eight doctrinal subjects
- Presentation: use of Bible and Spirit of Prophecy
- To include questions and answers

BEGINNING DATE: February 2007

COST: $50.00 (to copy materials)

B. **Daniel and Revelation Seminar (October 2007)**

1. Organize an annual Daniel and Revelation Seminar

2. Announce at Sabbath School, Divine Hour, in church bulletin, and forward communication on matter to surrounding churches and neighborhood.

3. To be conducted within a month after the conclusion of the doctrinal Bible study. If there is an extension of the studies, this seminar should not interfere with it since it should be conducted on Friday nights and Sabbath afternoons. May be arranged differently.

OBJECTIVES:

1. To outline and teach in detail all prophetic events and their interpretations as are recorded in the books of Daniel and Revelation.

2. To conduct this seminar in such a way as to lead all visitors who are not Adventists to Jesus and current Adventists into a deeper spiritual relationship with Jesus.

ORGANIZER: Personal Ministry

TEACHER: Pastor

CENTRAL SUCCESS INDICATORS (CSIs):

- Attendance: number in attendance
- Regularity: conducted on designated days as planned
- Teacher Performance: teacher survey performance to class members for class perception on the teacher's delivery
- Number of visitors led to Jesus and a place in His earthly family

BEGINNING DATE: October 1, 2007

ENDING DATE: October 31, 2007

COST: $1,500.00

C. **Relationship Building Seminar**

1. Organize Christian relationship cultivation/building seminar

2. Announce at Sabbath School, Divine Hour, in church bulletin, and inform surrounding churches and neighborhood

3. To be conducted on Friday nights and Sabbath mornings and afternoons

4. Seminar content expectations should be shared with the presenter

OBJECTIVE: To teach church members the principles of cultivating/building healthy Christian relationships and how to apply those principles in our daily lives—how to maintain such relationships. Developing and maintaining trust and confidentiality should be important aspects of this seminar.

ORGANIZER: Sabbath School/Women's Ministry

TEACHER/PRESENTER: Christian Professional Counselor; Maria will contact the counselor

CENTRAL SUCCESS INDICATORS (CSIs):

- Attendance: number to be determined
- Coverage of principles
- Clarity of presentation
- Level of involvement/interaction of presenter with audience.

BEGINNING DATE: April 30, 2007

COST: $1,500.00

D. Leadership Training Seminar

1. Organize at least two church leadership training seminars for 2007
2. To be conducted on Friday nights and/or Sabbath mornings and afternoons
3. If possible, develop flyers and mail to surrounding churches
4. Announce dates and time at Sabbath School, Divine Hour, and place in church bulletin

OBJECTIVES:

1. To prepare our members to effectively lead out in various capacities in the church.
2. To present in a systematic way the context within which church leadership takes place, Jesus' leadership, and secular leadership versus church leadership principles

ORGANIZER: Board of Elders/Pastor

TEACHER/PRESENTER: Dr. Guiste and other presenter

CENTRAL SUCCESS INDICATORS (CSIs):

- Attendance: To be decided
- Key concepts/principles presented

Appendix Plan Development in Local Churches

- Clarity of presentation
- Response of audience
- Interest generated (interaction of audience and presenter)

BEGINNING DATE: May 2007

COST: $2,000.00

E. **Services (Revivals, Communions, Week of Prayer, Wednesday Night meetings, Net 2007 etc.)**
   1. These are special and regular services that should be geared toward leading all members into a deeper and richer experience with Jesus
   2. Foci should be on teaching scripture, power of prayer, and leading members into a redemptive relationship with Jesus
   3. Attempts should be made to make the services as solemn as possible
   4. A thematic approach should be employed

   OBJECTIVES:
   1. To provide members with a clearer and more in-depth understanding of the Word of God and the power of prayer
   2. To assist members in the cultivation of redemptive relationships with Jesus and one another

   ORGANIZER: Board of Elders

   LEADERS: To be determined

   CENTRAL SUCCESS INDICATORS (CSIs).
   - Attendance: At least 10 percent above normal
   - Systematic presentation of presenter
   - Content of presentation
   - Response of audience

   BEGINNING DATE: January 2005

   COST: $500.00

Goal #2: To increase our membership by a minimum of 10 percent.

PROGRAMS/SEMINARS/ACTIVITIES

A. **Personal Ministry/Evangelism Seminar**

　1.　Jesus' method should be given the greatest of emphasis in this seminar

　2.　Books on winning friends and influencing people should be recommended

　OBJECTIVE: To provide information/principles and their application to members on how to approach family members, friends, strangers, etc. in reference to leading them to Jesus.

　ORGANIZER: Personal Ministry Leader/Department

　CENTRAL SUCCESS INDICATORS (CSIs):

　- Number in attendance: to be determined
　- Information presented: helpful?
　- Audience feedback

　DATE: 2007

　COST: $500.00

B. **Community Visitation Program**

　1.　Church members are to go at least two by two and make contact with community members and establish redemptive friendships as a means of showing Christian concern for them

　2.　Specific areas are to be identified for visitation on a systematic basis until the whole area is covered (a map of Brockton is needed).

　3.　Inquiry should be made concerning people's needs. Names and addresses should be collected for future use.

　4.　Self-introduction example: "My name is _____, and I am a member of the Gethsemane Church. We are visiting the area to get to know the community members. I have a small gift for you." (Materials: Christian literature, Spirit of Prophecy books, etc.)

5. Invitations should be issued to attend special services/programs. Also issue a general invitation in the event some people have or are not attending any church. If they do not have a church, invite them to be part of our family.

OBJECTIVE: To make group visits to the community in order to establish and cultivate healthy Christian relationships with its members, supply needs as warranted and eventually lead them to Jesus and a place in His earthly family.

ORGANIZER: Personal Ministry Leader/Department

CENTRAL SUCCESS INDICATORS (CSIs):

- Number of church members involved in this program
- Number of visits made/contacts
- Number of literature distributed
- Number of positive responses received

BEGINNING DATE: January 2007

COST: $300.00

C. **Visitors' Ministry Program**

1. Ushers/Greeters:

- Continue to assign ushers/greeters to welcome all people passing through our church door.
- Punctuality is essential.
- Visitors are to be encouraged to sign the guest book. Names and addresses are to be stored for future use.
- Guidelines for appropriate greetings should be written, memorized, and rehearsed. Nothing is to be left to chance.
- Make sure that all ushers and greeters know what to say and how to say it.

ORGANIZER: Usher Board/Leader

BEGINNING DATE: January 2007

2.   Pulpit Welcome:

- Special care is to be given to how visitors are welcomed

- Visitors are to feel the warmth, love, care, and genuine interest conveyed by the person doing the welcome

- They should be made to feel at home, encouraged to return, and should want to return in a hurry

- Follow-up calls should be made and cards sent to thank them for coming to our church

- Invitations should be issued to them for especially special programs

- If lunch is served, they should be invited to dine with the church family and to join a Bible study class

- It is important that we do all that which is necessary to make our guests feel as comfortable as possible in our church

- Visitors are to sense, through us, that they are in the presence of Jesus

ORGANIZER: Board of Elders, Head Usher, Clerks

BEGINNING DATE: January 2007

D. Public Evangelistic Efforts

- Community members who attend and demonstrate a commitment to follow Jesus should be baptized at the end of the effort

- Those showing any interest should be referred to a Bible study class for further study prior to baptism

- Such efforts should be conducted in or near to a residential area in which residents have expressed an interest

- This requires much preparatory and sustained work far in advance in order to prepare the "soil," "plant the seed," and "reap" the benefits of the labor through the power of the Holy Spirit

- An effort of this nature should not be undertaken unless the necessary work is done in advance

OBJECTIVE: To reach and teach community members about the gospel of Jesus and lead them into a deep spiritual relationship with Him and

Appendix Plan Development in Local Churches

membership into His earthly family. (This is a process designed to make disciples for Jesus.)

ORGANIZER: Board of Elders/Pastor

CENTRAL SUCCESS INDICATORS (CSIs):

- Attendance: to be decided
- How conducted: organization, operation, and follow up
- Number attend regularly
- Number committed for baptism
- Number who stay in church and become disciples

BEGINNING DATE: To be decided

ENDING DATE: To be decided

COST: To be decided

ULTIMATE SUCCESS INDICATOR: If our membership is increased by 10 percent or more at the end of 2005 based on our 2004 membership, the goal would have been realized. Time to establish another for 2006.

Goal #3: To clean the entire church building/property and raise $12,000.00 for some repairs and beauty restoration.

PROGRAMS/SEMINARS/ACTIVITIES

A. **Cleanup/Repair Days**
- Money raised may be used to purchase building materials. There are a few skilled people in the church who are able to perform certain repair work without pay. This will save us thousands.
- One general repair/cleanup day should be organized every two others to clean up for the simultaneous realization of both objectives
- Invitations may be issued to workmen/women in our sister churches for the cleanup/repair day

- Meals should be prepared (at least lunch)
- Specific work areas for cleaning and repair should be determined prior to the work day
- Cleaning and repair materials should be bought and made available for use prior to and on the day of cleaning/repairs.

OBJECTIVE: To keep God's house/church structure in a healthy physical condition that is pleasing to Him and all who enter it.

ORGANIZER: Board of Deacons/Deaconesses

BEGINNING DATE: To be decided

B. Fundraising Drive

1. Second offering for building funds
2. Individual contributions
3. Bake sales
4. International food fair
5. Christmas concert
6. Banquet (annual)
7. Solicit conferences

OBJECTIVE: To raise sufficient funds to cover the cleaning and repair costs.

ORGANIZER: Women's Ministry

CENTRAL SUCCESS INDICATORS (CSIs):

- Number of members participating
- Amount of money raised

BEGINNING DATE: To be decided

ULTIMATE SUCCESS INDICATOR: If the entire church is cleaned up as is predetermined and the stated amount of funds are raised, the goal would be considered fulfilled or realized.

Appendix Plan Development in Local Churches

Goal #4: To increase our members' financial giving by a minimum of 10 percent.

PROGRAMS/SEMINARS/ACTIVITIES

A. **Stewardship Seminar (two for 2007)**
- Four presentations during each seminar: Friday nights, Sabbath mornings (Sabbath School), Divine Hour, Sabbath afternoons

OBJECTIVE: To introduce and explain in some detail the concept and associated principles, and their application in the lives of church members.

ORGANIZER: Stewardship Leader/Committee

CENTRAL SUCCESS INDICATORS (CSIs):

- Number of members in attendance
- Presentation of concepts (systematic)
- Concepts learned
- Questions asked (indication of interest)

DATES: To be decided

B. **Stewardship Minutes**
- Five-minute presentation on concepts and principles during the Divine Hour

OBJECTIVES:

- To reinforce those principles and methods of application taught in the seminars, as well as to add to the principle pool, and cover in greater detail all principles and precepts related to stewardship.
- To demonstrate that the principles of stewardship are designed by God for the benefit of His people and the continuation of His work on earth.

ORGANIZER: Stewardship Leader/Committee

CENTRAL SUCCESS INDICATORS (CSIs):

- Positive feedback from members

- Consistency in presentation
- Increased giving

DATES: January 2007; to be decided

C. **Church Bulletin**

OBJECTIVE: Stewardship information included in the church bulletin will serve as an affirmation of our belief and reinforcement of the principles presented in the seminars and Sabbath morning presentations.

D. **Sermons**
- At least two sermons, in addition to the ones preached during the seminars, should be preached from the pulpit for the year or annually.

ORGANIZER: Stewardship Leader

PRESENTERS: Pastor/Elders/Invitee

DATES: To be decided

ULTIMATE SUCCESS INDICATOR: Calculate the percentage of giving at the end of 2007 to determine the percentage increase over that of 2006. If it is at least 10 percent greater, the goal would have been realized and a new one should be established for 2008.

CONCLUSION

It is now the responsibility of the church board and the church in business session to read, examine, analyze, scrutinize, and evaluate the value relevance of this information to take our church from where it is to where it needs to go. All suggestions are to be collected and given to the planning committee for further improvement of this plan before it is presented to the church at large for final approval. The final plan will be that which the church owns (psychological ownership is critical) and decides it needs to move forward to a better state in Jesus Christ.

Bibliography

Adair, Talbot. *Not Bosses But Leaders: How to Lead the Way to Success*. England: The Talbot Adair Press, 1987.

Adams, Jay. *Shepherding God's Flock*. Grand Rapids, MI: Baker Book House, 1980.

Anderson, Lynn. *They Smell Like Sheep: Spiritual Leadership for the 21st Century*. West Monroe, LA: Howard Publishing Company, 1997.

Barclay, William. *The Mind of St. Paul*. London: Harper & Row, 1975.

Bauer, Walter. *Greek-English Lexicon of the New Testament and Other Early Christian Literature*. Grand Rapids, MI: Zondervan, 1974

Bean, William C. *Strategic Planning That Makes Things Happen*. Amherst, MA: Human Resource Development Press Inc., 1993.

Beausay II. William. *The Leadership Genius of Jesus*. Nashville, TN: Thomas Nelson, 1997.

Bennis, Warren. *Why Leaders Can't Lead*. San Francisco, CA: Jossey-Bass Publishers, 1989.

Bondi, Richard. *Leading God's People*. Nashville, TN: Abingdon Press, 1989.

Bubna, Donald L., and Sarah Ricketts. *Building People*. Wheaton, IL: Tyndale House Publishers, 1978.

———. *Developing People Through A Caring Sharing Fellowship*. Wheaton, IL: Tyndale House Publishers, 1983.

Burns, James MacGregor. *Leadership*. New York, NY: Harper & Row, 1978.

Burrill, Russell. *Radical Disciples for Revolutionary Churches*. Fallbrook, CA: Hart Research Center, 1996.

———. *Rekindling a Lost Passion*. Fallbrook, CA: Hart Research, 1999.

———. *Revolution in the Church: Unleashing the Awesome Power of Lay Ministry.* Fallbrook, CA: Hart Research Center, 1993.

Clark, Stephen B. *Building Christian Communities.* Notre Dame, IN: Ave Maria Press, 1972.

Coleman, Robert E. *Dry Bones Can Live Again.* Old Tappan, NJ: Fleming H. Revell Company, 1969.

Campolo, Anthony. *The Power Delusion.* Wheaton, IL: Victor Books, 1984.

Conger, Jay A., and Beth Benjamin. *Building Leaders: How Successful Companies Develop the Next Generation.* San Francisco, CA: Jossey-Bass Publishers, 1999.

Conger, Jay A. *Learning to Lead: The Art of Transforming Managers Into Leaders.* San Francisco, CA: Jossey-Bass Publishers, 1992.

———. *The Charismatic Leader.* San Francisco, CA: Jossey-Bass Publishers, 1989.

Davis, James H., and Woodie W. White. *Racial Transition in the Church.* Nashville, TN: Abingdon Press, 1980.

DePree, Max. *Leadership Is an Art.* New York, NY: Bantam Doubleday Dell Publishing Group, 1989.

Donnithorne, Larry R. *The West Point Way of Leadership.* New York, NY: Doubleday, 1993.

Draper, James T. *Titus, Patterns for Church Living.* Wheaton, IL: Tyndale House Publishers, 1978.

Edwards, Rex D. *Every Believer a Minister.* Nampa, ID: Pacific Press Publishing Association, 1979.

Engstrom, Ted, and Janus Draper Jr. *The Making of a Christian Leader.* Grand Rapids, MI: Zondervan, 1976.

Etizioni, Amitai. *Modern Organizations.* Englewood Cliffs, NJ: Prentice-Hall Inc., 1964.

Froom, Leroy E. *Movement of Destiny.* Washington, DC: Review and Herald Publishing Association, 1971.

Galpin, Timothy J. *Making Strategy Work: Building Sustainable Growth Capability.* San Francisco, CA: Jossey-Bass Publishers, 1997.

Gangel, Kenneth O. *Competent to Lead.* Chicago, IL: Moody Press, 1974.

Gardner, John W. *On Leadership.* New York, NY: Free Press, 1990.

———. *The Heart of the Matter: Leader-Constituent Interaction.* Washington, DC: Independent Sector, 1986.

Giber, David, Louis Carter, and Marshall Goldsmith. *Linkage Inc's Best Practices in Leadership Development Handbook.* San Francisco, CA: Jossey-Bass Publishers, 2000.

Goodstein, Leonard D., Timothy Nolan, and William Pfeiffer. *Applied Strategic Planning: A Comprehensive Guide.* New York, NY: McGraw-Hill Publishing Company Inc., 1993.

Gordon, Thomas. *Leader Effectiveness Training.* New York, NY: Wyden, 1977.

Halvorsen Sr., Ron. "Cities Under Siege." *Adventist Review*, January 1999.

Hampton, John J., ed. *AMA Management Handbook.* 3rd. ed. New York, NY: AMACOM, 1994.

Harris, John. *Stress, Power, and Ministry.* Washington, DC: Alban Institute, 1979.

Jefferson, Charles. *The Ministering Shepherd.* Paris: Young Men's Christian Association, 1972.

Kets de Vries, Manfred F. R. *Leaders, Fools and Impostors: Essays on the Psychology of Leadership.* San Francisco, CA: Jossey-Bass Publishers, 1993.

Kilinski, Kenneth K., and Jerry C. Wofford. *Organization and Leadership in the Local Church.* Grand Rapids, MI: Zondervan Publishing House, 1973, 1976.

Koestenbaum, Peter. *Leadership: The Inner Side of Greatness.* San Francisco, CA: Jossey-Bass Publishers, 1991.

Kouzes, James M., and Barry Z. Posner. *The Leadership Challenge.* San Francisco, CA: Jossey-Bass Publishers, 1995.

──────. *Credibility.* San Francisco, CA: Jossey-Bass Publishers, 1993.

Kraemer, Hendrick. *A Theology of the Laity.* Philadelphia, PA: Westminster Press, 1958.

Labovitz, George, and Victor Rosansky. *The Power of Alignment.* New York, NY: John Wiley and Sons Inc., 1997.

Lall, Bernard M. and Geeta R. Lall. *Dynamic Leadership.* Mountain View, CA: Pacific Press Publishing Association, 1979.

Leider, Richard J. *The Power of Purpose: Creating Meaning in Your Life and Work.* San Francisco, CA: Berrett-Koehler Publishers, Ltd., 1997.

Lencioni, Patrick. *The Five Temptations of a CEO: A Leadership Fable.* San Francisco, CA: Jossey-Bass Publishers, 1998.

Levinson, Harry. *Executive.* Cambridge: Harvard University Press, 1981.

Lindgren, Alvin. *Foundations For Purposeful Church Administration.* Nashville, TN: Abingdon Press, 1965.

Martin, Carlos G. Quoted in *Adult Sabbath School Study Guide.* July-September, 2000.

Maxwell, John. *Developing the Leader Within You*. Nashville, TN: Thomas Nelson, 1993.

McCauley, Cynthia, Russ Moxley, and Ellen Van Velsor. *The Center for Creative Leadership Handbook of Leadership Development*. San Francisco, CA: Jossey-Bassey Publishers, 1998.

McGavaran Jr., Donald, and Winfield C. Arn. *How to Grow a Church*. Glendale, CA: Regal Books, 1973

Means, James, E. *Leadership in Christian Ministry*. Grand Rapids, MI: Baker Book House, 1989.

Miller, Calvin. *The Empowered Leader: Ten Keys to Servant Leadership*. Nashville, TN: Broadman & Holman Publishers, 1995.

Nanus, Burt. *Visionary Leadership*. San Francisco: CA: Jossey-Bass Publishers, 1992.

Nolan, Timothy, Leonard Goodstein, and William Pffeiffer. *Plan or Die*. San Francisco, CA: Jossey-Bass Publishers, 1993.

Oncken Jr., William. *Colorado Institute of Technology Journal*, 22 (July 1976).

Pascarella, Perry, and Mark A. Frockman. *The Purpose-Driven Organization: Unleashing the Power of Direction and Commitment*. San Francisco, CA: Jossey-Bass Publishers, 1989.

Phillips, Bob. *Good Clean Jokes*. New York, NY: Galahad Books, 1998.

Richards, Lawrence O., and Clyde Hoeldtke. *A Theology of Church Leadership*. Grand Rapids, MI: Zondervan, 1980.

Robinson, Bill. *Incarnate Leadership*. Grand Rapids, MI: Zondervan, 2009.

Rokeach, M. *The Nature of Human Values*. New York: Free Press, 1973.

Sanders, J. Oswald. *Spiritual Leadership*. Chicago, IL: Moody Press, 1961.

Schein, Edgar H. *Organizational Culture and Leadership*. San Francisco: Jossey-Bass Publishers, 1992.

Seventh-day Adventist Bible Commentary. 12 Volumes. Hagerstown, MD: Review and Herald Publishing Association, 1976.

Seventh-day Adventist Church Manual. 15th ed. Hagerstown, MD: Review and Herald Publishing Association, 1995.

———. 16th ed. Hagerstown, MD: Review and Herald Publishing Association, 2000.

Spreitzer, Gretchen, and Robert Quinn. *A Company of Leaders*. San Francisco, CA: Jossey-Bass Publishers, 2001.

Stevenson, Burton, ed. *The Home Book of Quotations*. 10th ed. New York, NY: Dodd, Mead and Company, 1967.

Strauch, Alexander. *Biblical Eldership: An Urgent Call to Restore Biblical Church Leadership*. Littleton, CO: Lewis & Roth Pubishers, 1995.

Streiker, Lowell. *Big Book of Laughter*. Nashville, TN: Thomas Nelson, 2000.

Stewart, Thomas. "Allied-Signal Turnaround Blitz." *FORTUNE Magazine*, November 30, 1992.

Tan, Paul Lee. *Encyclopedia of 15,000 Illustrations*. Dallas, TX: Bible Communications Inc., 1998

Tichy, Noel M., and Eli Cohen. *The Leadership Engine: How Winning Companies Build Leaders at Every Level*. New York, NY: HarperCollins, 1997.

Tjosvold, Dean, and Mary M. Tjosvold. *Psychology for Leaders: Using Motivation, Conflict, and Power to Manage More Effectively*. New York, NY: John Wiley and Son Inc., 1995.

Trueblood, Elton. *Your Other Vocation*. New York, NY: Harper & Brothers, 1956.

Vine, W. E. *Vine's Complete Expository Dictionary of Old and New Testament Words*. Nashville, TN: Thomas Nelson, 1996.

Water, Mark. *The New Encyclopedia of Christian Quotations*. Grand Rapids, MI: Baker Books, 2000.

Webster's Third New International Dictionary. Merriam-Webster Inc., 1986.

Weems Jr., Lovett. *Church Leadership: Vision, Team, Culture and Integrity*. Nashville, TN: Abingdon Press, 1993.

Wheatley, Margaret J. *Leadership and the New Science*. San Francisco, CA: Berrett-Koehler Publishers, 1999.

White, Ellen G. *Colporteur Ministry*. Mountain View, CA: Pacific Press Publishing Association, 1953.

———. *Counsels on Stewardship*. Washington, DC: Review and Herald Publishing Association, 1940.

———. *Counsels to Parents, Teachers, and Students*. Mountain View, CA: Pacific Press Publishing Association, 1913.

———. *The Desire of Ages*. Mountain View, CA: Pacific Press Publishing Association, 1898.

———. *Early Writings*. Washington, DC: Review and Herald Publishing Association, 1882.

———. *Education*. Mountain View, CA: Pacific Press Publishing Association, 1903.

———. *Evangelism*. Washington, DC: Review and Herald Publishing Association, 1946.

———. *The Great Controversy*. Mountain View, CA: Pacific Press Publishing Association, 1911.

———. *The Ministry of Healing*. Mountain View, CA: Pacific Press Publishing Association, 1905.

———. "Notes of Travel—No. 3." *The Review and Herald*, February 9, 1905.

———. *Patriarchs and Prophets*. Washington, DC: Review and Herald Publishing Association, 1890.

———. *Prophets and Kings*. Mountain View, CA: Pacific Press Publishing Association, 1917.

———. *Selected Messages*. Book 1. Washington, DC: Review and Herald Publishing Association, 1958.

———. *Steps to Christ*. Mountain View, CA: Pacific Press Publishing Association, 1892.

———. *Testimonies for the Church*. Vol. 1. Mountain View, CA: Pacific Press Publishing Association, 1868.

———. *Testimonies for the Church*. Vol. 2. Mountain View, CA: Pacific Press Publishing Association, 1871.

———. *Testimonies for the Church*. Vol. 3. Mountain View, CA: Pacific Press Publishing Association, 1875.

———. *Testimonies for the Church*. Vol. 4. Mountain View, CA: Pacific Press Publishing Association, 1881.

———. *Testimonies for the Church*. Vol. 5. Mountain View, CA: Pacific Press Publishing Association, 1889.

———. *Testimonies for the Church*. Vol. 6. Mountain View, CA: Pacific Press Publishing Association, 1901.

———. *Testimonies for the Church*. Vol. 7. Mountain View, CA: Pacific Press Publishing Association, 1902.

———. *Testimonies for the Church*. Vol. 8. Mountain View, CA: Pacific Press Publishing Association, 1904.

———. *Testimonies for the Church*. Vol. 9. Mountain View, CA: Pacific Press Publishing Association, 1909.

———. *Testimonies to Ministers and Gospel Workers*. Mountain View, CA: Pacific Press Publishing Association, 1923.

Wofford, Jerry, and Kenneth Kilinski. *Organization and Leadership in the Local Church*. Grand Rapids, MI: Zondervan, 1973.

We invite you to view the complete
selection of titles we publish at:

www.TEACHServices.com

Scan with your mobile
device to go directly
to our website.

Please write or email us your praises, reactions, or
thoughts about this or any other book we publish at:

www.TEACHServices.com • (800) 367-1844

P.O. Box 954
Ringgold, GA 30736

info@TEACHServices.com

TEACH Services, Inc., titles may be purchased in bulk for
educational, business, fund-raising, or sales promotional use.
For information, please e-mail:

BulkSales@TEACHServices.com

Finally, if you are interested in seeing
your own book in print, please contact us at

publishing@TEACHServices.com

We would be happy to review your manuscript for free.

www.ingramcontent.com/pod-product-compliance
Lightning Source LLC
Chambersburg PA
CBHW082114230426
43671CB00015B/2695